Lecture Notes in Computer Science 3367

Commenced Publication in 1973
Founding and Former Series Editors:
Gerhard Goos, Juris Hartmanis, and Jan van Leeuwen

T0232826

Wee Siong Ng   Beng Chin Ooi
Aris Ouksel   Claudio Sartori (Eds.)

Databases, Information Systems, and Peer-to-Peer Computing

Second International Workshop, DBISP2P 2004
Toronto, Canada, August 29-30, 2004
Revised Selected Papers

 Springer

Volume Editors

Wee Siong Ng
National University of Singapore
Singapore-MIT Alliance
4 Engineering Drive 3, Singapore, Malaysia
E-mail: ngws@comp.nus.edu.sg

Beng Chin Ooi
National University of Singapore
Department of Computer Science
School of Computing
Kent Ridge, Singapore 117543, Malaysia
E-mail: ooibc@comp.nus.edu.sg

Aris Ouksel
University of Illinois at Chicago
Department of Information and Decision Sciences
601 South Morgan Street, Chicago, IL 60607, USA
E-mail: aris@uic.edu

Claudio Sartori
University of Bologna
Department of Electronics, Computer Science and Systems
Viale Risorgimento, 2, 40136 Bologna, Italy
E-mail: claudio.sartori@unibo.it

Library of Congress Control Number: 2005921896

CR Subject Classification (1998): H.2, H.3, H.4, C.2, I.2.11, D.2.12, D.4.3, E.1

ISSN 0302-9743
ISBN 3-540-25233-9 Springer Berlin Heidelberg New York

Springer is a part of Springer Science+Business Media

springeronline.com

© Springer-Verlag Berlin Heidelberg 2005
Printed in Germany

Typesetting: Camera-ready by author, data conversion by Scientific Publishing Services, Chennai, India
Printed on acid-free paper   SPIN: 11404033   06/3142   5 4 3 2 1 0

Preface

Peer-to-peer (P2P) computing promises to offer exciting new possibilities in distributed information processing and database technologies. The realization of this promise lies fundamentally in the availability of enhanced services such as structured ways for classifying and registering shared information, verification and certification of information, content-distributed schemes and quality of content, security features, information discovery and accessibility, interoperation and composition of active information services, and finally market-based mechanisms to allow cooperative and non-cooperative information exchanges. The P2P paradigm lends itself to constructing large-scale complex, adaptive, autonomous and heterogeneous database and information systems, endowed with clearly specified and differential capabilities to negotiate, bargain, coordinate, and self-organize the information exchanges in large-scale networks. This vision will have a radical impact on the structure of complex organizations (business, scientific, or otherwise) and on the emergence and the formation of social communities, and on how the information is organized and processed.

The P2P information paradigm naturally encompasses static and wireless connectivity, and static and mobile architectures. Wireless connectivity combined with the increasingly small and powerful mobile devices and sensors pose new challenges to as well as opportunities for the database community. Information becomes ubiquitous, highly distributed and accessible anywhere and at any time over highly dynamic, unstable networks with very severe constraints on the information management and processing capabilities. What techniques and data models may be appropriate for this environment, and yet guarantee or approach the performance, versatility, and capability that users and developers have come to enjoy in traditional static, centralized, and distributed database environments? Is there a need to define new notions of consistency and durability, and completeness, for example?

This workshop concentrated on exploring the synergies between current database research and P2P computing. It is our belief that database research has much to contribute to the P2P grand challenge through its wealth of techniques for sophisticated semantics-based data models, new indexing algorithms and efficient data placement, query processing techniques, and transaction processing. Database technologies in the new information age will form the crucial components of the first generation of complex adaptive P2P information systems, which will be characterized by their ability to continuously self-organize, adapt to new circumstances, promote emergence as an inherent property, optimize locally but not necessarily globally, and deal with approximation and incompleteness. This workshop examined the impact of complex adaptive information systems on current database technologies and their relation to emerging industrial technologies such as IBM's autonomic computing initiative.

The workshop was collocated with VLDB, the major international database and information systems conference. It offered the opportunity for experts from all over the world working on databases and P2P computing to exchange ideas on the more recent developments in the field. The goal was not only to present these new ideas, but also to explore new challenges as the technology matures. The workshop provided also a forum to interact with researchers in related disciplines. Researchers from other related areas such as distributed systems, networks, multiagent systems, and complex systems were invited.

Broadly, the workshop participants were asked to address the following general questions:

- What are the synergies as well as the dissonances between the P2P computing and current database technologies?
- What are the principles characterizing complex adaptive P2P information systems?
- What specific techniques and models can database research bring to bear on the vision of P2P information systems? How are these techniques and models constrained or enhanced by new wireless, mobile, and sensor technologies?

After undergoing a rigorous review by an international Program Committee of experts, including online discussions to clarify the comments, 14 papers were finally selected. The organizers are grateful for the excellent professional work performed by all the members of the Program Committee. The keynote address was delivered by Ouri Wolfson from the University of Illinois at Chicago. It was entitled "DRIVE: Disseminating Resource Information in Vehicular and Other Mobile Peer-to-Peer Networks." A panel, chaired by Karl Aberer from EPFL (Ecole Polytechnique Fédérale de Lausanne) in Switzerland, addressed issues on next-generation search engines in a P2P environment. The title of the panel was "Will Google2Google Be the Next-Generation Web Search Engine?"

The organizers would particularly like to thank Wee Siong Ng from the University of Singapore for his excellent work in taking care of the review system and the website. We also thank the VLDB organization for their valuable support and the Steering Committee for their encouragement in setting up this series of workshops and for their continuing support.

September 2004   Beng Chin Ooi, Aris Ouksel, Claudio Sartori

Organization

Program Chair

Beng Chin Ooi   National University of Singapore, Singapore
Aris M. Ouksel   University of Illinois, Chicago, USA
Claudio Sartori   University of Bologna, Italy

Steering Committee

Karl Aberer   EPFL, Lausanne, Switzerland
Sonia Bergamaschi   University of Modena and Reggio-Emilia, Italy
Manolis Koubarakis   Technical University of Crete, Crete
Paul Marrow   Intelligent Systems Laboratory,
     BTexact Technologies, UK
Gianluca Moro   University of Bologna, Cesena, Italy
Aris M. Ouksel   University of Illinois, Chicago, USA
Munindar P. Singh   North Carolina State University, USA
Claudio Sartori   University of Bologna, Italy

Program Committee

Divyakant Agrawal   University of California, Santa Barbara, USA
Boualem Benattallah   University of New South Wales, Australia
Peter A. Boncz   CWI, Netherlands and Alex Delis Polytechnic
     University, New York, USA
Fausto Giunchiglia   University of Trento, Italy
Manfred Hauswirth   EPFL, Switzerland
Vana Kalogeraki   University of California, Riverside, USA
Achilles D. Kameas   Computer Technology Institute, Greece
Peri Loucopoulos   UMIST Manchester, UK
Alberto Montresor   University of Bologna, Italy
Jean-Henry Morin   University of Geneva, Switzerland
Gianluca Moro   University of Bologna, Italy
Wolfgang Nejdl   Learning Lab Lower Saxony, Germany
Wee Siong Ng   Singapore-MIT Alliance, Singapore
Thu D. Nguyen   Rutgers University, USA
Evaggelia Pitoura   University of Ioannina, Greece

Dimitris Plexousakis	Institute of Computer Science, FORTH, Greece
Krithi Ramamritham	IIT, Bombay, India and Wolf Siberski University of Hannover, Germany
Peter Triantafillou	RA Computer Technology Institute and University of Patras, Greece
Ouri Wolfson	University of Illinois, Chicago, USA
Martin Wolpers	Learning Lab Lower Saxony, Germany
Aoying Zhou	Fudan University, China

Sponsoring Institutions

Microsoft Corporation, USA
Springer

Table of Contents

Information Sharing and Optimization

Data Management in Mobile Peer-to-Peer Networks[1]

Bo Xu and Ouri Wolfson

Department of Computer Science, University of Illinois at Chicago
{boxu, wolfson}@cs.uic.edu

Abstract. In this paper we examine the database management of spatio-temporal resource information in mobile peer-to-peer networks, where moving objects communicate with each other via short-range wireless transmission. Several inherent characteristics of this environment, including the dynamic and unpredictable network topology, the limited peer-to-peer communication throughput, and the need for incentive for peer-to-peer cooperation, impose challenges to data management. In this paper we propose our solutions to these problems. The proposed system has the potential to create a completely new information marketplace.

1 Introduction

A mobile peer-to-peer network is a set of moving objects that communicate via short-range wireless technologies such as IEEE 802.11, Bluetooth, or Ultra Wide Band (UWB). With such communication mechanisms, a moving object receives information from its neighbors, or from remote objects by multi-hop transmission relayed by intermediate moving objects. A killer application of mobile peer-to-peer networks is resource discovery in transportation. For example, the mobile peer-to-peer network approach can be used to disseminate the information of available parking slots, which enables a vehicle to continuously display on a map to the driver, at any time, the available parking spaces around the current location of the vehicle. Or, the driver may use this approach to get the traffic conditions (e.g. average speed) one mile ahead. Similarly, a cab driver may use this approach to find a cab customer, or vice versa. Safety information (e.g. a malfunctioning brake light in a vehicle) can also be disseminated in this fashion.

A mobile peer-to-peer network can also be used in matching resource producers and consumers among pedestrians. For example, an individual wishing to sell a pair of tickets for an event (e.g. ball game, concert), may use this approach right before the event, at the event site, to propagate the resource information. For another example, a passenger who arrives at an airport may use this approach to find another passenger for cab-sharing from the airport to downtown, so as to split the cost of the cab. Furthermore, the approach can be used in social networks; when two singles whose profiles match are in close geographic proximity, one can call the other's cell phone and suggest a short face-to-face meeting.

---

[1] Research supported by NSF Grants 0326284, 0330342, ITR-0086144, and 0209190.

W.S. Ng et al. (Eds.): DBISP2P 2004, LNCS 3367, pp. 1–15, 2005.

The approach can also be used for emergency response and disaster recovery, in order to match specific needs with expertise (e.g. burn victim and dermatologist) or to locate victims. For example, scientists are developing cockroach-sized robots or sensors that are carried by real cockroaches, which are able to search victims in exploded or earthquake-damaged buildings [4]. These robots or sensors are equipped with radio transmitters. When a robot discovers a victim, it can use the data dissemination among mobile sensors to propagate the information to human rescuers. Sensors can also be installed on wild animals for endangered species animal assistance. A sensor monitors its carrier's health condition, and it disseminates a report when an emergency symptom is detected. Thus we use the term moving objects to refer to all, vehicles, pedestrians, robots, and animals.

We would like to comment at this moment that in our model a peer does not have to be a moving object, and databases residing on the fixed network may be involved. In many cases there are both moving peers and fixed peers, and they collaborate in data dissemination. For example, a sensor in the parking slot (or the meter for the slot) monitors the slot, and, while unoccupied, transmits the availability information to vehicles nearby. Or all the slots in a parking lot may transmit the information to a fixed 802.11 hotspot via a wired network, and the hotspot announces the information. In either case, the vehicles that receive the information may propagate it to a wider area via the mobile peer-to-peer network approach. In such an environment the mobile peer-to-peer network serves as a supplement/extension to the fixed-site based solution.

Compared to static peer-to-peer networks and static sensor networks, mobile peer-to-peer networks have the following characteristics that present challenges to data management.

1. Dynamic, unpredictable, and partitionable network topology. In our environment the peers are physically mobile, and sometimes can be highly mobile (consider vehicles that move in opposite directions at 120 miles/hour relative speed). The traffic density can vary in a big range from rush hours to midnight. The underlying communication network is thus subject to topology changes and disconnections. Peer-to-peer or sensor network approaches that require pre-defined data access structures such as search routing tables used in Gridella [12], Chord [14] and spanning trees used in Cougar [15] and TinyDB [13, 21] are impractical in such an environment.

2. Limited peer-to-peer communication throughput. The communication throughput between two encountered peers is constrained by the wireless bandwidth, the channel contention, and the limited connection time. For example, previous investigations into Bluetooth links have suggested 2 seconds as a typical setup time between two unknown devices [22]. This gives less than 2 seconds for data transfer when two vehicles encounter each other at 120 miles/hour relative speed (assuming that the transmission range is 100 meters). The limited throughput requires that the communication be selective such that the most important data are communicated.

3. Need for incentive for both information supplier and information propagators. Like many other peer-to-peer systems or mobile ad-hoc networks, the ultimate success of mobile peer-to-peer networks heavily relies on cooperation among users. In P2P systems, incentive is provided for peers to participate as suppliers of data, compute cycles, knowledge/expertise, and other resources. In mobile ad-hoc networks, incentive is provided for mobile hosts to participate as intermediaries/routers. In mobile peer-to-peer networks, the incentive has to be provided for participation as both suppliers and intermediaries (namely brokers).

The objective of our Dissemination of Resource Information in Vehicular Environments (DRIVE) project is to build a software platform that addresses the above issues and can be embedded within a hardware device attached to moving objects such as vehicles, personal digital assistants (PDAs), and sensors. The DRIVE platform consists of the following components:

1. Data Model. We introduce a unified data model for spatio-temporal resources in mobile peer-to-peer applications related to transportation, disaster recovery, mobile electronic commerce, and social networks. We illustrate how the data model can be used to represent various resource types even though these resource types are utilized in quite different ways.

2. Data Dissemination. We propose an *opportunistic* approach to dissemination of reports regarding availability of resources (parking slot, taxi-cab customer, dermatologist, etc.). In this approach, a moving object propagates the reports it carries to encountered objects, i.e. objects that come within transmission range; and it obtains new reports in exchange. For example, a vehicle finds out about available parking spaces from other vehicles. These spaces may either have been vacated by these encountered vehicles or these vehicles have obtained this information from other previously encountered ones. We call this paradigm *opportunistic peer-to-peer* (or OP2P).

3. Total Ordering of Resources by Relevance. With OP2P, a moving object constantly receives reports from the objects it encounters. If not controlled, the number of availability reports saved by an object will continuously increase, which will in turn increase the communication volume in future exchanges. Thus, to deal with the throughput challenge, we investigate techniques that prioritize the reports exchanged. These techniques provide a total rank in terms of relevance for all the reports across all the resource types stored in a moving object's reports database. The key issue is how to quantify the tradeoffs between the contributions of different attributes to the utility of a report.

4. Query Language and Query Processing. With OP2P, each peer m maintains a local reports database. The collection of the local databases of all the peers forms a virtual database to the database application in m. So the query language component and the query processing component deal with how to query this virtual database and how the query is processed.

5. Economic Model. Our incentive mechanisms are based upon virtual currency [5]. Each peer carries virtual currency in the form of a coin counter that is protected from illegitimate manipulation by a trusted and tamper resistant hardware module [6]. Each coin is bought for a certain amount of real money but it cannot be cashed for real money. We analyze the requirements to the economic model and propose possible solutions.

6. Information Usage Strategy. This component deals with how a resource consumer should use the received reports to take possession of a resource. This is important when the resource can only be exclusively used by one object at one time. Consider for example a driver who is looking for a parking slot. The driver may receive reports of multiple parking slots, and these parking slots may be in different orientation and distance with respect to the driver's current location. Then the question is which parking slot the driver should go to (namely, pursue).

7. Transaction Management. This component aims to study a spectrum of solutions to transactional and consistency issues that arise in report dissemination, and minimize dependence on any centralized structure.

All the components are divided into three layers as shown in Figure 1. The bottom is the *data* layer, which implements the data model for the spatio-temporal resources. Above the data layer is the *support* layer. This layer defines how the data is disseminated and how queries are processed. It also contains transaction management. The top is the *utility* layer, which contains the modules relevant to utilization of the resource information, including relevance evaluation, query language, economic model, and usage strategies.

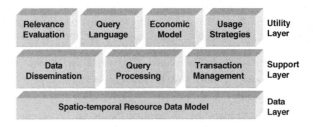

Fig. 1. The architecture of DRIVE

The rest of the paper is organized as follows. Section 2 introduces the data model and report ordering. Section 3 discusses OP2P data dissemination. Section 4 presents the query language and discusses query processing. Section 5 discusses the economic model. Section 6 discusses information usage strategies and transaction management. Section 7 discusses relevant work. Section 8 concludes the paper.

2   Data Model

2.1   Resource Model

In our system, resources may be spatial, temporal, or spatio-temporal. Information about the location of a gas station is a spatial resource. Information about the price of a stock on 11/12/03 at 2pm is temporal. There are various types of spatio-temporal resources, including parking slots, car accidents (reports about such resources provide traffic-jam information), taxi-cab requests, ride-sharing invitations, demands of expertise in disaster situations, and so on. Formally in our model there are *N resource* types T_1, T_2, ..., T_N. At any point in time there are M *resources* R_1, R_2, ..., R_M, where each resource belongs to a resource type. Each resource pertains to a particular point location and a particular time point, e.g. a parking slot that is available at a certain time, a cab request at a street intersection, invitation of cab-sharing from airport to downtown from a passenger wishing to split the cost of the cab, or the demand of certain expertise at a certain location at a certain time. We assume that resources are located at points in two-dimensional geospace. The location of the resource is referred to as the *home* of the resource. For example, the home of an available parking space is the location of the space, and the home of a cab request or a cab-sharing invitation is the location of the customer. For each resource there is a *valid duration*. For example, the valid duration of the cab request resource is the time period since the request is issued, until the request is satisfied or canceled. The valid duration of the cab-sharing invitation starts when the invitation is announced and ends when an agreement is reached between the invitation initiator and another passenger. A resource is *valid* during its valid duration.

Let us comment further about spatial resources, such as gas stations, ATM machines, etc. In these cases the valid duration is infinite. Opportunistic dissemination of reports about such resources is an alternative paradigm to geographic web searching (see e.g. [7]). Geographic web searching has generated a lot of interest since many search-engine queries pertain to a geographic area, e.g. find the Italian restaurants in the town of Highland Park. Thus instead of putting up a web site to be searched geographically, an Italian restaurant may decide to put a short-range transmitter and advertise via opportunistic dissemination. In mobile systems, this also solves some privacy concerns that arise when a user asks for the closest restaurant or gas station. Traditionally, the user would have had to provide her location to the cellular provider; but she does not need to do so in our scheme. In our scheme, the transmission between two vehicles can be totally anonymous.

2.2 Peers and Validity Reports

The system consists of two types of peers, namely fixed hotspots and moving objects. Each peer m that senses the validity of resources produces *validity reports*. Denote by $a(R)$ a report for a resource R. For each resource R there is a single peer m that produces validity reports, called the *report producer* for R. A peer may be the report producer for multiple resources. Each report $a(R)$ contains at least the following information, namely *resource-id*, *create-time*, and *home-location*. Resource-id is the identification of R that is unique among all the resources of the same type in the system; create-time is the time when report $a(R)$ is created (it is also the time when R is sensed valid); home-location is the home of R.

In the parking slots example, a sensor in the parking slot (or the meter for the slot) monitors the slot, and, when the slot becomes free, it produces a validity report. In the car accident example, the report is produced by the sensor that deploys the air-bag.

$a(R)$ may contain other information depending on the resource type of R. For example, a parking slot report may include the time limit of the parking meter; a single-matching request may include the sender's personal information such as occupation and age; and so on. We say that $a(R)$ is a type T_i report if R is a type T_i resource.

Let $a(R)$ be a type T_i report. At any point in time, a peer m is either a *consumer* or a *broker* of $a(R)$. m is a consumer of $a(R)$, and $a(R)$ is a *consumer report* to m, if m is attempting to discover or find a type T_i resource. m is a broker of $a(R)$ and $a(R)$ is a *broker report* to m, if m is not attempting to discover/find T_i but is brokering $a(R)$, i.e. the only purpose of m storing $a(R)$ is to relay it to other peers.

2.3 Reports Relations

There are two relations in the reports database of a peer m. One is the *consumer relation*, which stores all the reports that m knows about and for which m is a consumer. Another is the *broker relation*, which stores all the reports that m knows about and for which m is a broker. The two relations have a common object-relational schema. The schema contains three columns: (i) resource-type which indicates the type of the reported resource; (ii) resource-id; (iii) report-description, which is an abstract data type that encapsulates all the attributes of a report. All the report description data types inherit from a single data type called *AbstractReport*. AbstractReport contains two attributes, namely create-time and home-location. Thus every report description data type has these two attributes.

2.4 Report Relevance

Given the memory and communication-throughput constraints, it is desirable that the most important or useful reports are communicated during an encounter. One possible approach that appears to achieve this goal is that the receiver explicitly expresses the criteria for the reports it is interested in receiving. For example, "Give me all the reports $a(R)$ such that the distance between R and me is smaller than 1 mile and the age of $a(R)$ (i.e. the length of the time-period since the creation of $a(R)$) is less than 1 minute." However, this does not guarantee a total order of the reports; on the other hand such a total order is necessary to ensure that most relevant reports are exchanged first (such that if disconnection occurs before the exchange completes, the loss is minimal), and that the less relevant reports are purged from memory before more relevant ones.

Our approach is to rank all the reports in a peer's reports database in terms of their relevance or expected utility, and then the reports are communicated and saved in the order of their relevance. Or, the reports requested and communicated are the ones with a relevance above a certain threshold. The notion of relevance quantifies the importance or the expected utility of a report to a peer at a particular time and a particular location.

Let $a(R)$ be a type T_i report. The relevance of $a(R)$ to a <u>consumer</u> at time q and location p represents the importance or the expected utility of $a(R)$ to the consumer at q and p. The relevance of $a(R)$ to a <u>broker</u> at time q and location p represents the importance or the expected utility of $a(R)$ to future consumers of the report that the broker estimates it will encounter. The question is how to evaluate the relevance such as to provide a total order of all the reports across all the reports relations within a peer.

We consider reports ranking a multiple attribute decision making (MADM) problem [11]. We adopt a hierarchical weighting structure. At the first level of the weighting hierarchy, each resource type T_i is assigned a weight (priority) that represents the importance of T_i relative to other resource types. At the second level, each attribute of T_i is assigned a weight that represents the importance of that attribute relative to other attributes of T_i. When ordering reports, each report is assigned a score that is a weighted aggregation of the normalized values of each attribute. Then the reports are sorted based on their scores.

3 Data Dissemination

We assume that each peer is capable of communicating with the neighboring peers within a maximum of a few hundred meters. One example is an 802.11 hotspot or a PDA with Bluetooth support. The underlying communication module provides a mechanism to resolve interference and conflicts. Each peer is also capable of discovering peers that enter into or leave out of its transmission range. Finally, each peer is equipped with a GPS system so that (i) the peer knows its location at any point in time and (ii) the clock is synchronized among all the peers.

When two peers m_1 and m_2 encounter each other, m_1 first requests consumer reports from m_2 with relevance (according to the relevance metadata of m_1) above the lowest relevance in m_1's consumer relation. Then m_1 requests broker reports from m_2 with relevance above the lowest relevance in m_1's broker relation.

We would like to emphasize that in our model, the interactions among peers are completely self-organized. The association between a pair of peers is established when they encounter each other and is ended when they finish the exchange or when they are out of the transmission range of each other. Other than this there is no other procedure for a peer to join or leave the network.

4 The Economic Model

In this section we introduce an economic model that stimulates peers to participate in report dissemination even if they are not interested in using a resource. The economic model needs to satisfy the following requirements:

It should handle two categories of reports, depending on whether the producer or the consumer pays for the reports. Reports that the owner is interested in advertising are *producer-paid*. Reports that the consumer is interested in knowing are *consumer-paid*. A resource may have both producer-paid and consumer-paid reports, if both the producer and the consumer are willing to pay for the reports. For example, reports that include the location of a gas station may be producer-paid because the gas station wishes to advertise them to neighboring vehicles. They may also be consumer-paid because a consumer may be willing to pay for a gas station report if he really needs one. Similarly for taxi-cab requests and reports of available parking slots.

1. It should consider peers that may be producers, consumers, and brokers. For consumer paid reports, both producers and brokers should be incentivized. For producer paid reports, brokers should be incentivized.

2. It should allow any peer to turn-off the spatio-temporal information module. But if it turns on the spatio-temporal information module, then the module behaves according to the economic model.

3. It should protect from the following attacks: (i) A peer creates and sells fictitious validity reports; (ii) A propagator modifies a report; (iii) A consumer-paid report is overheard by an intruding-consumer that that does not pay; in other words, an intruder overhears the legitimate transfer of the report to a consumer; (iv) A peer illegitimately increases its virtual currency counter.

Now we present our solution that satisfies the above requirements. Section 4.1 introduces two fundamental components of our economic model, namely virtual currency and the security module. Section 4.2 discusses producer-paid reports. Section 4.3 discusses consumer-paid reports.

4.1 Virtual Currency and the Security Module

The system circulates a virtual currency called *coins*. The coins owned by each peer is represented by a coin counter that is physically stored in that peer. The coin counter is decreased when the peer pays out for buying validity reports and increased when the peer earns in for selling. Each peer has a trusted and tamper resistant hardware module called the *security module*. A common example of a low-cost security module is smart card with an embedded one-chip computer [6]. The coin counter is stored in the security module and thus is protected from illegitimate manipulation. Each coin is bought for a certain amount of real money but it cannot be cashed for real money, and therefore the motivation for breaking into the security module is significantly reduced. The validity reports database, including the consumer relation and the broker relation, are stored in the security module.

When two moving objects m_1 and m_2 encounter each other, if both m_1 and m_2 have their security module open, then m_1 and m_2 start a secure session to trade validity reports[2]. The trading policy is implemented in the security module. For each resource type T, the owner/user of a moving object may decide not to participate in the exchange of type T reports. The owner/user may also turn off the security module. However, if it participates in the game, then security module behaves according to the economic model.

4.2 Producer-Paid Reports

In our prior work [19], we studied producer-paid reports. At a high level, the producer-paid model works as follows. When a resource R is announced by its producer, the producer loads with the report $a(R)$ a certain number of coins, C, called the *initial budget* of $a(R)$. When $a(R)$ is received by a peer, it carries a certain budget C_0. A peer earns a flat commission fee f each time it transmits the report to another peer. The remaining budget of the report is divided between the sender and receiver (in order for both to keep propagating the report).

---

[2] The secure session is established based on some public key infrastructure that is omitted in this paper due to space limitations.

Intuitively, the higher the initial budget, the more peers can be reached. In [19] we determined the tradeoff between the initial budget and the effect of advertisement (i.e. the percentage of peers reached by the advertisement).

4.3 Consumer-Paid Reports

Each report $a(R)$ is acquired by the security module of a peer in one of the following two modes:

1. *Consumer.* In consumer mode, the report $a(R)$ is saved in the consumer relation. The consumer relation is accessible by the user so the user can read $a(R)$. The consumer buys new reports according to some strategy (see section 6) but cannot sell them. The price of a report is a function of the relevance of the report.

2. *Broker.* In broker mode the report $a(R)$ is saved in the broker relation. The broker relation is not accessible by the user so the user cannot read $a(R)$. Thus the user in broker mode cannot directly benefit from $a(R)$. The security module simply stores $a(R)$ and forwards it to other peers. A broker pays a percentage of the price of the report. It is paid the same percentage when selling the report to another broker, and it is paid the full price when selling the report to a consumer. How to setup the percentage to maximize the incentive is a subject of our future work. The received payment constitutes the incentive of the broker to participate in the game. A broker may sell $a(R)$ to multiple consumers or brokers. A producer always operates in broker mode for the reports it transmits.

Validity reports acquired in consumer mode are consumer reports, and reports acquired in broker mode are broker reports. At a particular peer a report cannot switch between broker and consumer.

For reports which both the producer and the consumer are willing to pay for, the producer-paid policy and the consumer-paid policy can be combined. For example, initially the report is producer-paid. After the carried budget is used out, the report becomes consumer-paid.

5 Query and Query Processing

With OP2P, each peer m maintains a local reports database. The collection of the local databases of all the peers forms a virtual database to the database application in m. In this section we discuss the query interface to this virtual database and the query processing issue.

5.1 Query Language

In order to motivate the design of our query language, first let us give several typical example queries a user may issue in our environment. These queries are expressed in natural language.

Example 1: Consider a transportation application where a passenger needs to transfer from one bus route to another. Assume that buses can wait for transfer passengers for certain amount of time. Now a transfer passenger Bob wants to transfer to route #8 at a certain intersection P. Bob expects to arrive at P at 10:10. Usually a bus driver is willing to wait at a stop for a transfer passenger for at most 2 minutes. So Bob wants to notify a route #8 bus to wait him if the bus arrives at *P* between 10:08 and 10:10.

Example 2: A hotspot collects the average traffic speed on the inbound 2-miles stretch of the I-290 highway that is centered at the hotspot.

Example 3: Alert when more than 50 taxi cabs are within a certain area at the same time.

Example 4: A driver wants to know all the parking slots located inside the downtown area and the relevance of which is higher than 0.5.

We believe that declarative languages like SQL are the preferred way of express such queries. DRIVE uses the following query template.

SELECT *select-list* [FROM **reports**] WHERE *where-clause*
[GROUP BY *gb-list* [HAVING *having-list*]]
[EPOCH DURATION *epoch* [FOR *time*]]
[REMOTE *query-destination-region* [BUDGET]]

The SELECT, FROM, WHERE, GROUP BY and HAVING clauses are very similar to the functionality of SQL. The relation name **reports** represents the virtual database.

The optional EPOCH DURATION clause specifies the time between successive samplings and for how long the query lasts (see [21]).

The optional REMOTE clause specifies whether the query is to be answered by the local database or is to be evaluated in a remote geographic region. If the REMOTE clause is used, then a query-destination-region should be further specified; it indicates that the query should be disseminated to all the peers in the specified region. If the REMOTE clause is omitted, then the query is processed locally.

BUDGET specifies how much budget in virtual currency the user is willing to spend for disseminating the query and collecting the answers. If BUDGET is omitted, then the database system automatically sets a budget based on the distance to the query-destination-region, the size of the query-destination-region, the peer density, and so on.

Our query template is similar to that provided by TinyDB [21] or Cougar [15]. The difference is that we have the REMOTE...BUDGET clause discussed above.

Finally, we define a member function Rel() for each report description data type. This function takes as input a set of attributes and it returns the relevance using the input as the relevance attributes.

Now we illustrate how our query template can be used to express the query examples given at the beginning of section 4.1 (Queries for examples 2-4 are omitted due to space limitations).

Example 1: The following query notifies a route #8 buses to wait if the bus arrives at *P* between 10:08 and 10:10.

SELECT resource_id
FROM **reports**
WHERE   resource-type=BUS   and   report-description.route_no=8   and
WITHIN_DISTANCE_   SOMETIME_BETWEEN(report-description.Traj,   P,   0,
10:08, 10:10)
REMOTE route_of_bus_ #8

route_no and Traj are two attributes of a bus report. Traj is the *trajectory* of the bus moving object; it defines the object's future location as a piece-wise linear function from time to the two-dimensional geography. WINTIN_DISTANCE_SOMETIME_BETWEEN(a,b,c,d,e) is a predicate introduced in [17]. It is true iff the distance between moving object a and point location b is within c some time between d and e. In our example it is true iff the bus arrives at P some time between 10:08 and 10:10.

If a route #8 bus receives the query and it will wait, then the bus sends Bob an answer to the query.

5.2 Query Processing

We focus on remote query processing. A remote query from moving object m is processed in three steps. First, the trajectory of the querying moving object is attached to the query, so that the answering objects know where to return answers. As explained earlier, the trajectory defines the object's future location as a piecewise linear function from time to the two-dimensional geography. It may be constructed based on the shortest path between the origin and the destination of the object, and the traffic speeds on each road segment along the path. The origin and destination are provided, for example, by the car navigation system. In the second step, the query is disseminated from m to the moving objects in the query-destination-region (given in the REMOTE clause). Finally the answers are returned to m. We concentrate on the query dissemination step and the answer delivery step in the rest of this section.

Query dissemination. Simple flooding can always be used for query dissemination, but this may unnecessarily incur a high communication cost. For example, if the receiving object is moving away from the query destination region, then propagating the query to it may be wasteful. So the question is: when a moving object m_1 that is carrying a query encounters another moving object m_2, how m_1 decides whether to forward the query to m_2? The objective is to reach an optimal tradeoff between communication cost and accuracy of answers. We postulate that the decision should depend on the location and the moving direction of m_2 relative to the query-destination-region, the shape of the query-destination-region, the density of moving objects, and the budget of the query.

Answer Delivery. There can be several strategies to propagate the answer back to the query originator m. First, each moving object can send m the answers it is aware of; in turn, m consolidates the results (e.g. eliminates duplicates). The second possibility is that a leader is elected in the query-destination-region; the leader collects and consolidates the answers of the responding objects, before delivering them to m. The third possibility is a hybrid, hierarchical solution, in which leaders of small sub-areas propagate to leaders of larger areas.

6 Information Usage Strategies and Transactional Issues

Information Usage Strategies
When multiple consumers hear about the same competitive resource (such as a parking slot or a cab customer), they may all head to that resource, leading to

contention. In order to address this phenomenon of "herding", a consumer needs to be selective when buying and acting on reports. In our prior work [1] we proposed an approach called Information Guided Searing (IGS) strategy to address this issue. In this approach, a consumer goes to a resource only when the relevance of the report is higher than an adaptive threshold. We compared by simulations the above information usage with the naive resource discovery approach where information is not used. The results showed that in some cases IGS cuts discovery time by more than 75%. We are studying strategies for using information to capture (i.e. reach before other competitors) geospatially distributed resources.

Transactional Issues

The transaction between two peers consists of a handshake initiation that includes the types of resources each one is interested in consuming/brokering, followed by the report exchange and coin charge/credit for each report. Observe that these operations must be executed as a distributed atomic transaction. For example, the credit of one account should be committed only if the debit of the other account is committed; and in turn, this should occur if and only if the corresponding report was received properly. Therefore, the transaction must be followed by a commit protocol. The problem is that, due to the high mobility at which the transaction occurs, the commit protocol between two peers may not begin or may not complete.

We propose to resolve this problem by a Mobile Peer-to-Peer Transaction (MOPT) mechanism which is a combination of an audit trail (or log) maintained online in the security module, and a central bank to which the audit trails of all peers are transmitted periodically, e.g. once a day. Our proposed MOPT mechanism has an online component that executes at the security module for each transaction, and an offline component.

The online component of MOPT at a security module S performs the following functions. It keeps a log of the reports that have been exchanged and the credit/debit charged for each one. The records of this log correspond to the log records in database transaction recovery. When a transaction completes unsuccessfully, then the user of S is still charged and can use the reports it received, and gets credit for the reports it (thinks it) sold. So if a broker B sent a report to a consumer C, but didn't receive the commit message, it still gets (temporary) credit.

The offline component of MOPT, at the end of the day sends to a central bank the logs of the transactions that completed unsuccessfully during the day. After receiving all the logs from all the peers, the central bank does the following for the transactions that completed unsuccessfully at one or both participants (thus it ignores transactions that completed successfully at both participants). If the same transaction completed unsuccessfully at both participants, then the traces from the respective security modules are used to settle the credit/charge to both accounts. In the example above, if C didn't receive the report, B's credit will be reversed. If the transaction completed unsuccessfully at only one of the participants, i.e. the transaction is absent from the other security module trace, this fact indicates how the account at the unsuccessful participant should be settled. In this case, in the example above, B's credit will be made permanent.

Observe that our MOPT mechanism needs to remember only the logs of unsuccessfully completed transactions, but can forget successfully completed transactions. Considering that peers may execute thousands of transaction per day, this is an important property.

Observe that this offline banking mechanism violates to some extent our principle of a completely decentralized economy. We will examine the framework/principles that can be enforced for a given level of decentralization. For example, assume that it is tolerable that occasionally peers may receive reports without paying, and some other peers may transmit resources without being paid. However, the system should provide integrity for the total amount of virtual currency in the system, namely virtual currency should not be lost or created. What is the maximum amount of decentralization allowed by this framework? Can the central bank be eliminated by doing so? In other words, we consider the semantic properties of our mobile peer-to-peer application to enable maximum decentralization; and this distinguishes our research from the extensive body of existing work on transactions/serializability issues.

7 Relevant Work

Traditional Peer-to-Peer Approaches
A traditional peer-to-peer approach like Gnutella [20] could be used to search spatio-temporal resources, the problem addressed in this paper. In Gnutella, a query for a resource type (expressed by key words) is flooded on the overlay network (within predefined hops), and replies are routed back to the querying node along the same path as the query message. In other words, resource information is *pulled* by the querying node from the resource producer. This generates two problems in our context. First, since resources are transient and consumers do not know when they are generated, a consumer will have to constantly flood its query in order to catch resource information. Second, this does not work if there is not a path between the querying node and the resource producer. In our approach, a resource report is *pushed* by the resource producer to consumers via opportunistic dissemination and the dissemination area is automatically bounded by information prioritization. Gridella [12] and DHT systems such as Chord [14] have similar problems as Gnutella in that they use a *pull* model. In addition, Gridella and DHT systems require that the complete identifier (or key) of the searched data item be provided in a query, whereas in our case a consumer does not know a priori the keys of the searched resources.

Resource Discovery and Data Dissemination in Mobile Distributed Environments
Resource discovery and data dissemination in mobile distributed environments have been repeatedly studied (see e.g. [3, 16, 8]). Some use the gossiping/epidemic paradigm [16, 8] which is similar to our OP2P approach. All this work considers dissemination of regular data items rather than spatio-temporal information. None of them discusses information prioritization and incentive mechanisms.

Static Sensor Networks
A database approach has been applied to static sensor networks in Cougar [15], TinyDB [13], and direct diffusion [2]. All these methods require that a certain graph structure such as a tree be established in the network such that each node aggregates the results returned by its downstream nodes and its own result, and forwards the aggregation result to its upstream node. However, in our environment, due to the

dynamic and unpredictable network topology, such a graph structure is hard to maintain. Our distributed query processing relies on opportunistic interactions between mobile nodes and therefore is totally different than Cougar and TinyDB.

Incentive Mechanisms for P2P and MANET

Our economic model, including virtual currency, security module, and consumer-paid policy, is inspired by the work of Buttyan and Hubaux [5] on stimulating packet forwarding in MANET. In their work, a node receives one unit of virtual currency for forwarding a message of another node, and such virtual currency units (nuglets) are deducted from the sender (or the destination). In our model, however, the amount of virtual currency charged by an intermediary node (broker) for forwarding a report is proportional to the expected benefit of the report, the latter depending on the dynamic spatio-temporal properties of the report (age and distance) as well as various system environmental parameters.

To the best of our knowledge, our work is the first one that attempts to quantify the relevance of spatio-temporal information and to price based on the benefit of information to the consumer rather than the cost of forwarding it. This distinguishes our work from many other incentive mechanisms (see e.g. [9, 10]) which concentrate on compensating forwarding cost in terms of battery power, memory, CPU cycles. In a vehicular network such cost is negligible.

8 Conclusion

In this paper we devised a platform for dissemination of spatial and temporal resource-information in a mobile peer-to-peer network environment, in which the database is distributed among the moving objects. The moving objects also serve as routers of queries and answers. The platform includes spatio-temporal resource data model, database maintenance via opportunistic peer-to-peer interactions, relevance evaluation for information prioritization, query language and query processing, economical model that provides incentive for peers to participate as information suppliers and intermediaries, information usage strategies, and transaction management.

In general, we feel that the P2P paradigm is a tidal wave that has tremendous potential, as Napster and Gnutella have already demonstrated for entertainment resources. Mobile P2P is the next step, and it will revolutionize dissemination of spatial and temporal resources. For example, location based services have been considered a hot topic for quite some time, and it has been assumed that they have to be provided by a separate commercial entity such as the cellular service providers. The approach outlined in this paper can provide an alternative that bypasses the commercial entity.

References

1. O. Wolfson, B. Xu, Y. Yin, Dissemination of Spatial-Temporal Information in Mobile Networks with Hotspots, *DBISP2P* 2004.
2. C. Intanagonwiwat, et al. Directed Diffusion: A Scalable and Robust Communication Paradigm for Sensor Networks. *Proceedings of MobiCOM*, 2000.

3. A. Helmy. Efficient Resource Discovery in Wireless AdHoc Networks: Contacts Do Help. Book Chapter in *Resource Management in Wireless Networking* by Kluwer Academic Publishers, May 2004.
4. http://firechief.com/ar/firefighting_roborescuers_increase_disaster/
5. L. Buttyan and J.P. Hubaux. Stimulating Cooperation in Self-Organizing Mobile Ad Hoc Networks. ACM/Kluwer Mobile Networks and Applications (MONET), 8(5), October 2003.
6. A. Pfitzmann, B. Pfitzmann, and M. Waidner. Trusting Mobile User Devices and Security Modules. *IEEE Computer*, February 1997.
7. A. Markowetz, et al. Exploiting the Internet As a Geospatial Database, *International Workshop on Next Generation Geospatial Information*, 2003.
8. M. Papadopouli et al. Effects of Power Conservation, Wireless Coverage and Cooperation on Data Dissemination Among Mobile Devices. *MobiHoc 2001*, Long Beach, California.
9. S. Zhong, et al. Sprite: A Simple, Cheat-Proof, Credit-Based System for Mobile Ad-Hoc Networks. In *Proceedings of IEEE INFOCOM* 2003.
10. R. Krishnan, et al. The economics of peer-to-peer networks, Carnegie Mellon University, 2002.
11. K. Yoon and C. Hwang. *Multiple Attribute Decision Making: An Introduction.* Sage Publications, 1995.
12. K. Aberer, et al. Improving Data Access in P2P Systems, *Internet Computing*, 6(1), 2002.
13. J. Hellerstein, et al. Beyond Average: Toward Sophisticated Sensing with Queries. *The Second International Workshop on Information Processing in Sensor Networks*, 2003.
14. I. Stoica, R. Morris, et al. Chord: A Scalable Peer-to-Peer Lookup Service for Internet Applications. In *Procs. ACM SIGCOMM*, 2001.
15. Y. Yao, J. Gehrke. Query Processing in Sensor Networks. *First Biennial Conference on Innovative Data Systems Research*, 2003.
16. K. Rothermel, C. Becker, and J. Hahner. Consistent Update Diffusion in Mobile Ad Hoc Networks. *Technical Report 2002/04*, CS Department, University of Stuttgart, 2002.
17. M. Vazirgiannis, O. Wolfson. A Spatiotemporal Query Language for Moving Objects. *Proceedings of the 7th International Symposium on Spatial and Temporal Databases*, 2001.
18. T. Michael. *Machine Learning.* McGraw-Hill, 1997.
19. O. Wolfson, B. Xu, P. Sistla. An Economic Model for Resource Exchange in Mobile Peer-to-Peer Networks. *Proceedings of SSDBM 2004.*
20. Gnutella website. http://gnutella.wego.com
21. S. Madden, et al. *TinyDB: In-Network Query processing in TinyOS*, Intel Research, October 15, 2002.
22. B. Wilcox-O'Hearn. Experiences Deploying a Large Scale Emergent Network. *International Workshop on Peer-toPeer Systems*, 2002.

On Using Histograms as Routing Indexes in Peer-to-Peer Systems*

Yannis Petrakis, Georgia Koloniari, and Evaggelia Pitoura

Department of Computer Science,
University of Ioannina, Greece
{pgiannis, kgeorgia, pitoura}@cs.uoi.gr

Abstract. Peer-to-peer systems offer an efficient means for sharing data among autonomous nodes. A central issue is locating the nodes with data matching a user query. A decentralized solution to this problem is based on using routing indexes which are data structures that describe the content of neighboring nodes. Each node uses its routing index to route a query towards those of its neighbors that provide the largest number of results. We consider using histograms as routing indexes. We describe a decentralized procedure for clustering similar nodes based on histograms. Similarity between nodes is defined based on the set of queries they match and related with the distance between their histograms. Our experimental results show that using histograms to cluster similar nodes and to route queries increases the number of results returned for a given number of nodes visited.

1 Introduction

The popularity of file sharing systems such as Napster, Gnutella and KaZaA has spurred much current attention to peer-to-peer (p2p) computing. Peer-to-peer computing refers to a form of distributed computing that involves a large number of autonomous computing nodes (the peers) that cooperate to share resources and services [11]. A central issue in p2p systems is identifying which peers contain data relevant to a user query. There two basic types of p2p systems with regards to the way data are distributed among peers: structured and unstructured ones.

In *structured p2p* systems, data items (or indexes) are placed at specific peers usually based on distributed hashing (DHTs) such as in CAN [13] and Chord [6]. With distributed hashing, each data item is associated with a key and each peer is assigned a range of keys and thus items. Peers are interconnected via a regular topology where peers that are close in the key space are highly interconnected. Although DHTs provide efficient search, they compromise peer autonomy. The DHT topology is regulated since all peers have the same number of neighboring peers and the selection of peers is strictly determined by the DHTs semantics. Furthermore, sophisticated load balancing procedures are required.

---

* Work supported in part by the IST programme of the European Commission FET under the IST-2001-32645 DBGlobe project.

W.S. Ng et al. (Eds.): DBISP2P 2004, LNCS 3367, pp. 16–30, 2005.

In *unstructured p2p* systems, there is no assumption about the placement of data items in the peers. When there is no information about the location of data items, flooding and its variation are used to discover the peers that maintain data relevant to a query. With flooding (such as in Gnutella), the peer where the query is originated contacts its neighbor peers which in turn contact their own neighbors until a peer with relevant data is reached. Flooding incurs large network overheads, thus to confine flooding, indexes are deployed. Such indexes can be either centralized (as in Napster) or distributed among the peers of the system providing for each peer a partial view of the system.

In this paper, we use a form of distributed index called routing index [3]. Each peer maintains a local index of all data available locally. It also maintains for each of its links, one routing index that summarizes the content of all peers reachable through this link within a given number of hops. We propose using histograms as local and routing indexes. Such histograms are used to route range queries and maximize the number of results returned for a given number of peers visited.

In addition, we use histograms to cluster peers that match the same set of queries. The similarity of two peers is defined based on the distance of the histograms used as their local indexes. The motivation for such clustering is that once in the appropriate cluster, all relevant to a query peers are a few links apart. In addition, we add a number of links among clusters to allow inter-cluster routing. Our clustering procedure is fully decentralized.

Our experimental results show that our procedure is effective: in the constructed clustered peer-to-peer system, the network distance of two peers is proportional to the distance of their local indexes. Furthermore, routing is very efficient, in particular, for a given number of visited peers, the results returned are 60% more than in an unclustered system.

Preliminary versions of a clustering procedure based on local indexes appears in [12] where Bloom filters are used for keyword queries on documents. The deployment of histograms as routing indexes for range selection queries, the routing procedure and the experimental results are new in this paper. As opposed to Bloom filters that only indicate the existence of relevant data, histograms allow for an ordering of peers based on the estimated results they provide to a query. This leads to a clustered p2p system in which the network distance of two peers is analogous to the estimated results.

The remainder of this paper is structured as follows. In Section 2, we introduce histograms as routing indexes and appropriate distance metrics. In Section 3, we describe how histograms are used to route queries and to cluster relevant peers. In Section 4, we present our experimental results. Finally, in Section 5, we compare our work with related research, and in Section 6 offer our conclusions.

2   Histograms in Peer-to-Peer Systems

We assume a p2p system with a set N of peers n_i. The number of peers changes as peers leave and join the system. Each peer is connected to a small number of other peers called its *neighbors*. Peers store data items. A query q may be posed at any of the peers, while data items satisfying the query may be located at many peers of the system. We call the peers with data satisfying the query *matching* peers. Our goal is to route the query to its matching peers efficiently.

2.1   Histograms as Routing Indexes

We consider a p2p system where each peer stores a relation R with a numeric attribute x and focus on routing range selection queries on x. Our approach is based on using local indexes to describe the content of each peer. In particular, each peer n maintains a summary, called local index, that describes its content. A property of the index is that we can determine, with high probability, whether the peer matches the query based on the index of the peer, that is, without looking at the actual content of the peer. We propose using histograms as local indexes.

A histogram on an attribute x is constructed by partitioning the data distribution of x into b (≥ 1) mutually disjoint subsets called *buckets* and approximating the frequencies and values in each bucket. Histograms are widely used as a mechanism for compression and approximations of data distributions for selectivity estimation, approximate query answering and load balancing [7]. In this paper, we use histograms for clustering and query routing in p2p systems. We consider *equi-width* histograms, that is, we divide the value set of attribute x into ranges of equal width and keep the percentage of x's occurrences for each bucket. In addition, we maintain the total number of all tuples (the histogram *size*).

We denote by $LI(n)$ the histogram used as the local index of peer n. Besides its local index, each peer n maintains one routing index $RI(n, e)$ for each of its links e. $RI(n, e)$ summarizes the content of all peers that are reachable from n using link e at a distance at most R. The routing indexes are also histograms defined next.

We shall use the notation $H(n)$ to denote a histogram (used either as a local index $LI(n)$ or as a routing index $RI(n, e)$), $H_i(n)$ to denote its i-th bucket, $0 \leq i \leq b - 1$, and $S(H(n))$ to denote its size. Then,

Definition 1 (Histogram-Based Routing Index). *The histogram-based routing index $RI(n, e)$ of radius R of the link e of peer n is defined as follows: for $0 \leq i \leq b - 1$, $RI_i(n, e) = (\Sigma_{p \in P} LI_i(p) * S(LI(p))/\Sigma_{p \in P} S(LI(p))$ and $S(RI(n, e)) = \Sigma_{p \in P} S(LI(p))$ where P is the set of all peers p within distance R of n reachable through link e.*

An example is shown in Fig. 1. The set of peers within distance R of n is called the *horizon* of radius R of n.

As usual, we make the *uniform frequency* assumption and approximate all frequencies in a bucket by their average. We also make the *continuous values* assumption, where all possible values in the domain of x that lie in the range of the bucket are assumed to be present. However, there is a probability that although a value is indicated as present by the histogram, it does not really exist in the data (false positive). This is shown to depend on the number of buckets,

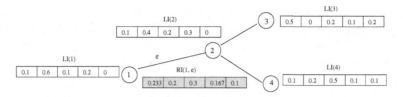

Fig. 1. The local indexes of peers 1, 2, 3, and 4 and the routing index of link e of peer 1 for radius $R = 2$, assuming that local indexes $LI(2)$, $LI(3)$ and $LI(4)$ have the same size

the number of tuples and the range of the attribute. Details can be found in the Appendix.

For a given query q, the local histogram $LI(n)$ of peer n provides an estimation of the number of results (matching tuples) of peer n, while the routing index $RI(n, e)$ provides an estimation of the number of results that can be found when the query is routed through link e. We denote by $results(n, q)$ the actual number of results to query q and by $hresults(H(n), q)$ the number of results estimated by the histogram $H(n)$. Let a query $q_k = \{x: a \leq x \leq a + k * d\}$, where d is equal to the range of each bucket, $0 \leq k \leq b$ and $a = c * d$, where $0 \leq c \leq b - 1$. We also consider the queries $q_< = \{x: x \leq a\}$ and $q_> = \{x: x \geq a\}$. Note that query $q_>$ is the same with query q_b.

We can estimate $results(n, q)$ using the histogram $H(n)$ of peer n based on the type of the query q as follows:

- q_k: $hresults(H(n), q_k) = S(H(n)) * \Sigma_{i=a/d}^{((a+k*d)/d)} H_i(n)$
- $q_<$: $hresults(H(n), q_<) = S(H(n)) * \Sigma_{i=0}^{a/d} H_i(n)$
- $q_>$: $hresults(H(n), q_>) = S(H(n)) * \Sigma_{i=a/d}^{b} H_i(n)$

We defined the query q_k as starting from the lower limit of a bucket ($a = c * d$), for simplicity.

2.2 Using Histograms for Clustering

Ideally, we would like to route each query q only through the peers that have the most number of results (top-k matching peers). To express this, we define *PeerRecall* as our performance measure. *PeerRecall* expresses how far from the optimal a routing protocol performs. Let V be a set of peers ($V \subseteq N$), by $Sresults(V, q)$ we denote the sum of the numbers of results (i.e., matching tuples) returned by each peer that belongs to V.

$$Sresults(V, q) = \Sigma_{v \in V} results(v, q) \tag{1}$$

Definition 2 (PeerRecall). *Let Visited (Visited $\subseteq N$) be the set of peers visited during the routing of a query q and Optimal (Optimal $\subseteq N$) be the set of peers such that $|Optimal| = |Visited|$ and $v \in Optimal \Leftrightarrow results(v, q) \geq results(u, q), \forall u \notin Optimal$. We define PeerRecall as: $PeerRecall(q) = Sresults(Visited, q)/Sresults(Optimal, q)$.*

Intuitively, to increase *Peer Recall*, peers that match similar queries must be linked to each other. This is because, if such peers are grouped together, once we find one matching peer, all others are nearby. The network *distance* between two peers n_i and n_j, $dist(n_i, n_j)$ is the length of the shortest path from n_i to n_j. In general, peers that match similar queries should have small network distances. Our goal is to cluster peers, so that peers in the same cluster match similar queries. The links between peers in the same cluster are called *short-range* links. We also provide a few links, called *long-range* links, among peers in different clusters. Long-range links serve to reduce the maximum distance between any two peers in the system, called the *diameter* of the system. They are used for inter-cluster routing.

To cluster peers, we propose using their local indexes. That is, we cluster peers that have similar local histograms. For this to work, the distance (d) between two histograms must be descriptive of the difference in the number of results to any given query.

Property 1. Let $LI(n_1)$, $LI(n_2)$ and $LI(n_3)$ be the local indexes of three peers n_1, n_2 and n_3. If $d(LI(n_1), LI(n_2)) \geq d(LI(n_1), LI(n_3))$, then $|results(n_1, q)/S(LI(n_1)) - results(n_2, q)/S(LI(n_2))| \geq |results(n_1, q)/S(LI(n_1)) - results(n_3, q)/S(LI(n_3))|$.

That is, we want the distance of two histograms to be descriptive of the difference in the number of results they return for a given query workload. In the following, as a first step we consider how two well-known distance metrics perform with respect to the above property.

Histogram Distances. The L_1-distance of two histograms $H(n_1)$ and $H(n_2)$ is defined as:

Definition 3 (L_1 Distance Between Histograms). *Let two histograms $H(n_1)$ and $H(n_2)$ with b buckets, their L_1 distance, $d_{L_1}(H(n_1), H(n_2))$ is defined as:* $d_{L_1}(H(n_1), H(n_2)) = \Sigma_{i=0}^{b-1} |H_i(n_1) - H_i(n_2)|$.

Let us define as

$$L1(i) = H_i(n_1) - H_i(n_2). \tag{2}$$

then

$$d_{L_1}(H(n_1), H(n_2)) = \Sigma_{l=0}^{b-1} |L1(l)| \tag{3}$$

The histograms we study are *ordinal* histograms, that is, there exists an ordering among their buckets, since they are built on numeric attributes. For ordinal histograms, the position of the buckets is important and thus, we want the definition of histogram distance to also take into account this ordering. This property is called *shuffling dependence*. For example, for the three histograms of Fig. 2, the distance between histograms $H(n_1)$ and $H(n_2)$ that have all their values at adjacent buckets ($H_i(n_1)$ and $H_{i+1}(n_2)$ respectively) should be smaller than the distance between histograms $H(n_1)$ and $H(n_3)$ that have their values at buckets further apart. This is because, the difference of results for peers n_1

Fig. 2. Intuitively, the distance between $H(n_1)$ and $H(n_2)$ should be smaller than the distance between $H(n_1)$ and $H(n_3)$

and n_2 is smaller for a larger number of range queries than for peers n_1 and n_3. The shuffling dependence property does not hold for d_{L_1}, since the three histograms have the same pair-wise distances.

We now consider an edit distance based similarity metric between histograms for which the shuffling dependence property holds. The edit distance between two histograms $H(n_1)$ and $H(n_2)$ is the total number of all necessary minimum movements for transforming $H(n_1)$ to $H(n_2)$ by moving elements to the left or right. It has been shown that this is expressed by the following definition [2]:

Definition 4 (Edit Distance Between Histograms). *Let two histograms* $H(n_1)$ *and* $H(n_2)$ *with b buckets, their edit distance,* $d_e(H(n_1), H(n_2))$ *is defined as:* $d_e(H(n_1), H(n_2)) = \Sigma_{i=0}^{b-1}|\Sigma_{j=0}^{i}(H_j(n_1) - H_j(n_2))|.$

Let us define as

$$pref(l) = \Sigma_{i=0}^{l}H_i(n_1) - \Sigma_{i=0}^{l}H_i(n_2) \qquad (4)$$

then

$$d_e(H(n_1), H(n_2)) = \Sigma_{l=0}^{b-1}|pref(l)| \qquad (5)$$

Let a query $q_k = \{x: a \leq x \leq a + k * d$, where d is equal to the range of each bucket and $0 \leq k \leq b\}$.

Given that a is chosen uniformly at random from the domain of x, then the difference in the results is equal to:

$$|hresults(H(n_1), q_k)/S(H(n_1)) - hresults(H(n_2), q_k)/S(H(n_2))| =$$
$$\Sigma_{j=0}^{b-1}|pref(j + k) - pref(j - 1)| \qquad (6)$$

where $pref(j) = 0$ for $j \geq b - 1$ and $j < 0$.

From Equation 6, for $k = b - 1$ that is for queries $x \geq a$ Property 1 holds. It also holds for $x \leq a$. It does not hold however, in general.

To summarize, the L_1 distance satisfies Property 1 for q_0 (that is for queries that cover one bucket), while the edit distance satisfies Property 1 for $q_<$ and $q_>$ (which is the same with q_b).

3   Query Routing and Network Construction

We describe next how histogram-based indexes can be used to route a query and to cluster similar peers together. We distinguish between two types of links:

short-range or *short* links that connect similar peers and *long-range* or *long* links that connect non-similar peers. Two peers belong to the same *cluster* if and only if there is a path consisting only of short links between them. We describe first how queries are routed and then how long and short links are created.

3.1   Query Routing

A query q may be posed at any peer n. Our goal is to route the query q through peers that give a large number of results for q. Ideally, we would like to visit only those peers that provide the most results. To maximize *PeerRecall*, we use a greedy query routing heuristic: each peer that receives a query propagates it through those of its links whose routing indexes indicate that they lead to peers that provide the largest number of results. The routing of a query stops either when a predefined number of peers is visited or when a satisfactory number of results is located. Specifically, for a query q posed at peer n:

1. First, n checks its local index and if the index indicates that there may be matching data locally, it retrieves them.
2. Then, n checks whether the maximum number of visited peers ($MaxVisited$) has been reached or the desired number of matching data items (results) has been attained. If so, the routing of the query stops.
3. Else, n propagates the query through the link e whose routing index gives the most matches ($hresults(RI(n,e),q) > hresults(RI(n,l),q)$, $\forall$ link $l \neq e$) and e has not been followed yet. If $hresults(RI(n,e),q) = 0$, $\forall$ link e that has not been followed, query propagation stops.

By following the link e whose $hresults(RI(n,e),q)$ returns the largest value, the query is propagated towards the peers with the most results and thus *PeerRecall* is increased.

When a query reaches a peer that has no links whose routing indexes indicate a positive number of results, or when all such links have already been followed, backtracking is used. This state can be reached either by a false positive or when the desired number of results has not been attained yet. In this case, the query is returned to the previous visited peer that checks whether there are any other links with indexes with results for the query that have not been followed yet, and propagates the query through one or more of them. If there are no such matching links, it sends the query to its previous peer and so on. Thus, each peer should store the peer that propagated the query to it. In addition, we store an identifier for each query to avoid cycles. Note that this corresponds to a Depth-First traversal.

To avoid situations in which all routing indexes indicate that there are no results, initially we use the following variation of the routing procedure. If no matching link has been found during the routing of the query, and the current peer n has no matching links ($hresults(RI(n,e), q) = 0$ $\forall$ link e of n), which means that the matching peers (if any) are outside the radius R of n, then the long-range link of this peer is followed (even if it does not match the query). The idea is that we want to move to another region of the network, since the current region (bounded by the horizon) has no matching peers. In the case that the peer has no long-range link or we have already followed all long-range links, the query is propagated through a short link to a neighbor peer and so on until a long-range link is found.

3.2   Clustering

We describe how routing indexes can be used for distributed clustering. The idea is to use the local index of each new peer as a query and route this towards the peers that have most similar indexes.

In particular, each new peer that enters the system tries to find a relevant cluster of peers. Then, it links with a number SL of peers in this cluster through short links. Also, with probability P_l, it links with a peer that does not belong to this cluster through a long link. Short links are inserted so that peers with relevant data are located nearby in the p2p system. Long links are used for keeping the network diameter small. The motivation is that we want to be easy to find both all relevant results once in the right cluster, and the relevant cluster once in another cluster, thus increasing *PeerRecall*.

When a new peer n wishes to join the system, a join message that contains its local index $LI(n)$ is posed as a query to a well known peer in the system. The join message also maintains a list L (initially empty) with all peers visited during the routing of the join message. The join message is propagated until up to $JMaxVisited$ peers are visited.

Whenever the join message reaches a peer p the procedure is the following:

1. The distance $d(LI(n), LI(p))$ between local indexes $LI(n)$ and $LI(p)$ is calculated.
2. Peer p and the corresponding distance are added to list L.
3. If the maximum number of visited peers $JMaxVisited$ is reached, the routing of the join message stops.
4. Else, the distances $d(LI(n), RI(p, e))$ between the local index $LI(n)$ of the new peer n and the routing indexes $RI(p, e)$ that correspond to each of the links e of peer p are calculated.
5. The message is propagated through the link e with the smallest distance that has not been followed yet, because there is a higher probability to find the relevant cluster through this link. When the message reaches a peer with no other links that have not been followed, backtracking is used.

When routing stops, the new peer selects to be linked through short links to the SL peers of the list L whose local indexes have the SL smallest distances from the local index of the new peer. It also connects to one of the rest of the peers in the list through a long link with probability P_l.

An issue is how the peer that will be attached to the new peer through the long link is selected. One approach is to select randomly one of the rest of the peers within the list (that does not belong to the SL peers selected to be linked through short links). Another approach is to select one of the rest of the peers within the list with a probability based on their distances from the new peer. Thus, we rank these peers based on their distances, where the first in the ranking is the one with the smallest distance and has $rank = 0$. The second in the ranking has $rank = 1$ and so on. The probability that a specific peer from the list is selected with respect to its ranking is: $\alpha * (1 - \alpha)^{rank}$, where $0 < \alpha < 1$. The smaller the value of α, the greater the probability to create a long link with a more dissimilar peer.

4   Experimental Results

We implemented a simulator in C to test the efficiency of our approach. The size of the network varies from 500 to 1500 peers and the radius of the horizon from 1 to 3. Each new peer creates 1 to 2 short links ($SL = 1$ or 2) and one long link with probability $P_l = 0.4$. The routing of the join message stops when a maximum number ($JMaxVisited$) of peers is visited. The routing of a query stops when a maximum number ($MaxVisited$) of peers is visited. Both numbers are set to 5% of the existing peers. Each peer stores a relation with an integer attribute $x \in [0, 499]$ with 1000 tuples. The tuples are summarized by a histogram with 50 buckets. 70% of the tuples of each peer belong to one bucket, and the rest are uniformly distributed among the remaining buckets. The tuples in each bucket also follow the uniform distribution. The input parameters are summarized in Table 1.

Table 1. Input parameters

Parameter	Default Value	Range
Number of peers	500	500-1500
Radius of the horizon	2	1-3
Number of short links (SL)	2	1-2
Probability of long link (P_l)	0.4	
Perc of peers visited during join ($JMaxVisited$)	5	
Perc of peers visited during search ($MaxVisited$)	5	
Histogram-related parameters		
Number of buckets (b)	50	
Domain of x	[0, 499]	
Tuples per peer	1000	
Range of queries	2	0-4

We compare first the two distance metrics. Then, we evaluate the clustering and the query routing procedures.

4.1   Histogram Distance Metrics

We run a set of experiments to evaluate the performance of the two histogram distance metrics (the L_1 and the edit distance). For simplicity of presentation, in the reported experiment, we use histograms with 10 buckets and $x \in [0, 99]$. We used a workload with queries having range (k) varying from 0 (covering data in 1 bucket) to 4 (covering data in 5 buckets). We use 10 histograms $H(i)$ $0 \leq i < 10$ with 10 buckets each, that have 70% of their data in bucket i and the rest uniformly distributed among the other buckets. We compute the distance of each histogram with $H(0)$ using the two distance metrics. Our performance measure is the difference in the number of results for each histogram with $H(0)$, that is:

$$|hresults(H(n), q_k)/S(H(n)) - hresults(H(0), q_k)/S(H(0))|, \ 1 \leq n < 10$$

with respect to the distance of the respected histograms (that is, whether Property 1 is satisfied).

Figure 3(left) shows the results when the L_1 distance is used. Due to the nature of the data, all compared histograms have the same distance. The distance of the histograms has no relation with the difference in the number of results. This is because the L_1 distance compares only the respective buckets of each histogram without taking into account their neighboring buckets which however influence the behavior of queries with ranges larger than 0.

The edit distance (Fig. 3(right)) outperforms L_1. In particular, as the distance between the histograms increases, their respective differences in the results also increases. However, for each query range this occurs until some point after which the difference in the results becomes constant irrespectively of the histogram distance. This is explained as follows. The edit distance between two histograms takes into account the ordering of all buckets, while a query with range r involves only $r + 1$ buckets, and thus it does not depend on the difference that the two histograms may have in the rest of their buckets. For example, for a query with range 0, the difference in the results remains constant while the histogram distances increase. This is because the query involves only single buckets while the edit distance considers the whole histogram. Thus, the edit distance works better for queries with large ranges.

We also calculated the average performance of the two distance metrics for a mixed query workload of queries with range from 0 to 4 (Fig. 4). L_1 has the worst overall performance since although the distance between the various

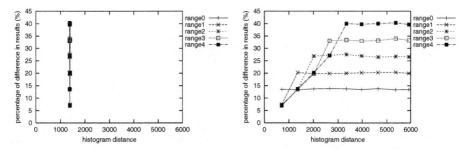

Fig. 3. Relation of the number of results returned with the histogram distance using (left) the L_1 distance and (right) the edit distance

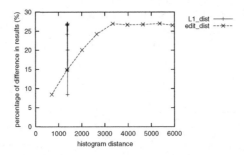

Fig. 4. Comparison of histogram distances

histograms is constant, the difference in the number of results increases. The edit distance behaves better. The difference in results increases until a point and then it becomes constant. If we continue with ranges larger than 4, this point occurs later.

4.2   Cluster Quality

In this set of experiments, we evaluate the quality of clustering. For these experiments, we assume a query workload with range 2 (whose results occupy 3 buckets). We compare the constructed clustered network with a randomly constructed p2p system, that is a p2p system in which each new peer connects randomly to an existing peer (random construction and routing) (*random*).

We measure the average histogram distance between the peers that are at various network distances from each other in the created p2p network. We use a network of 500 nodes and radius 2, and conduct the same experiment for $SL = 1$ (Fig. 5(left)) and $SL = 2$ (Fig. 5(right)). As the network distance between two peers increases, their histogram distance increases too, for both histogram distance metrics and for both 1 and 2 short links. This means that the more similar two peers are, the closer in the network they are expected to be. The rate of increase of the histogram distance is large when the network distance is small and decreases as the network distance increases, due to the

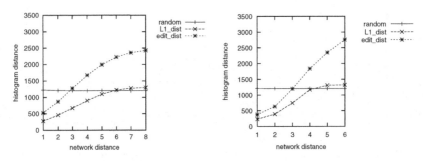

Fig. 5. Cluster quality with (left) $SL = 1$ and (right) $SL = 2$

denser clustering of similar peers in a particular area of the network (e.g., the formation of clusters of similar peers). The edit distance has a larger increase rate for large network distances (4 and above for 2 short links and 6 and above for 1 short link) than the L_1 distance (which remains nearly constant for these network distances). The conclusion is that in the network built using the edit distance, some kind of ordering among the peers in different clusters is achieved. For the random network, the histogram distance is constant for all network distances, since there is no clustering of similar peers.

4.3   Query Routing

In this set of experiments, we evaluate the performance of query routing using as our performance measure *PeerRecall* (as defined in Def. 2). We compare the constructed clustered network with a randomly constructed p2p, that is a p2p system in which each new peer connects randomly to an existing peer (random construction and routing) (*random*). We also consider a randomly constructed p2p system that uses histograms only for query routing (*random_join*).

We use a network of 500 peers and examine the influence of the horizon in the query routing performance for $SL = 1$ (Fig. 6(left)) and $SL = 2$ (Fig. 6(right)). The radius varies from 1 to 3; we use queries with range = 2. Using histograms for both clustering and query routing results in much better performance than using histograms only for routing or not using histograms at all. For radius 2 and for 2 short links, we have the best performance. For 1 short link, *PeerRecall* increases as the radius of the horizon increases, since each peer has information about the content of more peers. For 2 short links, *PeerRecall* decreases for radius greater than 2. The reason is that there are more links, and thus, much more peers are included within the horizon of a particular peer (when compared with the network built using 1 short link). Thus, a very large number of peers correspond to each routing index. This results in losing more information than when using radius 2. Thus, for each type of network there is an optimal value of the radius that gives the best performance.

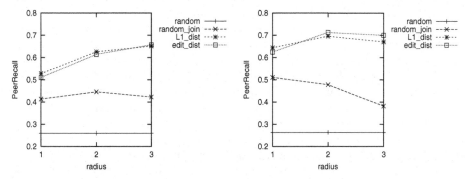

Fig. 6. Routing for different values of the radius and with (left) $SL = 1$ and (right) $SL = 2$

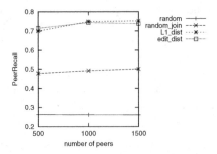

Fig. 7. Varying the number of nodes

Next, we examine how our algorithms perform with a larger number of peers. We vary the size of the network from 500 to 1500. Radius is set to 2 and we use 2 short links and queries with range = 2. As shown in Fig. 7, *PeerRecall* remains nearly constant for both histogram distance metrics and outperforms the *random_join* and the *random* networks.

5   Related Work

Many recent research efforts focus on organizing peers in clusters based on their content. In most cases, the number or the description of the clusters is fixed and global knowledge of this information is required. In this paper, we describe a fully decentralized clustering procedure that uses histograms to cluster peers that answer similar queries. In [1], peers are partitioned into topic segments based on their documents. A fixed set of C clusters is assumed, each one corresponding to a topic segment. Knowledge of the C centroids is global. Clusters of peers are formed in [17] based on the semantic categories of their documents; the semantic categories are predefined. Similarly, [4] assumes predefined classification hierarchies based on which queries and documents are categorized. The clustering of peers in [10] is based on the schemes of the peers and on predefined policies provided by human experts. Besides clustering of peers based on content, clustering on other common features is possible such as on their interests [8].

In terms of range queries, there has been a number of proposals for supporting them in structured p2p systems. In [15], which is based on CAN, the answers of previous range queries are cached at the appropriate peers and used to answer future range queries. In [16], range queries are processed in Chord by using an order-preserving hash function. Two approaches for supporting multidimensional range queries are presented in [5]. In the first approach, multi-dimensional data is mapped into a single dimension using space-filling curves and then this single-dimensional data is range-partitioned across a dynamic set of peers. For query routing, each multi-dimensional range query is first converted to a set of 1-d range queries. In the second approach, the multi-dimensional data space is broken up into "rectangles" with each peer managing one rectangle using a kd-tree whose leaves correspond to a rectangle being stored by a peer.

Routing indexes were introduced in [3] where various types of indexes were proposed based on the way each index takes into account the information about the number of hops required for locating a matching peer. In the attenuated Bloom filters of [14], for each link of a peer, there is an array of routing indexes. The i-th index summarizes items available at peers at a distance of exactly i hops. The peer indexes of [9] use the notion of horizon to bound the number of peers that each index summarizes.

6   Conclusions and Future Work

In this paper, we propose using histograms as routing indexes in peer-to-peer systems. We show how such indexes can be used to route queries towards the peers that have the most results. We also present a decentralized clustering procedure that clusters peers that match similar queries. To achieve this, we use the histograms of each peer and test how the L_1 and the edit histogram distances can be used to this end. Our experimental results show that our clustering procedure is effective, since in the constructed clustered peer-to-peer system, the network distance of two peers is proportional to the distance of their histograms. Furthermore, routing is very efficient, since using histograms increases the number of results returned for a given number of peers visited.

This work is a first step towards leveraging the power of histograms in peer-to-peer systems. There are many issues that need further investigation. We are currently working on defining more appropriate distance metrics and multi-attribute histograms. We are also developing procedures for dynamically updating the clusters. Another issue is investigating the use of other types of histograms (besides equi-width ones).

References

1. M. Bawa, G. S. Manku, and P. Raghavan. SETS: Search Enhanced by Topic Segmentation. In *SIGIR*, 2003.
2. S-H Cha and S. N. Sribari. On Measuring the Distance Between Histograms. *Patern Recognition*, 35:1355–1370, 2002.
3. A. Crespo and H. Garcia-Molina. Routing Indices for Peer-to-Peer Systems. In *ICDCS*, 2002.
4. A. Crespo and H. Garcia-Molina. Semantic Overlay Networks for P2P Systems. Technical report, 2002. Submitted for publication.
5. P. Ganesan, B. Yang, and H. Garcia-Molina. One Torus to Rule Them All: Multidimensional Queries in P2P Systems. In *ICDE*, 2004.
6. R. Morris I. Stoica, D. Karger, M. F. Kaashoek, and H. Balakrishnan. Chord: A Scalable Peer-to-Peer Lookup Service for Internet Applications. *IEEE/ACM Trans. on Networking*, 11(1):17–32, 2003.
7. Y. Ioannidis. The History of Histograms. In *VLDB*, 2003.
8. M.S. Khambatti, K.D. Ryu, and P. Dasgupta. Efficient Discovery of Implicitly Formed Peer-to-Peer Communities. *International Journal of Parallel and Distributed Systems and Networks*, 5(4):155–164, 2002.

9. Y. Wang. S. R. Jeffrey L. Galanis and D. J. DeWitt. Processing Queries in a Large Peer-to-Peer System. In *Caise*, 2003.

10. A. Loser, F. Naumann, W. Siberski, W. Nejdl, and U. Thaden. Semantic Overlay Clusters within Super-Peer Networks. In *International Workshop on Databases, Information Systems and Peer-to-Peer Computing*, 2003.

11. D. S. Milojicic, V. Kalogeraki, R. Lukose, K. Nagaraja, J. Pruyne, B. Richard, S. Rollins, and Z. Xu. Peer-to-Peer Computing. Technical Report HPL-2002-57, HP Laboratories Palo Alto, 2002.

12. Y. Petrakis and E. Pitoura. On Constructing Small Worlds in Unstructured Peer-to-Peer Systems. In *EDBT International Workshop on Peer-to-Peer Computing and Databases*, 2004.

13. S. Ratnasamy, P. Francis, M. Handley, R. Karp, and S. Schenker. A Scalable Content-Addressable Network. In *SIGCOMM*, 2001.

14. Sean C. Rhea and J. Kubiatowicz. Probabilistic Location and Routing. In *INFOCOM*, 2002.

15. O. D. Sahin, A. Gupta, D. Agrawal, and A. El Abbadi. A Peer-to-peer Framework for Caching Range Queries. In *ICDE*, 2004.

16. P. Triantafillou and T. Pitoura. Towards a Unifying Framework for Complex Query Processing over Structured Peer-to-Peer Data Networks. In *DBISP2P*, 2003.

17. P. Triantafillou, C. Xiruhaki, M. Koubarakis, and N. Ntarmos. Towards High Performance Peer-to-Peer Content and Resource Sharing Systems. In *CIDR*, 2003.

Appendix

False Positive Probability for a Histogram. Let H be a histogram for an integer attribute $x \in [Dmin, Dmax]$ (x can take $D = Dmax - Dmin + 1$ distinct values). H has b buckets. Let a query $x = A$. We assume that each peer has n tuples that follow uniform distribution. Then in each bucket we have n/b tuples. The probability that we do not have a query match, that is, there does not exist a tuple with value $x = A$ in the data summarized by H is $P(query\_no\_match) = ((D - 1)/D)^n$. The probability that the histogram indicates a match is: $P(hist\_match) = 1 - ((b - 1)/b)^n$ (it is sufficient that one tuple falls into the bucket that A falls into as well). The range of each bucket is D/b. Thus the probability of having a $query\_no\_match$ while we had a histogram match is: $P_1 = ((D/b - 1)/(D/b))^{n/b} = ((D - b)/D)^{n/b}$. Thus, the false positive probability is according to the formula of Bayes:
$P(fp) = P(hist\_match \ / \ query\_no\_match) = P_1 * P(hist\_match)/P(query\_no\_match) \Rightarrow$

$$P(fp) = (((D - b)/D)^{n/b} * (1 - ((b - 1)/b)^n))/((D - 1)/D)^n. \qquad (7)$$

Processing and Optimization of Complex Queries in Schema-Based P2P-Networks

Hadhami Dhraief[2], Alfons Kemper[3], Wolfgang Nejdl[1,2], and Christian Wiesner[4]

[1] L3S Research Center, University of Hannover, Germany
nejdl@l3s.de
[2] Information Systems Institute, University of Hannover, Germany
{hdhraief, nejdl}@kbs.uni-hannover.de
[3] Computer Science Department, Technical University of Munich, Germany
kemper@in.tum.de
[4] Computer Science Department, University of Passau, Germany
wiesner@db.fmi.uni-passau.de

Abstract. Peer-to-Peer infrastructures are emerging as one of the important data management infrastructures in the World Wide Web. So far, however, most work has focused on simple P2P networks which tackle efficient query distribution to a large set of peers but assume that each query can be answered completely at each peer. For queries which need data from more than one peer to be executed this is clearly insufficient. Unfortunately, though quite a few database techniques can be re-used in the P2P context, P2P data management infrastructures pose additional challenges caused by the dynamic nature of these networks. In P2P networks, we can assume neither global knowledge about data distribution, nor the suitableness of static topologies and static query plans for these networks. Unlike in traditional distributed database systems, we cannot assume complete information schema and allocation schema instances but rather work with distributed schema information which can only direct query processing tasks from one node to one or more neighboring nodes.

In this paper we first describe briefly our super-peer based topology and schema-aware distributed routing indices extended with suitable statistics and describe how this information is extracted and updated. Second we show how these indices facilitate the distribution and dynamic expansion of query plans. Third we propose a set of transformation rules to optimize query plans and discuss different optimization strategies in detail, enabling efficient distributed query processing in a schema-based P2P network.

1   Introduction and Motivation

P2P computing provides a very efficient way of storing and accessing distributed resources, as shown by the success of music file sharing networks such as Gnutella, where simple attributes are used to describe the resources. A lot of effort has been put into refining topologies and query routing functionalities of these networks. A new breed of P2P applications inspired from earlier systems like Napster and Gnutella has more efficient infrastructures such as the ones based on distributed hash tables. Less effort

W.S. Ng et al. (Eds.): DBISP2P 2004, LNCS 3367, pp. 31–45, 2005.
© Springer-Verlag Berlin Heidelberg 2005

has been put into extending the representation and query functionalities offered by such networks. Projects exploring more expressive P2P infrastructures [17, 2, 1, 10] have only slowly started the move toward schema-based P2P networks.

In the Edutella project [7, 17] we have been exploring several issues arising in that context, in order to design and implement a schema-based P2P infrastructure for the Semantic Web. Edutella relies on the W3C metadata standards RDF and RDF Schema (RDFS) to describe distributed resources, and uses basic P2P primitives provided as part of the JXTA framework [9]. In the ObjectGlobe project [5, 15] we have designed and implemented a distributed data network consisting of three kinds of suppliers: *data-providers*, which supply data, *function-providers*, that offer (an extensible set of) query operators to process data, and *cycle-providers*, which are contracted to execute query operators. ObjectGlobe enables applications to execute complex queries which involve the execution of operators from multiple function providers at different sites (cycle providers) and the retrieval of data and documents from multiple data sources. Both systems, Edutella and ObjectGlobe, have to deal with complex queries in a highly dynamic, distributed, and open environment.

Although distributed query optimization and execution are well known issues investigated in database research, distributed query processing in schema-based P2P networks is novel. Middleware systems, e.g., Garlic [12], have been used to overcome the heterogeneity faced when data are dispersed across different data sources. In [16] central mapping information of all participating is used to provide access to distributed data sources. [19] introduces so called mutant query plans, which encapsulate partially evaluated query plans and data. Loss of pipelining during execution limits the general applicability for distributed query processing, and no user-defined operators are supported. AmbientDB [3] executes SQL queries over a P2P network. The approach is based on distributed hash tables and does not take into account user-defined operators.

Very recent work of Stuckenschmidt et al. [25] exploits schema paths for optimizing queries on distributed RDF repositories. Their approach constructs the overall query plan in a mediator-like manner and uses replicated schema paths (which serve as a global allocation schema of the data) to determine which portions of the query plan can be pushed to the data sources. The approach does not handle the case that individual portions of the pushed query plan can be further distributed. In a highly distributed environment like a P2P network it is, however, a scalability concern to assume global knowledge of the allocation schema. For example, the update behavior of the join indices will be a problem in such an environment, as new data sources with new RDF properties joining the network will lead to an enormous growth of all join indices and huge transfer costs. Our approach addresses in particular load balancing strategies during query plan generation and mechanisms for the dynamic placement of operators. Their query processing facilities are limited to joins and selections. User-defined operators are not considered but needed in case multiple resources contribute data to the same property, which potentially leads to an enormous explosion of the search space.

To enable dynamic, extensible, and distributed query processing in schema-based P2P networks, where we need to evaluate complex queries requiring data from several peers and where both standard query operators and user-defined code can be executed nearby the data, we have to distribute query processing to the (super-)peers. Since each peer in a P2P network usually has varying resources available, e.g., regarding bandwidth or processing power, exploiting the different capabilities in a P2P network can lead to an efficient network architecture, where a small subset of peers, called super-peers [27], takes over specific responsibilities for peer aggregation, query routing, and mediation.

In such an architecture, super-peers can, on the one hand, provide query processing capabilities, and on the other hand functionality for the management of index structures and for query optimization. Super-peer based P2P infrastructures are usually based on a two-phase routing architecture, which first routes queries in the super-peer backbone, and then distributes them to the peers connected to the super-peers. Our routing mechanism is based on two distributed routing indices storing information to route within the super-peer backbone and between super-peers and their respective peers [18]. The query processors at the super-peers can be dynamically extended by special-purpose query operators that are shipped to the query processor as part of the query plan. In this way, query evaluation plans (QEPs for short) with user-defined code, e.g., selection predicates, compression functions, join predicates, etc., can be pushed from the client to the (super-) peers where they are executed.

Furthermore, super-peers have to provide an optimizer for dynamically generating good query plans from the queries they receive. We utilize these distributed query processing capabilities at the super-peers and distribute the user's query to the corresponding super-peers. This distribution process is guided by the (dynamic) distributed routing indices, which correspond to the (static) data allocation schema in traditional distributed DBMSs. However, as the index is dynamic and itself distributed over the super-peers, static query optimization as used in distributed DBMSs is not possible. Query optimization must be therefore be dynamic and based on the data allocation schema known at each super-peer.

This paper is based on the framework presented in [6] and focuses on appropriate query optimization in P2P networks. First, we describe our super-peer based topology and schema-aware distributed routing indices enriched with additional statistics. Second, we describe how these statistics are extracted and updated. In section 3, we describe how these indices facilitate the distribution and dynamic expansion of query plans. In section 4 , we propose transformation rules to optimize query plans and discuss different optimization strategies. Finally, we conclude with a short overview of the implemented systems and future work.

2   Distributed Routing Indices

Efficient query routing is one of the corner stones of advanced P2P systems. We rely on a super-peer topology with "schema-aware" routing indices.

The HyperCuP Topology. Super-peers are arranged in the HyperCuP topology. The HyperCuP algorithm as described in [21] is capable of organizing super-peers of a P2P network into a recursive graph structure called a hypercube that stems from the family of Cayley graphs. Super-peers join the HyperCuP topology by asking any of the already integrated super-peers which then carries out the super-peer integration protocol. No central maintenance is necessary for changing the HyperCuP structure. The

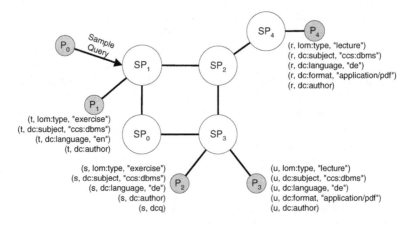

Fig. 1. Routing Example Network

basic HyperCuP topology enables efficient and non-redundant query broadcasts. For broadcasts, each node can be seen as the root of a specific spanning tree through the P2P network. Peers connect to the super-peers in a star-like fashion. Figure 1 shows an example super-peer based P2P network.

Routing Indices. Our super-peers [18] employ routing indices which explicitly acknowledge the semantic heterogeneity of schema-based P2P networks, and therefore include schema information as well as other possible index information. The indices are local in the sense that all index entries only refer to direct neighbors (peers and super-peers). Network connections among the super-peers form the super-peer backbone that is responsible for message routing and integration/mediation of metadata.

Our super-peer network implements a routing mechanism based on two indices storing information to route within the P2P backbone and between super-peers and their respective peers. The super-peer/peer routing indices (SP/P indices) contain information about each peer connected to the super-peer, including schema and attribute information from the peers. On registration the peer provides this information to its super-peer. In contrast to other approaches (Gnutella, CAN [20]), our indices do not refer to individual content elements but to peers (as in CHORD [24]). The indices can contain information about peers at different granularities: schemas, schema properties, property value ranges and individual property values. Details are described in [18]. Using indices with different granularities enables us to state queries at different levels of accuracy. In order to avoid backbone broadcasting we use super-peer/super-peer routing indices (SP/SP indices) to forward queries among the super-peers. These SP/SP indices are essentially extracts and summaries from all local SP/P indices maintained in the super-peers. Similar to the SP/P indices they contain schema information at different granularities, but refer to the super-peers' neighbors in the super-peer backbone. Queries are forwarded to super-peer neighbors based on the SP/SP indices, and sent to connected peers based on the SP/P indices.

Statistics in the Routing Indices. The routing indices as described so far enable the efficient routing of queries. Nevertheless, additional information (statistics, physical

Table 1. SP/P Index of SP_1 at Different Granularities

Granularity	SP/P Index of SP_1		
Schema	dc		P_1, P_0
	lom		P_1, SP_3
Property	dc:subject		$P_1 [13], P_0 [16]$
	dc:language		$P_1 [15]$
	lom:type		$P_1 [10]$
Property	lom:type	"exercise"	$P_1 [10]$
Value	dc:language	"de"	$P_0 [15]$

parameters of the network, etc.) both in the SP/P and the SP/SP routing indices are necessary to enhance the optimization process and enable the choice of the best query execution plan. As mentioned in the introduction we aim at using approved techniques and methods in databases, particularly from distributed database systems. The most important parameters for query optimization in this context are number and size of the stored documents at the different peers. This information is provided by the peers during the registration process. The following piece of the RDF-Schema *PeerDescription* shows the definition of the property elementCount, used for the documents count at a given peer at the property-value level.

```
(...)

<rdf:Property rdf:ID="elementCount">
        <rdfs:isDefinedBy rdf:resource="http://www.learninglab.de/~brunkhor/rdf
        /PeerDescription#"/>
        <rdfs:label>elementCount</rdfs:label>
        <rdfs:comment>An integer that specifies how often an element has occured.
                    Used in conjunction with hasPropertyValues.</rdfs:comment>
        <rdfs:range rdf:resource="http://www.w3c.org/2000/01/rdf_schema#Literal"/>
        <rdfs:domain rdf:resource="#Peer"/>
</rdf:Property/>

(...)
```

If we register documents only at the property value level, we can derive the information for the property level by accumulating the number and size of documents for each property. Multi-valued properties like dc:author complicate this aggregation. Histograms [11] can help to obtain more precise estimates. For this paper, we assume that the registration occurs at property level, property value level, and property value range level. The schema level can be considered as meta-level, which can be used to answer general queries (e.g. "Which standards are used to annotate documents at Peer x?"). Thus, the information about the number and size of documents are not relevant at this level. Table 1 shows the SP/P routing index of super-peer SP_1 including statistics at different granularities. In the following we will restrict the discussion on the size (si) and the number (n) of available documents. However, it is easily possible to add further useful statistics such as minimum, maximum, and average values and the total number of documents at each peer. If a peer P_y (re-)registers or leaves a given super-peer SP_x with a schema element set including document statistics $S_y(s_1(n_1, si_1), \ldots, s_m(n_m, si_m))$, an update of the SP/P and the SP/SP indices is needed. The algorithm for building and updating the SP/P routing indices described before remains unmodified. The peers simply register including their statistics information in addition to the schema elements. The update information of the SP/SP indices propagated via messages however must be extended as follows:

1. SP_x derives the total number and size of the documents (and potentially further statistics) registered by the peers for each schema element $s_i \in S_y$ and sends these statistics combined with s_i to its neighbors in its spanning tree.
2. Any other super-peer in the spanning tree of SP_x updates its SP/SP index and derives the total number and size of the documents in its SP/SP index at each $s_i \in S_y$ and forwards the data to its neighbors.

3   Plan Generation, Distribution and Optimization

Using the indices described in the previous section we can now describe how query plan generation and distribution proceeds in our P2P network.

3.1   Distributed Plan Generation

In contrast to traditional distributed query optimization approaches, we cannot generate the query plan statically at one single host. Therefore we have to generate an abstract query plan at a super-peer which is partially executed locally and where we push other parts of the query plan to its neighbors. The plan generation at each super-peer therefore involves five major steps as depicted in Figure 2 and is described in details in [6].

First, the received query (stated in our SQL dialect) is parsed and transformed into an internal representation which is a decomposition of the query into its building blocks. Then, the local indices are consulted to determine the location of the required resources. For this purpose we have to distinguish between resource directions (RDs) and physical resources (PRs). Users specify the desired information by giving properties and property-values restricting logical resources (LRs). These LRs are bound to RDs resp. PRs where all levels of granularity of the indices have to be considered. Multiple RDs and PRs can contribute data for the same LR. Based on the bindings, a local query plan is generated. As super-peers have a very limited view of the whole P2P network (only the neighbors are known), it is obvious that no comprehensive static plan in the traditional sense can be produced. Therefore, we determine which sub-plans have to be delegated to the neighboring (super-)peers. The remaining parts constitute the input to the local

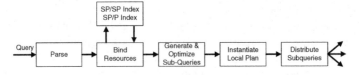

Fig. 2. Plan Generation at a Super-Peer

plan. To perform cost based optimization, the optimizer uses statistics of the input data, the network topology, and the hosts. The optimizer may collect and use response times, transfer rates, and even result sizes from previous query executions. Finally, the local query plan is instantiated at the super-peer, all user-defined code is loaded, the communication path to the super-peer which uses this part of the query plan as input is established, and the remaining sub-queries are distributed to the corresponding super-peers, where they are processed further.

3.2   Query Optimization

Let us now describe some of the details involved in the optimization process at a super-peer. We employ a transformation-based optimizer starting with an initial query plan. The optimizer applies equivalence transformations and determines the cost of the generated alternatives using a cost model. In contrast to bottom-up approaches employed in traditional dynamic programming based optimization we can stop at any time with a complete and valid query plan. In our implementation we use iterative improvement to enumerate plan alternatives. Superior techniques as shown in [22] are applicable.

In the following we present the set of the most important transformation rules, focusing on the ones relevant to processing joins and unions within the P2P context. Further rules can be added easily. Furthermore we extend conventional cost models taking the special requirements of P2P query processing into account. During the optimization process we employ heuristics that favor query plans with few sub-plans as this leads to more robust distributed query execution. A huge number of wide spread sub-plans accessing the same documents would be more error-prone and often inefficient to execute. Our decision also implies, that less messages are exchanged between the (super-) peers and less data is transferred.

The Initial Query Plan. The initial (canonical) query plan accesses only logical resources and is constructed in the following way: Use all join predicates and join the logical resources. If logical resources could not be joined due to a lack of join predicates, the Cartesian product includes them into the query plan. Thereafter, all remaining selection predicates and user-defined filters are applied on top of the query plan. Finally, the result is submitted to the client.

The Transformation Rules. The initial query plan is optimized top-down using a transformation-based optimizer. In such an approach we apply a set of transformation rules to the query plan and generate alternatives, which are then ranked using our cost model. The best (local) query plan is executed. Transformation rules are represented as

$$\frac{\{\text{inputQEP}\} \quad [\text{condition/action}]}{\{\text{outputQEP}\}}$$

where one input query plan is transformed into an output query plan. The condition/action part may be omitted. We assume that the transformations are executed at host H_L. If H_L is a super-peer, we have access to the local routing indices *SPP* and *SPSP*.

Basic Transformation Rules. We can express the *Bind Resources* step explained in the previous subsection as the following *Binding Transformation*:

$$[.5\text{em}] \frac{\{LR\} \quad [PR_j@P_j \in match(SPP), RD_k@SP_k \in match(SPSP)]}{\left\{ \bigcup_j PR_j@P_j \cup \bigcup_k RD_k@SP_k \right\}}$$

The function *match* consults the local indices and determines the location of the matching resources. The LRs are bound to RDs, if a corresponding data source is found in the SP/SP index. Using the SP/P index, LRs are bound to PRs, i.e., the URIs of registered resources. Multiple RDs and PRs can contribute data for the same LR. This is expressed by the union of RDs and PRs. $PR_j@P_j$ denotes that the j-th bound PR belongs to the corresponding LR and references a resource at peer P_j. A similar argument applies for the RDs.

Applying the following two transformations to a query plan pushes selections and user-defined filters down towards the data sources. This enables us to reduce the amount of transferred data early.

$$\frac{\{\sigma(A \ op \ B)\}}{\{\sigma(A) \ op \ \sigma(B)\}} \qquad \frac{\{\sigma(op(A))\}}{\{op(\sigma(A))\}}$$

Here, A and B are arbitrary sub-plans.

The next two rules apply the associative and commutative laws to unions, joins, and Cartesian products.

$$\frac{\{(A \ op \ B) \ op \ C\} \quad [op \in \{\cup, \ , \times\}]}{\{A \ op \ (B \ op \ C)\}} \qquad \frac{\{A \ op \ B\} \quad [op \in \{\cup, \ , \times\}]}{\{B \ op \ A\}}$$

Again, A, B, and C denote arbitrary sub-plans.

Finally, each operator is annotated with the host where it is to be executed. This is done bottom up from the leaves of the operator tree which constitute PRs and RDs. The annotations of the leaves are given by the first transformation rule. An operator can be executed on host H_L, if all its inputs are computed at H_L.

$$\frac{\{A@H_1 \ op \ B@H_2\} \quad [H_1 \neq H_2]}{\{A@H_1 \ op@H_L \ B@H_2\}} \quad \frac{\{A@H_1 \ op \ B@H_2\} \quad [H_1 = H_2]}{\{A@H_1 \ op@H_1 \ B@H_1\}} \quad \frac{\{op(A@H_1)\}}{\{op@H_1(A@H_1)\}}$$

A and B are sub-plans and $op@H_1$ indicates that the operator op is executed at host H_1. This rule enables us to execute mobile code at remote hosts, e.g., to push selective filter predicates, complex join predicates, or compression functions to the data sources.

The plans generated by the rules so far typically have one union operator for each logical resource. The degree of parallelism can be increased and distributed computing resources can be utilized better if operators are distributed over the P2P network.

Optimization Strategy: Union of Joins. As shown above, several PRs and RDs can contribute data for the same LRs. The simplest way for incorporating the data for such an LR would be to union all the accessed physical resources before any other operation is considered for that LR. This would be done by the binding transformation. This naive strategy would produce good plans in some cases, but query optimization would be limited and possibly better plans might never be considered. Thus, several alternatives for the naive query plan must be considered by applying equivalence transformations.

Table 2. Explosion of the Search Space

configuration	number of plans
$UJ([2,2])$	8
$UJ([3,3])$	385
$UJ([4,4])$	144705
$UJ([5,5])$	913749304

To increase the degree of distribution, the query plan can be transformed using the following transformation which turns the join of unions into a union of joins:

$$\frac{\{(A_1 \cup \ldots \cup A_n) \quad (B_1 \cup \ldots \cup B_m)\}}{\{(A_1 \quad (B_1 \cup \ldots \cup B_m)) \cup \ldots \cup (A_n \quad (B_1 \cup \ldots \cup B_m))\}}$$

If many RDs and PRs are bound to LRs and when this rule is applied recursively in combination with the associative and commutative laws the number of plans which have to be considered during query optimization is huge. [4] has derived a lower bound for the number of alternatives when joining two LRs, consisting of n_1 and n_2 bound resources:

$$\mathrm{UJ}(n_1, n_2) = \sum_{j=1}^{n_1} \left(\left\{ {n_1 \atop j} \right\} \mathrm{bell}(n_2)^j \right) + \sum_{j=1}^{n_2} \left(\left\{ {n_2 \atop j} \right\} \mathrm{bell}(n_1)^j \right) - \mathrm{bell}(n_1)\mathrm{bell}(n_2)$$

In this definition $\left\{ {m \atop k} \right\}$ denotes the Stirling number of the second kind which represents the number of ways a set with m elements can be partitioned into k disjoint, non-empty subsets. The term $\mathrm{bell}(m)$ denotes the Bell number which represents the number of ways a set with n elements can be partitioned into disjoint, non-empty subsets. The definition of *UJ* follows the construction of a query plan starting from its canonical form. First we have to select a LR constituting of different bindings. Each such binding has to be joined with an expression which is equivalent to the other LR. All these expressions are counted by the call to the function for the Bell numbers. At the end we have to consider duplicate QEPs which are generated when for every appearance of a LR in a QEP the same partitioning is selected. If the same partitionings are selected, the order in which the LRs are used in the construction of a QEP does not matter anymore. Therefore, the last term of the definition of *UJ* includes the number of QEPs with that property. Table 2 gives an impression of the search space explosion, the generated plan may have a huge number of sub-queries.

Optimizing by Collecting Resources. A very promising heuristics in a distributed environment is to collect as many bindings of one LR as possible at one host. To implement this strategy, the optimizer determines one "collecting host" to collect all data of one logical resource. Other hosts are informed to send all data to the collecting host (in the following this is done by the CollectSend Operator). In contrast to the canonical query plan this collecting host is determined dynamically and may change during query execution, i.e., we can place the resource-collecting union at an arbitrary (super-) peer.

$$\frac{\left\{\bigcup_j PR_j@P_j \cup \bigcup_k RD_k@SP_k\right\} \quad \left[H_C \in \bigcup_j P_j \cup \bigcup_k SP_k\right]}{\left\{CR(LR)@H_C \cup \overset{H_C \neq H_j}{\underset{j}{\bigcup}} CollectSend(H_C, LR)@P_j \cup \overset{H_C \neq H_k}{\underset{k}{\bigcup}} CollectSend(H_C, LR)@SP_k\right\}}$$

(a) Collecting Host Selection

$$\frac{\left\{CollectSend(H_C, LR)\right\} \quad \left[\begin{array}{l} PR_j@P_j \in match(SPP), \\ RD_k@SP_k \qquad\qquad \in \\ match(SPSP) \end{array}\right]}{\left\{CollectSend(H_C, LR)@P_j, \ldots, CollectSend(H_C, LR)@SP_k\right\}}$$

(b) Propagate CollectSend

$$\frac{\left\{CollectSend(H_C, LR)\right\} \left[\begin{array}{l} PR_j@P_j \in match(SPP), \\ RD_k@SP_k \qquad\qquad \in \\ match(SPSP) \end{array}\right]}{\left\{Send(H_C, \bigcup_j PR^j@P_j \cup \bigcup_k RD_k@SP_k)@H_L\right\}}$$

(c) Execute CollectSend

$$\frac{\left\{CR(LR)\right\} \left[\begin{array}{l} PR_j@P_j \in match(SPP), \\ RD_k@SP_k \qquad\qquad \in \\ match(SPSP) \end{array}\right]}{\left\{Receive@H_L \cup \bigcup_j PR_j@P_j \cup \bigcup_k RD_k@SP_k\right\}}$$

(d) Execute Collect Resource At Host

$$\frac{\left\{CR(LR)\right\} \left[\begin{array}{l} PR_j@P_j \in match(SPP), RD_k@SP_k \in match(SPSP), \\ H_C \in \bigcup_j P_j \cup \bigcup_k SP_k, setForward(LR, H_C) \end{array}\right]}{\left\{\begin{array}{l} CR(LR)@H_C \cup \overset{H_C \neq H_j}{\underset{j}{\bigcup}} CollectSend(H_C, LR)@P_j \\ \cup \overset{H_C \neq H_k}{\underset{k}{\bigcup}} CollectSend(H_C, LR)@SP_k \end{array}\right\}}$$

(e) Forward Collect Resource

Fig. 3. Transformation Rules for the "Collect Resources" Strategy

In well clustered networks it is useful to place the collecting union operator nearby the majority of the data and to ship only a few resources.

To include this strategy in our query optimization, we introduce Collect Resources (CRs) which can be used in the previous rules like bound resources. Additionally, we propose the following five transformation rules (shown in Figure 3):

- First, the collecting host H_C is selected from the set of all referenced neighbors (taken from the PRs and RDs) (Figure 3(a)). Then, we replace all bound resources, i.e., PRs and RDs, of the input plan with a collect resource which is executed at H_C and CollectSend operators are pushed to the other neighbors. These CollectSend operators ship all data of the LR to the collecting host H_C.
- When a CollectSend operator is received by a host, it can be propagated to all its matching neighbors (Figure 3(b)) which are determined from the local indices. The plan is split into multiple parts which are distributed broadcast-like to the neighbors.
- Hosts can also execute the CollectSend operator (Figure 3(c)). This is treated as a binding transformation where results are sent back to the collecting host.
- A collecting host can execute the CR operator by accepting resources belonging to the given LR (Figure 3(d)). The results are sent from sub-plans built by the latter two transformations. Additionally, resources are bound using the local indices.

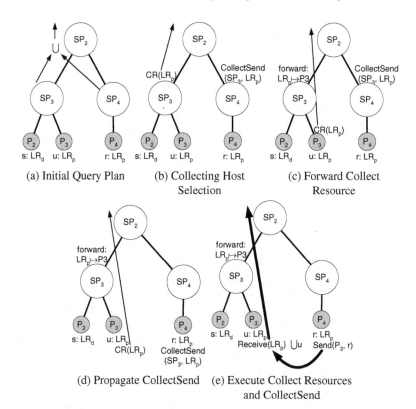

Fig. 4. Example Applications of "Collect Resources" Accessing LR_p
(Thin lines demonstrate the query plan during instantiation, bold lines show the flow of results.)

– Finally, the CR operator can also be forwarded to a neighbor (Figure 3(e)). This means that first, we choose the new collecting host H_C from the neighbors and set an appropriate forward. The CR is pushed to H_C and all matching neighbors are instructed to send their data for LR to H_C. During query instantiation a CollectSend operator follows the forwards and creates a proper Send operator with the actual collecting host as target. Thus, results are sent directly to the correct host.

Figure 4 illustrates the rules querying resources of LR_p, i.e., the documents r and u. Starting at SP_2 as the local host with the initial query plan (Figure 4(a)), SP_3 is selected as collecting host of LR_p (Figure 4(b)) and a CollectSend informs SP_4 to send all documents regarding LR_p to SP_3. SP_3 decides to forward the CR to P_3 where the results are sent directly back to the initial caller (bypassing SP_3 and SP_2) (Figure 4(c)). SP_4, on its part, propagates the CollectSend operator to P_4 (Figure 4(d)). Finally, P_4 finds out by considering SP_3 to send the local resource r to P_3 and P_3 executes the CR operator and returns u and the received document r (Figure 4(e)).

Splitting and Distributing the Query Plan. Valid query plans must be completely annotated and all resources must be bound. The best query plan is split into a local plan

---

Algorithm 1 Splitting the Query Plan

1: $Q_L = Q$
2: $Q_R = \emptyset$

3: **function** $splitPlan(op)$
4:    **for all** $childOp \in op.children$ **do**
5:       **if** $childOp.host == op.host$ **then**
6:          $splitPlan(childOp)$
7:       **else**
8:          $Q_R.put(childOp.host, Send(op.host, childOp))$
9:          $replace(Q_L, childOp, Receive(childOp.host))$
10:      **end if**
11:   **end for**
12: **end function**

---

and multiple remote query plans. The remote plans are shipped to the referenced hosts[1] where the optimization process continues on the smaller query plans. The local query plan is instantiated and combines the results of the remote query plans.

Algorithm 1 splits (in DFS manner) a QEP into the local plan Q_L and the remote plans. The remote plans are stored in the mapping Q_R from the host where to execute the remaining query parts onto the query plan itself. One remote host may execute multiple sub-plans. The recursive function is called with the top-level operator of the query plan. Then the child operators are examined. If a child is executed at the same host, i.e., the local host, the function is called recursively. Otherwise, this is the root of a remote sub-plan and a Send operator is put on top of the sub-plan including the child operator. The remote sub-plan is separated from the local plan and a Receive operator at the local host is responsible for the connection to the remote plan.

The Cost Model. Some of the parameters used for our cost model are stored within the local SP/P and SP/SP indices as described in Section 2, others are determined periodically by the runtime environment. In our distributed query processing environment we are interested in the plan with the lowest response time. Such a response time cost model was devised in [8] and explicitly takes parallelism and pipelining into account.

The most important parameters of query optimization in traditional databases are number and size of intermediary results. The same applies to P2P query processing, where we utilize the number of documents and the overall/maximum/minimum size of the registered resources for estimating the costs of a query plan. Our cost model also considers physical properties of the network, e.g., the network bandwidth, the latency, and the number of hops to the neighbors. But it is also important to know CPU and memory load of the local (super-) peer and the neighbors, as especially the super-peers are in danger of being overloaded, when too many queries execute operators at the super-peers. This would slow down query execution, so the optimizer should be aware of the current load situation of the local super-peer and the neighboring (super-) peers and generate alternative query plans, e.g. by using the "Collect" strategy, which enables the

---

[1] Note, that these are always neighboring hosts.

query optimizer to place operators on low loaded hosts. For these reasons, we utilize load information as one important parameter for the optimizer's cost model. Load collectors are used to collect data for the optimizer's view of the load situation of all relevant resources at the neighboring hosts. We measure the average CPU and memory load on (super-) peers and send the current situation to the neighbors. The optimizer's view of the load situation is updated at intervals of several seconds to prevent overloading the network. Using this information the optimizer at each (super-) peer can decide whether a sub-plan can be pushed to a neighbor, or—in the case of an overload—an alternative query plan would produce faster results.

Additionally, adapting the techniques presented in [23], our cost model can be extended to take the response time of "similar" queries, i.e., queries accessing the same index entries, into account.

4   Implementation

The discussed techniques for processing and optimizing complex queries in the highly dynamic and open environment of schema-based super-peer networks are already implemented in Edutella. The Edutella System [7] which constitutes an RDF-based metadata infrastructure for JXTA [13] is an open source project written in java.

The organisation of the super-peer backbone in the HyperCup-topology occurs dynamically. The distributed routing indices are also built and updated dynamically based on the registration files of the peers/super-peers.

We distinguish between *metadata statistics* such as document count and file size and *network statistic parameters*. The *metadata statistics* are automatically extracted from the registration files and stored in the SP/P and SP/SP routing indices. The *network statistic parameters* can be extracted at a given super-peer in an active way (e.g. memory load) by asking the neighboring super-peers or in a passive way by storing for example the response time of a given super-peer or peer. The statistics are currently used during the plan generation. The complex query processing modules are included in the package *net.jxta.edutella.complexquery*. We also implemented a subpackage *net.jxta.edutella.complexquery.graph* for the visualization of the QEPs. The subpackage *net.jxta.edutella.complexquery.work* includes all classes needed for the execution of the QEP's different steps.

The complex query processing techniques are also implemented in QueryFlow [14, 15] which is based on ObjectGlobe [5], building upon earlier work by some of the authors on distributed query processing. A demonstration of the QueryFlow-based implementation was given in [26].

5   Conclusion and Further Work

Peer-to-Peer data management infrastructures are emerging as one of the important infrastructures for data intensive networks on the World Wide Web. In this paper we have investigated query distribution and query optimization issues for schema-based peer-to-peer networks, which use complex and possibly heterogeneous schemas for describing the data managed by the participating peers. Specifically, we have focussed on addressing one particularly severe shortcoming of current peer-to-peer networks, i.e. that they are unable to handle queries which need data from several peers to compute answers.

Comparing P2P data management networks to conventional distributed and federated database systems, we have identified specific additional challenges which make it impossible to apply distributed database query planning and optimization techniques in a straightforward way. We have therefore specified an innovative query routing and planning architecture based on distributed routing indices managed by a suitably connected set of super-peers, which makes distributed query processing available also in P2P data management networks. We have discussed how to use transformation-based techniques for incremental query optimization at each super-peer, and specified a set of transformation rules, relevant for processing joins and unions in such a network. These techniques allow us to place query operators next to data sources and utilize distributed computing resources more effectively.

Future work will concentrate on the further investigation of simulations and experiments to evaluate and extend our current set of transformation rules. We will also evaluate the use of additional statistics useful as input to our query plan generation more intensively.

References

1. K. Aberer and M. Hauswirth. Semantic gossiping. In *Database and Information Systems Research for Semantic Web and Enterprises, Invitational Workshop*, University of Georgia, Amicalola Falls and State Park, Georgia, April 2002.
2. P. A. Bernstein, F. Giunchiglia, A. Kementsietsidis, J. Mylopoulos, L. Serafini, and I. Zaihrayeu. Data management for peer-to-peer computing: A vision. In *Proceedings of the Fifth International Workshop on the Web and Databases*, Madison, Wisconsin, June 2002.
3. P. Boncz and C. Treijtel. AmbientDB: Relational Query Processing over P2P Network. In *International Workshop on Databases, Information Systems and Peer-to-Peer Computing*, Berlin, Germany, September 2003.
4. R. Braumandl. *Quality of Service and Query Processing in an Information Economy*. PhD thesis, Universität Passau, Fakultät für Mathematik und Informatik, D-94030 Passau, 2001. Universität Passau.
5. R. Braumandl, M. Keidl, A. Kemper, D. Kossmann, A. Kreutz, S. Seltzsam, and K. Stocker. ObjectGlobe: Ubiquitous query processing on the Internet. *The VLDB Journal: Special Issue on E-Services*, 10(3):48–71, August 2001.
6. I. Brunkhorst, H. Dhraief, A. Kemper, W. Nejdl, and C. Wiesner. Distributed queries and query optimization in schema-baed p2p-systems. In *International Workshop On Databases, Information Systems and Peer-to-Peer Computing, VLDB 2003*, Berlin, Germany, September 2003.
7. The Edutella Project. http://edutella.jxta.org/, 2002.
8. S. Ganguly, W. Hasan, and R. Krishnamurthy. Query optimization for parallel execution. In *Proc. of the ACM SIGMOD Conf. on Management of Data*, pages 9–18, San Diego, CA, USA, June 1992.
9. L. Gong. Project JXTA: A technology overview. Technical report, SUN Microsystems, April 2001. http://www.jxta.org/project/www/docs/TechOverview.pdf.
10. A. Y. Halevy, Z. G. Ives, P. Mork, and I. Tatarinov. Piazza: Data management infrastructure for semantic web applications. In *Proceedings of the Twelfth International World Wide Web Conference (WWW2003)*, Budapest, Hungary, May 2003.

11. Y. E. Ioannidis. The History of Histograms. In *Proc. of the Conf. on Very Large Data Bases (VLDB)*, pages 19–30, 2003.
12. V. Josifovski, P. Schwarz, L. Haas, and E. Lin. Garlic: A New Flavor of Federated Query Processing for DB2. In *Proc. of the ACM SIGMOD Conf. on Management of Data*, Madison, USA, June 2002.
13. Project JXTA Homepage. http://www.jxta.org/.
14. A. Kemper and C. Wiesner. HyperQueries: Dynamic Distributed Query Processing on the Internet. In *Proc. of the Conf. on Very Large Data Bases (VLDB)*, pages 551–560, Rom, Italy, September 2001.
15. A. Kemper, C. Wiesner, and P. Winklhofer. Building Dynamic Market Places using Hyper-Queries. In *Proc. of the Intl. Conf. on Extending Database Technology (EDBT)*, volume Lecture Notes in computer Science (LNCS), pages 749–752, Prague, Czech Republic, March 2002. Springer Verlag.
16. A. Y. Levy, D. Srivastava, and T. Kirk. Data Model and Query Evaluation in Global Information Systems. *Journal of Intelligent Information Systems (JIIS)*, 5(2):121–143, 1995.
17. W. Nejdl, B. Wolf, C. Qu, S. Decker, M. Sintek, A. Naeve, M. Nilsson, M. Palmér, and T. Risch. EDUTELLA: A P2P Networking Infrastructure based on RDF. In *Proceedings of the 11th International World Wide Web Conference*, Hawaii, USA, May 2002. http://edutella.jxta.org/reports/edutella-whitepaper.pdf.
18. W. Nejdl, M. Wolpers, W. Siberski, C. Schmitz, M. Schlosser, I. Brunkhorst, and A. Loser. Super-peer-based routing and clustering strategies for RDF-based peer-to-peer networks. In *Proceedings of the International World Wide Web Conference*, Budapest, Hungary, May 2003. http://citeseer.nj.nec.com/nejdl02superpeerbased.html.
19. V. Papadimos and D. Maier. Distributed Query Processing and Catalogs for Peer-to-Peer Systems. Asilomar, CA, USA, January 2003.
20. S. Ratnasamy, P. Francis, M. Handley, R. Karp, and S. Shenker. A scalable content addressable network. In *Proceedings of the 2001 Conference on applications, technologies, architectures, and protocols for computer communications*. ACM Press New York, NY, USA, 2001.
21. M. Schlosser, M. Sintek, S. Decker, and W. Nejdl. HyperCuP—Hypercubes, Ontologies and Efficient Search on P2P Networks. In *International Workshop on Agents and Peer-to-Peer Computing*, Bologna, Italy, July 2002.
22. M. Steinbrunn, G. Moerkotte, and A. Kemper. Heuristic and randomized optimization for the join ordering problem. *The VLDB Journal*, 6(3):191–208, August 1997.
23. M. Stillger, G. M. Lohman, V. Markl, and M. Kandil. LEO - DB2's LEarning Optimizer. In *Proc. of the Conf. on Very Large Data Bases (VLDB)*, pages 19–28, Rom, Italy, September 2001.
24. I. Stoica, R. Morris, D. Karger, M. F. Kaashoek, and H. Balakrishnan. Chord: A scalable peer-to-peer lookup service for internet applications. In *Proceedings of the 2001 Conference on applications, technologies, architectures, and protocols for computer communications*. ACM Press New York, NY, USA, 2001.
25. H. Stuckenschmidt, R. Vdovjak, G-J. Houben, and J. Broekstra. Index structures and algorithms for querying distributed rdf repositories. In *Proceedings of the 13th International World Wide Web Conference (WWW2004)*, New York, USA, May 2004.
26. C. Wiesner, A. Kemper, and S. Brandl. Dynamic, Extendible Query Processing in Super-Peer Based P2P Systems (Demonstration). In *Proc. IEEE Conf. on Data Engineering*, Boston, USA, March 2004.
27. B. Yang and H. Garcia-Molina. Improving search in peer-to-peer systems. In *Proceedings of the 22nd International Conference on Distributed Computing Systems*, Viena, Austria, July 2002. http://dbpubs.stanford.edu:8090/pub/2001-47.

Using Information Retrieval Techniques to Route Queries in an InfoBeacons Network

Brian F. Cooper

College of Computing, Georgia Institute of Technology
cooperb@cc.gatech.edu

Abstract. We present the InfoBeacons system, in which a peer-to-peer network of beacons cooperates to route queries to the best information sources. The routing in our system uses techniques adapted from information retrieval. We examine routing at two levels. First, each beacon is assigned several sources and routes queries to those sources. Many sources are unwilling to provide more cooperation than simple searching, and we must adapt traditional information retrieval techniques to choose the best sources despite this lack of cooperation. Second, beacons route queries to other beacons using techniques similar to those for routing queries to sources. We examine alternative architectures for routing queries between beacons. Results of experiments using a beacon network to search 1,000 information sources demonstrates how our techniques can be used to efficiently route queries; for example, our techniques require contacting up to 70 percent fewer sources than random walk techniques.

1 Introduction

There is an explosion of useful data available from dynamic information sources, such as "deep-web" data sources, web services, web logs and personal web servers [3]. The Internet and web standards make it possible and easy to contact a source and retrieve information. But the proliferation of sources creates a challenge: how to find the right source of information for a given query? Peer-to-peer search mechanisms are useful for finding information in large scale distributed systems, but such mechanisms often rely on the explicit cooperation of information sources to export data, data summaries or data schemas to aid in searching. Many data sources are unwilling to provide this cooperation, either because they do not want to export valuable information, or because they do not want to modify their service software and expend the resources necessary to cooperate with a peer-to-peer system.

How can we build a peer-to-peer system that is useful for searching large numbers of distributed sources when those sources will not provide more cooperation than simple searching? Our approach is to build a network of peers, called *InfoBeacons*, that are loosely-coupled to the information sources: beacons connect to sources and utilize their existing search interface, but do not expect tight schema integration, data summary export, or any other high-level cooperation from the source. InfoBeacons act to guide user keyword queries to information sources, where the actual processing of queries is done, and then retrieve results and return them to the user. As such, the InfoBeacons

W.S. Ng et al. (Eds.): DBISP2P 2004, LNCS 3367, pp. 46–60, 2005.

network is similar to a super-peer network, except that the beacons do not expect the same level of cooperation from sources (i.e. exporting their indexes) that super-peers expect. In order to choose appropriate sources for a given query, we adapt techniques from networked information retrieval [14, 16, 13]. These techniques allow us to gather information about a source's content, and then predict how good that source will be for a given query. As a result, we can route queries through the system to the most appropriate sources, and avoid overburdening sources with irrelevant queries.

In this paper, we describe how the InfoBeacons system uses IR techniques to perform query routing. In particular, we describe routing at two levels. First, each beacon is responsible for several sources, and uses IR-style ranking to route a query to the best sources. A beacon cannot rely on sources to export a summary of their content, so the beacon builds up its own summary by caching the results of previous queries. The beacon then uses this cache to determine how to route future queries. Second, multiple beacons are connected in a peer-to-peer network, and IR-style ranking is used to determine how queries are routed through the beacon network. Many beacons can cooperate in this way to provide a system that searches a very large number of sources, while keeping the resource requirements low for each individual beacon. We examine two approaches to inter-beacon routing. In the *hierarchical* approach, a "superbeacon" uses IR-style ranking to choose among beacons, in the same way that beacons use ranking to choose among sources. In the *flat* approach, beacons treat each other as regular sources, forming a flat topology composed of both beacons and sources. A beacon routes queries to the most promising "neighbor," which may be a source or another beacon.

We have implemented an InfoBeacons prototype to route queries to information sources using our techniques. Experiments using our prototype to route queries to sources containing information downloaded from the Internet demonstrate that our techniques perform better than random walks, an efficient and scalable peer-to-peer routing mechanism [23, 1]. In ongoing work we are comparing our techniques to other routing approaches, such as those in [32, 20].

Content searching using information retrieval in peer-to-peer networks has been studied before [27, 26, 30]. Our work goes beyond these existing systems to examine using IR for routing between peers in addition to content searching. Moreover, our system focuses on searching over frequently-changing, uncooperative sources. Existing techniques, such as [26], assume that sources will export inverted lists for their content, and that these inverted lists do not require too many updates. General routing in peer-to-peer networks has also been studied extensively (for example, [32, 20, 23, 1, 28, 10, 21]). Some of these systems use a limited form of content-based routing based on document identifiers [28] or on keywords in document metadata (such as the title) [21]. Our work focuses on full-text content-based searching and routing, which presents new performance challenges. Other systems are not based on content, and instead route queries based on network topology [32, 23, 1] or peer processing capacity [10]. Routing approaches based on content, topology and capacity can be complementary, and it may be possible to combine these approaches. More related work is discussed in Section 5.

In this paper, we examine how information retrieval techniques can be adapted to route queries in a peer-to-peer system. Specifically, we make the following contributions:

- We show how a beacon can route queries to appropriate sources using a ranking we have developed called *ProbResults*. (Section 2)
- We discuss how beacons can also use ProbResults to route queries to other beacons. We examine both *hierarchical* and *flat* approaches for inter-beacon routing. (Section 3)
- We present results from a preliminary experimental study comparing our routing techniques to existing techniques. Our study shows that ProbResults outperforms existing source selection techniques, and that both the hierarchical and flat approaches outperform random walk-based routing in our beacon network. (Section 4)

We examine related work in Section 5, and discuss our conclusions and future work in Section 6.

2   Routing Queries to Information Sources

In the InfoBeacons system, *beacons* connected in a peer-to-peer network work together to guide user queries to useful information sources. Beacons accept user keyword queries, connect to sources, submit the queries to sources, retrieve results, and return them to the user. The user is therefore shielded from the complexity of choosing and searching many different sources. A beacon is like a *meta-querier* such as GlOSS [16] or CORI [13], but adapted to work in a peer-to-peer manner with uncooperative sources. The differences between a beacon and existing meta-queriers are summarized in Section 5, and quantitative comparisons are presented in Section 4. User queries in our system are conjunctions of multiple terms, although our techniques can be extended to deal with general boolean queries.

In this section, we focus on the techniques a single beacon uses to route queries among its information sources. While each each beacon is only responsible for a few sources (say, 100 or so), the system scales to large numbers of sources by routing queries between multiple beacons (as described in Section 3). In this way, the resource requirements on each beacon are kept low. In fact, beacons are designed to be very lightweight peers, so that they can run in the background on a PC-class machine. Beacons can be run by users, data sources, libraries, ISPs, and so on.

It is too expensive to send every query to every source, so the beacon must determine the most appropriate sources for each query. Ideally, each source would export a summary of its content to help the beacon route queries. However, many Internet information sources are willing to accept queries and return results, but are unwilling to provide more cooperation by exporting their contents, content summaries, or schema information. As a result, a beacon must learn which sources are good for each queries, while relying only on the sources' basic search interface. We say in this case that the beacon is *loosely coupled* to the information sources.

Beacons learn about sources by caching results from previous queries, and then use these results to choose appropriate sources for future queries. The architecture that the beacon uses to carry out this process is shown in Figure 1. This figure shows four main components:

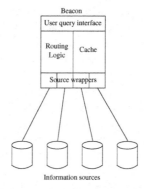

Information sources

Fig. 1. Beacon architecture

- The *user query interface*, which accepts queries from users and returns results.
- The *source wrappers*, which submit queries to different information sources and retrieve results.
- The *cache*, which caches results from information sources.
- The *routing logic*, which uses the cache to choose which sources to route new queries to.

The source wrappers are lightweight: they only handle the task of connecting to the source, submitting a keyword query, and retrieving results. They do not perform complex schema translation or use advanced features of the source API. Techniques for generation of source wrappers have been studied by others; see for example [31]. This loose coupling ensures that it is cheap to integrate a new source, so that the system is tolerant to sources constantly appearing and disappearing.

We have developed a function, called *ProbResults*, to determine where to route queries. ProbResults uses the beacon cache to predict the number of results that a source will return containing the given query words; this predicted number is called the *ProbResults score*. The user specifies a desired number of results, and sources are contacted in order of decreasing ProbResults score until enough results have been found. (If the local sources cannot supply enough results, other beacons are contacted; see Section 3.) The ProbResults function uses several values:

- n_Q: the number of terms in the query Q
- R_i^s: the number of past results from source s that contained query word i
- tq_s: the total number of times that source s has been queried by the beacon

The ProbResults score for site s for a query Q is calculated by:

$$ProbResultsScore_Q^s = \prod_{i=1}^{n_Q} R_i^s / tq_s$$

Each R_i^s / tq_s term represents the expected number of results (for any query) from s that contain query word i. Multiplying the R_i^s / tq_s values produces an aggregate score for all of the query words. We experimented with other ways of combining the R_i^s/tq_s terms (such as addition or taking the max) but found that multiplication worked best because it gave a higher score to sources that return results containing all of the query terms than to sources that return results containing several instances of just some of the query words.

In order to keep the beacon lightweight, the beacon cache does not contain whole documents, but instead only retains statistics about the word distributions in the results returned from each source. In fact, the only information that is needed for each source s is the R_i^s value for each word and the tq_s value for the source. To cache a new result document, the beacon parses the document, extracts the words, and increments the R_i^s values for each word for the source s. The result is that the beacon cache is very compact, and experiments show that a beacon responsible for 100 sources needs only a few tens of megabytes of cache. If necessary, the cache size can be bounded, resulting in graceful degradation in performance. Detailed results on the cache size are presented in [11].

Consider two sources s_1 and s_2 that are managed by the same beacon B. Source s_1 contains chemistry papers, while s_2 contains retail customer survey responses. After several queries, a portion of the beacon cache might contain:

	exothermic	oxygen	reactions	product	consumer	tq_s
s_1	70	80	120	0	40	100
s_2	10	15	80	130	210	150

The numbers in this table represent the R_i^s counts for each word and source. Now imagine that a user submits a query for "exothermic reactions" to B. The ProbResults score for s_1 is $(70/100) \times (120/100) = 0.84$, while the score for s_2 is $(10/150) \times (80/150) = 0.036$. Thus, the beacon B would first contact s_1 to search for "exothermic reactions." This makes sense, since site s_1 contains chemistry literature, and the beacon cache reflects that more previous results from s_1 contain "exothermic" and "reactions" than those from s_2. On the other hand, if the user searches for "consumer reactions," we would expect s_2 to receive a higher ProbResults score, and it does, scoring 0.75 (compared to 0.48 for s_1).

The ProbResults function is adapted from the Ind metric used in the bGlOSS information retrieval system [16]. ProbResults differs from Ind in several key ways in order to work in a loosely-coupled, dynamic peer-to-peer architecture. First, ProbResults tries to characterize both the behavior and the content of a source, while Ind focuses only on the content. For example, the R_i^s value used by ProbResults counts documents once per time they are returned as a query result, not just once overall (as in Ind). Thus, ProbResults gives higher weight to documents that are returned multiple times, better characterizing the behavior of the source in response to queries. Characterizing a source's behavior helps compensate for the inexact picture a loosely-coupled beacon has of the source's content. Another difference is that both the tq_s and R_i^s values are constantly updated in the beacon cache, unlike in GlOSS, where a static source summary is constructed. As a result, ProbResults produces scores that are tuned to the current behavior of the source, unlike Ind, whose scores can become stale over time. Results in Section 4 show that ProbResults produces better predictions in our system than the Ind ranking.

Two optimizations are useful to significantly improve the accuracy of the ProbResults function. First, if the beacon cache contains no information for a particular query word i for a given source s, a non-zero minimum value P_{min} is used, instead of zero, for R_i^s/tq_s. This minimum probability addresses the fact that the cache is an incomplete summary of a source's content. In the example above, the $R_i^{s_1}$ value for "product" for s_1 might be zero because s_1 does not have any documents containing the term "product," or because the documents containing "product" have not yet been cached; the beacon does not know which case is correct. Without P_{min}, a source for which only some of the query words appeared in the cache would have a score of zero. Given a query for "product exothermic reactions," we still would prefer source s_1 over some source s_3 for which $R_i^{s_3}$ is zero for all three query terms. Using P_{min} instead of $0/100$ for "product" ensures that the ProbResults score for s_1 for this query is non-zero.

The second optimization, called *experience weighting*, weights the R_i^s values in the beacon cache to reflect the beacon's experience with word i as a query word. If a query containing word i is sent to source s and the source returns results, the R_i^s value is multiplied by a constant *experience factor* EF. If a query containing word i returns no results from s, then R_i^s is divided by EF. Experience weighting allows the beacon to refine its cache statistics based on the behavior of the source, and to make better predictions despite having incomplete information about the source's query model or content changes at the source.

Due to space limitations, both of these optimizations, as well as experimental results demonstrating their utility, are described elsewhere [11].

3   Routing Queries Between Beacons

Different sources contain widely varying information, and a single beacon may not have the right sources to answer a given query. Even though a user initially submits his query to a single beacon, that beacon may have to forward the query to several other beacons in order to retrieve results. The simplest approach would be for the beacon to send the query to all of its neighbor beacons, but this flooding approach is too expensive in a large scale system. In this section we examine how a beacon can intelligently route queries to other beacons.

One approach is to use existing peer-to-peer routing techniques. For example, a beacon could forward each query to a randomly selected neighbor. Such "random walks" [23, 1] have been shown to be an effective and scalable way of routing queries in a peer-to-peer network. However, no content information is used during the routing process, and such information could be used in routing to reduce the number of contacted peers while still returning high quality results.

Beacons use the ProbResults ranking to route queries to information sources. We can extend this approach to use ProbResults to route queries between beacons. In particular, we study two mechanisms for routing queries between beacons:

- *Hierarchical*: A "superbeacon" caches results from beacons, and uses this cache along with ProbResults to choose beacons for a given query.

- *Flat*: Each beacon's neighbor beacons are treated as regular sources, and ProbResults produces a single ranking of both information sources and neighbor beacons.

An example of the *hierarchical* approach is shown in Figure 2(a). As the figure shows, the superbeacon is connected to the rest of the system's beacons, who are in turn connected to the system's sources. Each query is submitted to the superbeacon, which

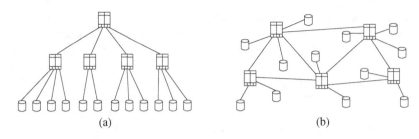

Fig. 2. Beacon network topologies: (a) hierarchical, (b) flat

uses ProbResults to rank the beacons for that query. The superbeacon routes the query to beacons in decreasing order of ProbResultsScore, until it has received enough results to satisfy the user's threshold. As with regular beacons, the superbeacon caches the results it receives for use in routing future queries.

One alternative approach we examined was to have each beacon send a copy of its cache to the superbeacon, and have the superbeacon evaluate the query against each cache to determine which beacon is best. This approach may result in more accurate routing, since the superbeacon would have more information about each beacon. However, while each beacon's cache is small, in a large scale system there are likely to be many beacons, and a large amount of space would be required to store a copy of every beacon's cache. Our goal is to keep beacons, even the superbeacon, as lightweight as possible, and therefore it is infeasible to expect the superbeacon to store copies of all of the beacon caches. As a result, we chose the approach described above, where the super-beacon keeps its own compact cache of results from the beacons and uses ProbResults to perform the routing.

Unfortunately, the hierarchical approach still may not be scalable enough. The super-beacon must know about all of the beacons in the system, and must perform processing on every user query. This degree of centralization is contrary to the decentralized philos-ophy of peer-to-peer systems, since the superbeacon can quickly become a bottleneck hindering the performance of the system.

A more scalable approach is to maintain the routing information in a decentralized manner, which is the goal of the *flat* architecture. An example of the flat architecture is shown in Figure 2(b). As this figure shows, a beacon's neighbors consist of both information sources and other beacons, forming a one-level "flat" topology. Each beacon caches results both from information sources and from other beacons. For each query, ProbResults is used to produce a single ranking of neighbors, and these neighbors are contacted in order of decreasing ProbResults score until enough results have been found. For example, a beacon might first route the query to an information source with a score of 0.9, then to a neighbor beacon that has a score of 0.8, then to another information source with a score of 0.7, and so on.

The flat approach avoids the centralization of the hierarchical approach, since there is no beacon that has to process every query or know about every other beacon. A disadvantage of the flat approach is that each beacon has less information than the superbeacon would, and thus prediction accuracy may suffer.

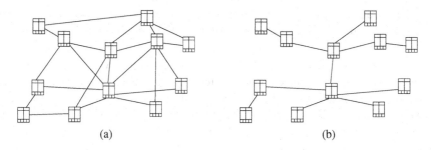

(a)   (b)

Fig. 3. Flat topologies: (a) random, (b) spanning tree. (Information sources omitted for clarity)

In experiments with our beacon prototype, we found that the topology of the flat network had a large impact on performance. Initially, we constructed a random topology, connecting each beacon with a randomly chosen set of beacon neighbors. An example of this topology is shown in Figure 3(a). In this topology, a given beacon has a path to all of the other beacons (and sources) along each of its beacon neighbor links. This means that the same documents can appear as results from any of these neighbor links, and, after a while, the ProbResults ranking begins to assign the same score to all of the beacon neighbors. This prevents the beacon from making effective routing decisions and performance suffers.

If we instead use a spanning tree topology, as in Figure 3(b), the inter-beacon routing performs better. A distinct set of beacons and sources is reachable along any given beacon neighbor link. The result is that the beacon's ProbResults scores effectively distinguish between the information available along each of the neighbor links, improving routing accuracy. Results in Section 4 demonstrate the performance improvement of the spanning tree topology.

It is possible that other peer-to-peer routing strategies might be used to route queries among beacons, including other strategies reported in the literature [32, 20]. As part of our ongoing work we are conducting experiments to compare these strategies to our ProbResults-based routing techniques.

4   Experimental Results

We have conducted a set of experiments to test the performance of our techniques. In these experiments, we used the beacon network to route keyword queries to information sources, and counted the total number of information sources contacted for each query. Our goal is to minimize the number of unnecessary sources contacted, so that we can reduce the load on sources, improve response time and enhance overall scalability.

Our results can be summarized as follows:

- The ProbResults function is more effective than a random-walk routing strategy in routing queries to a beacon's information sources, reducing the number of sources contacted per query by 90 percent. ProbResults is also more effective than routing strategies developed in non-peer-to-peer systems, such as GlOSS and CORI, reducing the number of contacted sources per query by at least 35 percent.

- Using a spanning tree topology to connect beacons in the *flat* architecture provides higher performance than a random graph topology, reducing the number of contacted sources per query by 23 percent.

- The *hierarchical* architecture provides the best performance overall; beacons in this architecture contact 70 percent fewer sources per query compared to beacons using a random walk strategy. The *flat* architecture, which avoids the potential bottlenecks of a centralized superbeacon, also provides good performance, with 31 percent fewer sources contacted per query compared to random walks.

We describe these results in more detail in this section.

4.1   Experimental Setup

In our experiments, we used a beacon network to route queries among 1,000 Internet information sources. To ensure our experiments were repeatable, we created our own information sources on machines in our lab, and populated them with HTML documents downloaded from 1,000 .com, .net, .gov, .edu and .org websites. Each information source managed documents downloaded from one website, and processed keyword searches using the vector space model with TF/IDF weighting. The total number of documents at all sources was 166,145, for a total of 4.0 GB. Each source had between 1 and 2,303 documents. Some sources had many documents and some had few, just as in the actual Internet.

We used synthetically generated keyword queries so that we could evaluate our system with a large query set. The distribution of query terms in our generated queries matched the observed distribution of several real query sets as reported in [7], namely, that the most frequent query terms are terms that are neither too common nor too rare in the document corpus. Queries had between one and six terms.

We assume that each user specifies a threshold T: the number of desired document results. This is similar to a search engine, where users usually only look at the first page or two of results. Here, we used $T = 10$, although other experiments (omitted here) show that our results and techniques generalize to other values of T.

Our beacon prototype is implemented in C++, and uses XML messages carried over HTTP to communicate between beacons. Also, a beacon accepts user queries and returns results via XML over HTTP, and queries information sources using HTTP.

4.2   Routing Queries Between Information Sources

First, we conducted an experiment to examine the performance of our techniques for routing queries between information sources. In this experiment, we used our beacon prototype to route queries between 100 sources selected randomly from our total set of 1,000. We used 40,000 queries generated from the terms in the content of these 100 sources. We compared several routing mechanisms:

- *ProbResults*: Our ranking function, described in Section 2.
- *Ind*: The Ind ranking function, used in the bGlOSS system [16].
- *Max*: The Max ranking function, used in the vGlOSS system [16].

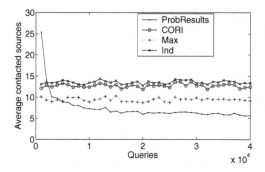

Fig. 4. Routing queries to information sources

- *CORI*: The ranking function used in the CORI system [13].
- *Random*: Queries are routed to randomly selected sources.

The Ind, Max and CORI ranking functions are defined in [16, 13]. The GlOSS and CORI systems require that sources export their data to a central index to aid in routing, a requirement that is not feasible if sources are uncooperative. In such a case, query probing can be used instead: a set of randomly chosen queries are sent to the source and the results are used to substitute for the full source content [8]. This is the approach we use in our experiments.

The results are shown in Figure 4. The horizontal axis in this figure shows the number of queries submitted to the beacon, and the vertical axis shows the average number of sources contacted per query. Initially the beacon using ProbResults performs poorly, but as the cache warms up, the performance improves. Eventually (after about 5,000 queries), the beacon using ProbResults performs better than a beacon using the other techniques. With a warm cache, a beacon using ProbResults contacts 52 percent fewer sources than one using CORI, 35 percent fewer than one using Max, 55 percent fewer than one using Ind, and 90 percent fewer than one using Random (62.3 sources per query, not shown). ProbResults performs well because it effectively tracks the behavior of sources in response to queries. The warm-up time of the beacon cache is a disadvantage compared to existing techniques; in ongoing work, we are examining using query probing to accelerate the warming time.

We have also examined the quality of returned information, and experimented with smaller and larger numbers of sources per beacon, with sources that have larger content databases, and with sources that have frequently changing content. In each case, a beacon using ProbResults performs better than one using Ind, Max, CORI or Random. These results are discussed in detail in [11].

4.3   Beacon Network Topologies in the Flat Architecture

Next, we examined the impact of the beacon network topology in the flat architecture. Recall that in this architecture, each beacon treats its neighbor beacons as regular sources, and produces a single ProbResults ranking of beacons and sources in order to route queries. We used a network of 50 beacons to route queries to 1,000 information

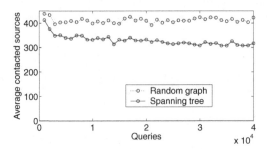

Fig. 5. Flat architecture topologies

sources. In general, we expect beacons to be assigned to 100 or so sources, but we felt that a network of only ten beacons was too small for our experiments. In ongoing work we are conducting experiments with larger numbers of beacons and sources. A total of 40,000 queries generated from content at all sources were submitted to randomly chosen beacons.

We examined two topologies for the connections between beacons:

- *Random network*: connections were made between randomly chosen beacons to form a general graph. Each beacon had an average of 5 beacon neighbors.
- *Spanning tree*: connections were made between randomly chosen beacons to form a spanning tree. Each beacon had up to 4 beacon neighbors.

In both cases, the links between beacons were bi-directional.

The results are shown in Figure 5. As the figure shows, under both topologies, the performance of the network improves as the beacon caches warm up. However, the improvement is most noticeable with the spanning tree topology. After about 20,000 queries the beacon network only needs to contact 316 sources per query in order to find results, compared to 412 with the random topology (30 percent more than the spanning tree topology). With the random network, the warming of the beacon caches produces improvements in routing to information sources, but this improvement is cancelled by the ineffective routing to other beacons. In contrast, with the spanning tree topology, beacons route queries to other beacons more effectively, and thus overall the routing improves as the beacon caches warm up.

The spanning tree topology is used with the flat architecture for the rest of the results reported in this paper. In ongoing work, we are examining other topologies and techniques to further optimize the flat routing architecture.

4.4   Routing Queries Between Beacons

We conducted an experiment to examine the performance of our techniques for routing queries between beacons. We used a network of 50 beacons to route queries to 1,000 information sources. As before, we submitted 40,000 queries to randomly chosen beacons. We compared the following techniques:

- *Hierarchical architecture*: A superbeacon used ProbResults to route queries to beacons, who then routed them to information sources.

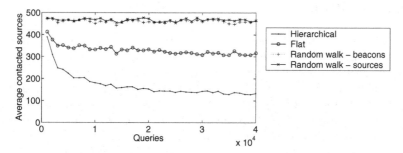

Fig. 6. Routing queries between beacons

- *Flat architecture*: Beacons used ProbResults to route queries to their neighbors in a flat topology of sources and beacons.

- *Random walk among beacons*: Beacons were organized into a network with a random topology (with an average of 5 neighbors), and random walking was used to route queries between beacons.

- *Random walk among sources*: Information sources were organized into a network with a random topology (with an average of 5 neighbors), and random walking was used to route queries between sources.

The two random walk approaches allowed us to examine different aspects of our techniques: *random walk among beacons* uses beacons but not IR-style routing between them, while *random walk among sources* uses a traditional unstructured peer-to-peer architecture instead of the beacon network.

The results are shown in Figure 6. As the figure shows, the best performance is achieved using the hierarchical architecture. The superbeacon, despite having limited information about the data accessible at each beacon, still has enough information to make informed routing decisions using the ProbResults metric.

The beacon network using the flat architecture contacts 2.3 times as many sources compared to the hierarchical approach (after the caches are warm). Unlike the superbeacon, which processes all 40,000 queries, each beacon in the flat architecture only sees a fraction of the queries. As a result, beacons in the flat architecture cache fewer results than the superbeacon, and have less information for making routing decisions. The result is less routing accuracy. The flat architecture may still be preferred, however, since it avoids the potential bottlenecks of the centralized superbeacon approach.

The flat architecture performs better than either random walk approach, contacting at least 31 percent fewer sources (after the caches are warmed). The beacons are able to use their cached information and the ProbResults ranking to make better routing decisions than the random walk. This demonstrates the value of information retrieval-style ranking to the query routing process.

Finally, the random walk among beacons approach performs only marginally better than the random walk among sources approach. This result demonstrates that the beacon routing among sources is not by itself sufficient in a network of distributed beacons; user queries must also be carefully routed to the proper beacons.

In ongoing work, we are examining further optimizations to our routing techniques, and comparing our techniques to other peer-to-peer routing strategies (such as [32, 20]).

5   Related Work

Several systems have been developed to perform information retrieval using a peer-to-peer architecture [27, 26, 30]. Beacons actually handle the "source selection" problem, while individual sources handle the "information retrieval" problem.

Meta-queriers such as GlOSS [16] and CORI [13] perform source selection, and beacons are similar to metaqueriers but adapted in several ways to work into a peer-to-peer architecture. First, the beacon is loosely coupled to the information source, while many existing systems require sources to export their contents or content summaries. This allows the beacons to work with sources that are not willing to provide more cooperation than simple searching. Loose coupling also makes it inexpensive to integrate a new source, addressing the high turnover observed in many peer-to-peer systems. Second, meta-queriers tend to be centralized, while in our system, sources are managed in a decentralized way by many beacons. Our approach enhances the scalability of the system. Third, existing systems usually build up a static characterization of the source contents, while a beacon constantly adapts its cache in response to new results. Our results show that continual adaptation improves source selection performance (especially when content is changing frequently; see [11]).

Several peer-to-peer systems have been developed to perform source selection [3, 15]. These systems, like metaqueriers, expect sources to export content summaries to aid in routing. The Harvest system is an early example, with "brokers" that are similar to our beacons [6]. Harvest combines source data export with search engine-style crawling of static content through modules called "gatherers." Unlike Harvest, our system requires neither source export, nor that the data be crawlable (as much hidden-web data is not).

Other systems that search multiple sources include data integration systems and search engines. Data integration systems, including traditional [9] and P2P systems [18, 17, 24] require tight schema integration. These systems construct complex schema mappings [4] or assume that most of the data has similar structure [18]. In a large scale system such as the Web, it is too expensive to construct all the required mappings, and data is structured in a wide variety of ways. Compared to these systems, our approach trades strong query semantics for enhanced scalability. Search engines [25] can search over HTML pages at many sites but do not deal well with uncrawlable or "hidden" data in web databases. Our approach uses sources' own query processors to search "hidden" data. Some search systems assume a consistent classification scheme or topic hierarchy to which sources can be assigned to aid in routing (such as in [19, 29]) but it is not clear that sources can always be assigned a single, unambiguous topic or that a single hierarchy is equally useful to all users.

Various approaches to routing in peer-to-peer systems have been proposed [32, 20, 23, 1, 28, 10, 21]. Our system uses the full text of content to aid in routing, while existing systems focus on document metadata, query statistics, network topology, or peer-processing capacity. It may be possible to combine our approach with existing approaches to achieve even more accuracy in routing.

Caching of data to improve performance has been well studied in many contexts, including the web [2], database systems [12], information retrieval [22] and peer-to-peer search [5]. Usually, data from a known source is cached to hide latency, not necessarily for source selection.

6   Conclusions and Future Work

We have examined how techniques adapted from information retrieval can be used to route queries in a peer-to-peer system. Our goal is to route queries to the best information sources, and allow those sources to perform the actual query processing. A network of beacons works together to perform the routing. In particular, we examined routing at two levels. First, individual beacons use ProbResults, a ranking adapted from information retrieval, to route queries to individual sources. Our techniques perform well despite limited cooperation from sources. Second, beacons also use ProbResults to route queries to other beacons. We presented two approaches for inter-beacon routing. In the hierarchical approach, a single superbeacon chooses among beacons, who then choose among sources. In the flat approach, beacons route queries to beacon neighbors if those neighbors have a higher ProbResults score than the beacon's sources. Experimental results demonstrate that our techniques are more effective than random walks for routing queries to information sources. These results show the value of using full-text content information when conducting peer-to-peer routing. In ongoing work, we are examining further routing optimizations, and comparing to other existing routing schemes.

References

1. L. Adamic, R. Lukose, A. Puniyani, and B. Huberman. Search in power-law networks. *Phys. Rev. E*, 64:46135–46143, 2001.
2. G. Barish and K. Obraczka. World wide web caching: Trends and techniques. *IEEE Communications Magazine*, May 2000.
3. M. Bawa, R. J. Bayardo Jr., S. Rajagopalan, and E. Shekita. Make it fresh, make it quick — searching a network of personal webservers. In *Proc. WWW*, 2003.
4. P.A. Bernstein, F. Giunchiglia, A. Kementsietsidis, J. Mylopoulos, L. Serafini, and I. Zaihrayeu. Data management for peer-to-peer computing: A vision. In *Proc. WebDB*, 2002.
5. B. Bhattacharjee. Efficient peer-to-peer searches using result-caching. In *Proc. IPTPS*, 2003.
6. C. M. Bowman, P. B. Danzig, D. R. Hardy, U. Manber, and M. F. Schwartz. The Harvest information discovery and access system. In *Proc. 2nd WWW Conference*, 1994.
7. B. Cahoon, K. S. McKinley, and Z. Lu. Evaluating the performance of distributed architectures for information retrieval using a variety of workloads. *ACM Transactions on Information Systems*, 18(1):1–43, January 2000.
8. J.P. Callan and M.E. Connell. Query-based sampling of text databases. *ACM TOIS*, 19(2):97–130, 2001.
9. S. Chawathe, H. Garcia-Molina, J. Hammer, K. Ireland, Y. Papakonstantinou, J. Ullman, and J. Widom. The TSIMMIS project: Integration of heterogeneous information sources. In *In Proc. of IPSJ Conference*, October 1994.
10. Y. Chawathe, S. Ratnasamy, L. Breslau, N. Lanham, and S. Shenker. Making Gnutella-like P2P systems scalable. In *Proc. ACM SIGCOMM*, 2003.
11. B.F. Cooper. Guiding users to information sources with InfoBeacons. In *Proc. ACM/IFIP/USENIX 5th International Middleware Conference*, 2004.
12. M.J. Franklin and M.J. Carey. Client-server caching revisited. In *Proc. Int'l Workshop on Distributed Object Management*, 1992.
13. J.C. French, A.L. Powell, J. Callan, C.L. Viles, T. Emmitt, K.J. Prey, and Y. Mou. Comparing the performance of database selection algorithms. In *Proc. SIGIR*, 1999.

14. N. Fuhr. A decision-theoretic approach to database selection in networked IR. *ACM TOIS*, 17(3):229–249, 1999.
15. L. Galanis, Y. Wang, S.R. Jeffrey, and D.J. DeWitt. Locating data sources in large distributed systems. In *Proc. VLDB*, 2003.
16. L. Gravano, H. Garcia-Molina, and A. Tomasic. GlOSS: Text-source discovery over the internet. *ACM TODS*, 24(2):229–264, June 1999.
17. A.Y. Halevy, Z.G. Ives, P. Mork, and I. Tatarinov. Piazza: Data management infrastructure for semantic web applications. In *Proc. WWW*, 2003.
18. R. Huebsch, J.M. Hellerstein, N. Lanham, B.T. Loo, S. Shenker, and I. Stoica. Querying the Internet with PIER. In *Proc. VLDB*, 2003.
19. P. Ipeirotis and L. Gravano. Distributed search over the hidden web: Hierarchical database sampling and selection. In *Proc. VLDB*, 2002.
20. V. Kalogeraki, D. Gunopulos, and D. Zeinalipour-Yazti. A local search mechanism for peer-to-peer networks. In *Proc. CIKM*, 2002.
21. B.T. Loo, R. Huebsch, I. Stoica, and J.M. Hellerstein. The case for a hybrid P2P search infrastructure. In *Proc. International Workshop on Peer-to-Peer Systems*, 2004.
22. Z. Lu and K. S. McKinley. Partial collection replication versus caching for information retrieval systems. In *Proc. SIGIR*, 2000.
23. Q. Lv, P. Cao, E. Cohen, K. Li, and S. Shenker. Search and replication in unstructured peer-to-peer networks. In *Proc. of ACM Int'l Conf. on Supercomputing (ICS'02)*, June 2002.
24. W. Nejdl, M. Wolpers, W. Siberski, C. Schmitz, M. Schlosser, I. Brunkhorst, and A. Loser. Super-peer-based routing and clustering strategies for RDF-based peer-to-peer networks. In *Proc. WWW*, 2003.
25. L. Page and S. Brin. The anatomy of a large-scale hypertext web search engine. In *Proc. WWW*, 1998.
26. P. Reynolds and A. Vahdat. Efficient peer-to-peer keyword searching. In *Proc. ACM/IFIP/USENIX International Middleware Conference*, 2003.
27. S. Shi, G. Yang, D. Wang, J. Yu, S. Qu, and M. Chen. Making peer-to-peer keyword searching feasible using multilevel partitioning. In *Proc. International Workshop on Peer-to-Peer Systems*, 2004.
28. I. Stoica, R. Morris, D. Karger, M. F. Kaashoek, and H. Balakrishnan. Chord: A scalable peer-to-peer lookup service for internet applications. In *Proc. SIGCOMM*, Aug. 2001.
29. A. Sugiura and O. Etzioni. Query routing for web search engines: Architecture and experiments. In *Proc. WWW*, 2000.
30. C. Tang, Z. Xu, and S. Dwarkadas. Peer-to-peer information retrieval using self-organizing semantic overlay networks. In *Proc. SIGCOMM*, 2003.
31. J. Wang and F. Lochovsky. Data extraction and label assignment for web databases. In *Proc. WWW*, 2003.
32. B. Yang and H. Garcia-Molina. Efficient search in peer-to-peer networks. In *Proc. Int'l Conf. on Distributed Computing Systems (ICDCS)*, July 2002.

Content-Based Similarity Search over Peer-to-Peer Systems*

Ozgur D. Sahin[1], Fatih Emekci[1], Divyakant Agrawal[1], and Amr El Abbadi[1]

Department of Computer Science, University of California Santa Barbara,
Santa Barbara, CA 93106
{odsahin, fatih, agrawal, amr}@cs.ucsb.edu

Abstract. Peer-to-peer applications are used to share large volumes of data. An important requirement of these systems is efficient methods for locating the data of interest in a large collection of data. Unfortunately current peer-to-peer systems either offer exact keyword match functionality or provide inefficient text search methods through centralized indexing or flooding. In this paper we propose a method based on popular Information Retrieval techniques to facilitate content-based searches in peer-to-peer systems. A simulation of the proposed design was implemented and its performance was evaluated using some commonly used test collections, including Ohsumed which was used for the TREC-9 Filtering Track. The experiments demonstrate that our approach is scalable as it achieves high recall by visiting only a small subset of the peers.

1   Introduction

Peer-to-peer systems [1, 2] have emerged as a powerful paradigm for exchanging data. They are used by millions of users for file sharing over the Internet. Typically, available systems use a centralized design or a flooding model for locating files and routing in the system. There have also been several academic peer-to-peer system proposals that offer very efficient key lookups. These systems are based on implementing a *Distributed Hash Table (DHT)* over the peers and they impose a certain structure on the overlay network constructed by the peers. In DHTs, a key lookup can typically be resolved by exchanging $O(logN)$ messages where N is the number of peers in the system. Examples of DHTs include Chord [3], CAN [4], Pastry [5] and Tapestry [6].

As the amount of data shared in peer-to-peer systems increases, it becomes very important to support content-based search of documents efficiently. Unfortunately, available systems do not provide efficient methods for keyword search. File sharing peer-to-peer systems use a central index or flooding to support keyword searches, neither of which is very desirable due to scalability and efficiency concerns. Different proposals have been made to improve the search efficiency in

---

* This research was funded in parts by NSF grants EIA 00-80134, IIS 02-09112, and CNF 04-23336.

W.S. Ng et al. (Eds.): DBISP2P 2004, LNCS 3367, pp. 61–78, 2005.

these systems [7, 8, 9, 10] based on selective query forwarding, notion of gossip, and topic segmentation. DHTs, on the other hand, only support *exact match* lookups since they use hashing to distribute the objects in the system. If the exact key is not known, the users cannot locate the objects they are looking for. Several methods have been proposed to provide *keyword search* capabilities for DHTs [11, 12, 13, 14]. However these methods, with the exception of [14], only provide keyword matching and are subject to load balancing problems as some *popular* keywords in real systems tend to appear and be queried more frequently than others. They are also susceptible to polysemy (words having multiple meanings) and synonymy (multiple words having the same meaning). However, these problems have been extensively addressed by the Information Retrieval community for centralized document retrieval. One popular solution is Latent Semantic Indexing (LSI) [15]. LSI facilitates the retrieval of relevant documents even when some of the query keywords do not appear in the documents. pSearch [14] is the first peer-to-peer system to use LSI to reduce the feature vectors of the documents, which are then used for distributing document information among the peers. pSearch requires the maintenance of a multidimensional CAN. As mentioned in [14], pSearch is less efficient as the size of the corpus increases. Alternatively, Zhu et al. [16] use Locality Sensitive Hash Functions to provide semantic search over DHTs, and Koloniari et al. [17] employ multi-level bloom filters to route XML path queries and to build content-based overlay networks.

Our design for content-based similarity search is similar to pSearch as we employ Information Retrieval techniques to extract feature vectors from documents and use them to determine the locations of the document indices in a DHT (Chord [3] in our case). This provides content-based search as it uses LSI for feature vector extraction. Unlike pSearch, our approach is independent of corpus size and hence is scalable. Any type of data, such as documents, images, or music files, can be queried with our design as long as there is a meaningful method to extract feature vectors from the objects. It can also be used to answer other types of queries such as *"Find the top k documents/images which are similar to a given sample."*, which are common in information retrieval and image retrieval systems. Another interesting possibility is to employ our design for searching the Web using a distributed model rather than a centralized one. For example, most commercial search engines crawl millions of web pages and build a centralized index to find the web pages that contain certain keywords. They typically index a small fraction of the Web and scalability will be a serious problem for such centralized systems considering the rapid growth of the Web. A peer-to-peer approach with scalability and decentralization properties would significantly improve performance. ODISSEA [18] investigates the issue of designing a P2P-based search engine for the Web. Li et al. [19] analyze the feasibility of peer-to-peer keyword search over the Web and conclude that it is feasible with certain optimizations and compromises. In general, a peer-to-peer approach provides the following benefits over a centralized design:

– Due to the underlying peer-to-peer architecture, the system is scalable, robust (no single point of failure), fault-tolerant, decentralized, and dynamic.

- Distributing the load over many peers is more cost effective than maintaining a dedicated site to handle the central index.
- When a new document is inserted into the system, the associated index information is created and becomes accessible to other peers immediately.

The rest of the paper is organized as follows: In Sect. 2 we present background to our work. Section 3 explains the basics of our document distribution model. Section 4 discusses some improvements to the basic design in order to provide load balancing. Experimental results are presented in Sect. 5, and the last section concludes the paper.

2   Background

In this section we introduce the Vector Space Model for document representation and Latent Semantic Analysis for reducing the size of vectors while preserving information related to synonymy and polysemy. Finally we present Chord, the underlying peer-to-peer structure used in our system.

2.1   Vector Space Model (VSM)

In this model, a document is represented as a term vector [20]. Each component of the vector represents the importance of the corresponding term within the document. Components are calculated using TFxIDF scheme, where TF (term frequency) is the frequency of the term within the document and IDF (inverse document frequency) is the inverse of the number of documents in which the term appears. The idea behind this scheme is that terms that appear more frequently in a document are good candidates for representing this document, whereas terms that appear in too many documents should be penalized.

A document set with d documents can be represented by a $t \times d$ term-document matrix, which is obtained by combining the vector representations of all documents, where t is the number of distinct terms appearing in the set.

Each query is also represented as a vector, which is the weighted sum of the vectors of the terms appearing in the query. A common similarity measure is *cosine similarity*, which is the cosine of the angle between the vectors. The cosine similarity between two n-dimensional vectors A and B is expressed as:

$$\cos \theta = \frac{A \cdot B}{|A||B|} = \frac{\sum_{i=1}^{n} A_i B_i}{\sqrt{\sum_{i=1}^{n} A_i^2} \sqrt{\sum_{i=1}^{n} B_i^2}}$$

2.2   Latent Semantic Indexing (LSI)

VSM suffers from synonymy and polysemy. LSI addresses this problem by trying to discover associations between terms and documents (implicit semantic structure) in the document set [15]. It uses Singular Value Decomposition (SVD) to approximate the original term-document matrix [21].

Consider a $t \times d$ dimensional term-document matrix, X, where d is the number of documents and t is the number of distinct terms in the document set. X can be decomposed into the product of 3 matrices: $X = U\Sigma V^T$. This is called the singular value decomposition of X. U and V are orthogonal matrices with dimensions $t \times m$ and $d \times m$ respectively, where m is the rank of X. Σ is an $m \times m$ diagonal matrix with the singular values of X in decreasing order along its diagonal. LSI uses a simple technique to reduce the sizes of the resulting matrices to get optimal approximations to X. Among the singular values in Σ, the first k largest ones are kept and the remaining ones are set to zero. The zero rows and columns of Σ are deleted and a new matrix, Σ_k, of dimensions $k \times k$ is obtained. By deleting the corresponding columns and rows from U and V, two new matrices U_k and V_k are obtained. The new matrix $X_k = U_k\Sigma_k V_k^T$ is of rank k and is an approximation of the original term-document matrix X. The rows of the $V_k\Sigma_k$ matrix can be considered as the reduced vector representations for the documents. Hence each document is represented by a vector of size k, rather than the original t dimensional vectors. Although t is very large, i.e., tens of thousands for a fairly large data set, it has been shown that selecting the value of k between $100 - 300$ for LSI yields good results [15, 22].

2.3   Chord

Chord [3] is a P2P system that implements a Distributed Hash Table. It uses an m-bit identifier ring, $[0, 2^m - 1]$, for routing and locating objects. Both the objects and the peers in the system are assigned m-bit keys through a uniform hash function and mapped to the identifier ring. An object is stored at the peer following it on the ring, i.e., its *successor*.

Each peer maintains a finger table for efficient routing. The finger table of a peer contains the IP addresses and Chord identifiers of $O(logN)$ other peers, i.e., its neighbors, that are at exponentially increasing distances from the peer on the identifier ring, where N is the number of peers in the system. Peers periodically exchange *refresh* messages with their neighbors to keep their finger tables up to date. Chord is designed for very efficient exact-key lookups. A lookup request is delivered to its destination via $O(logN)$ hops. At each hop, the request is forwarded to a peer from the finger table whose identifier most immediately precedes the destination point. In Fig. 1, peer $P1$'s request for document d is routed through $P2$ and $P3$ to d's successor $P4$, by following the links from the local finger tables.

Chord is a dynamic system in which peers can enter or leave the system at will. When a new peer wants to join, it is assigned an identifier and it sends a join request toward this identifier through an existing Chord peer. The affected finger tables are updated accordingly and the keys that are assigned to the new peer are transferred from its successor. Similarly, upon departure of a peer, its keys are assigned to its successor and the affected finger tables are updated.

3   Document Distribution Model

In this section, we describe our system which provides content-based document search over the Chord peer-to-peer system. We first introduce the general design

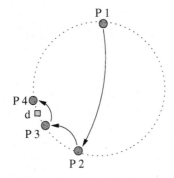

Fig. 1. An example Chord system

and then discuss each step in more detail. Possible improvements to the basic model are discussed in Sect. 4.

We use VSM to extract the feature vectors of the documents, which are then reduced to a lower dimensional space using LSI. Associated with each document is a document index which contains the location (IP address) and the vector of the document. Each document index is stored at multiple locations in the system. The document indices are distributed over the Chord system according to the document vectors in such a way that documents that are semantically similar to each other are mapped to nearby locations on the Chord ring. When a query is issued, its feature vector is computed. The queries are then routed in the system according to their vectors and the document indices stored at the destination peers are checked for possible results. A query may result in multiple lookups in order to improve accuracy.

3.1   Computing Document Vectors

The initial feature vectors of the documents are extracted using VSM. The calculated term-document matrix is then reduced using LSI to transform the document vectors into a low dimensional space, which is called the *LSI space*. However, this process requires global knowledge about the document collection, for example to compute the IDF of the terms. Since our system is designed for a dynamic distributed environment, it is not feasible to access all the documents. Fortunately, it has been shown that LSI works efficiently if it is provided with a small representative subset (sample set) of the whole document set [23, 24]. Hence the basis of the LSI space and the IDF of the terms are calculated only for the sample set. This information is called the *global information* and used by the peers to calculate the document vectors locally.

We assume that a well-known peer in the system is assigned the task of managing global information about the system. It uses a randomly sampled subset of the documents to compute the initial global information, which is then distributed to all peers in the system. This peer periodically samples some documents from the system and incrementally updates the global information accordingly in order to reflect the properties of the documents currently shared in the system [21]. If the change in the global information is above a certain threshold, the global information is recalculated and disseminated to the peers. Assuming that the general characteristics of the document set changes slowly over time, the global information needs not to be disseminated frequently. For sampling, a set of random Chord keys are generated and the peers responsible for these keys are contacted to retrieve sample documents. To disseminate information, an efficient P2P broadcast protocol can be used, such as the one proposed in [25].

The peers compute the vector representations of the documents locally using the global information. The vectors of the documents are computed by extracting the frequencies of the terms in the documents and then calculating the weighted sum of the term frequencies and the corresponding term vectors (*folding-in*).

3.2   Publishing Documents

The document indices need to be distributed among the different peers in the P2P environment[1]. The distribution scheme should satisfy the following requirements:

- Indices of similar documents are stored at the same peer,
- Given a query vector, it is possible to identify the peers that are likely to store the indices of documents that are similar to the query,
- Indices are distributed evenly among the peers.

The traditional Chord uniformly distributes objects on the peers regardless of content. Our main challenge is to develop a content-based hash function that maps the higher dimensional vectors to the single dimensional Chord ring. This content-based hash function needs to capture the notion of similarity used for retrieval. Due to the popularity of the cosine similarity measure, we distribute and retrieve documents based on this measure. Our hashing scheme is based on the similarity of a document to a set of preselected reference documents, which is called the *reference set*. The vectors of the reference documents are referred to as *reference vectors*. Reference vectors are selected only once at the system initiation time while computing the initial global statistics, and then used by every peer in the system. New peers can simply obtain the reference set from any other peer while joining the system. In our experiments, we used 2 different schemes for selecting the reference vectors. First, we picked them randomly from the initial sample set, and second we clustered the initial sample set and used the cluster centroids as references.

For each document, we compute the cosine of the angle between the document vector and each reference vector. The cosine of the angle between a document vector and a reference vector is called the *reference cosine* of the document with respect to this reference. The references are then sorted by reference cosine values in decreasing order. The sorted list of references is called the *reference list*

---

[1] The process of storing a document's index in the system will be referred to as *publishing* the document.

of the document. The top elements of the reference list of a document are the references that are closest to the document in terms of cosine similarity. Note that each document has a potentially different ordering of the references, which is one of the permutations of the reference set.

Example 1: We use a simple example to illustrate the above process. Consider a large set of documents. For simplicity, assume that each document is represented by a 2-d vector. We will focus on the following four documents:

$d_1=[0.45\ 0.89]$, $d_2=[0.56\ 0.83]$, $d_3=[0.41\ 0.91]$, $d_4=[0.95\ 0.32]$.

We get the following cosine similarity values between each pair of documents (corresponding angles in degrees are shown in parenthesis):

$\cos(d_1,d_2)=0.992\ (7.1)$ $\cos(d_1,d_3)=0.999\ (2.1)$ $\cos(d_1,d_4)=0.707\ (45.0)$
$\cos(d_2,d_3)=0.987\ (9.3)$ $\cos(d_2,d_4)=0.789\ (37.9)$ $\cos(d_3,d_4)=0.681\ (47.1)$

These values suggest that the first three documents, d_1, d_2, and d_3, are similar to each other, whereas d_4 is not similar to the other three documents.

Consider a reference set with 8 reference vectors: $R_0=[0.32\ 0.95]$, $R_1=[0.80\ 0.60]$, $R_2=[0.14\ 0.99]$, $R_3=[0.89\ 0.48]$, $R_4=[0.37\ 0.93]$, $R_5=[0.16\ 0.99]$, $R_6=[0.50\ 0.87]$, and $R_7=[0.94\ 0.35]$.

We start by computing the reference list of d_1. First, we calculate the reference cosine values for each reference, and then get the reference list of d_1 after sorting the reference vectors in decreasing order of the cosine values:

$RC(d_1)=\{0.990,0.845,0.949,0.800,0.997,0.956,0.999,0.733\}$
$RL(d_1) = R_6, R_4, R_0, R_5, R_2, R_1, R_3, R_7$.

Repeating the same steps, we obtain the reference lists for each document:

$RL(d_2) = R_6, R_4, R_0, R_1, R_5, R_2, R_3, R_7$.
$RL(d_3) = R_4, R_6, R_0, R_5, R_2, R_1, R_3, R_7$.
$RL(d_4) = R_7, R_3, R_1, R_6, R_4, R_0, R_5, R_2$.

We make two observations regarding the reference lists of the documents:

1. If two documents are similar, then they have many common references at the top positions of their reference lists. For example, d_1, d_2, and d_3 have the same set of vectors (R_6, R_4, and R_0) at the top three positions of their lists. However, these three documents do not share any of the top three references with d_4, which is in fact not similar. Thus the top vectors in the reference lists of the documents can be used to distribute documents among peers so that similar documents are mapped to close locations on the Chord ring.
2. Even if two documents are similar and share some top references in their lists, these references may appear in slightly different positions. For example, the top two references are (R_6,R_4) for d_1 and d_2, and (R_4,R_6) for d_3. Our design should be able to handle such mismatches so that even if two similar documents have common references at slightly different positions, they should be mapped to nearby locations.

Given the reference list of a document, we use it to determine where to store the document. Since documents tend to be large, a typical approach is to leave the actual document stored wherever it was created, and use the Chord peer to maintain a document index, which contains a pointer to the peer storing the document (IP address) and the vector of the document. Thus the peer storing the index can locally calculate the similarity of the document to a query during query lookup using the document vector.

The reference list is hashed to the Chord identifier space as follows: Pick the top K reference ID's in the reference list. Concatenate their binary representations, with the highest relevant reference as the high order bits. If there are any remaining bits in the Chord bit representation, fill it with zeros. In our experiments, we use $K = 2$, and hence use the top pair of references to hash a document to a peer in the Chord ring. Thus, for example, document d_1 and d_2 would hash to the same peer since they share the same top 2 references. However, d_3 will not map to the same peer although it does share a lot of similarity with d_1 and d_2.

In light of the above observations, we store multiple indices for each document based on multiple pairs chosen from the top reference vectors from a document's reference list. For example, d_1 in Example 1 can be published for the reference pairs (R_6, R_4), (R_6, R_0), and (R_4, R_0). The number of indices to be published for each document, *docPerm*, is a system parameter, and poses a tradeoff between the storage space and recall rate. Storing more replicas of a document's index requires more storage but also provides better chances of finding this document when it is in fact similar to a query. A peer can decide on the value of *docPerm* for a document depending on different criteria. For example if the document is considered important, its index can have more replicas. Another important decision is the choice of the different reference pairs. Our experiments suggest that choosing the reference pairs from the top five references of the reference list provides good results.

Example 2: We now continue Example 1 to demonstrate the index distribution process. Assume we publish d_1 for the pairs (R_6, R_4), (R_6, R_0), and (R_4, R_0) in a Chord system that uses 10-bit keys. Since there are 8 references, each reference number can be represented by 3 bits. The Chord key corresponding to (R_6, R_4) is 1101000000 because $6 = (110)_2$ and $4 = (100)_2$. Similarly, the keys corresponding to (R_6, R_0) and (R_4, R_0) are 1100000000 and 1000000000 respectively. The index of d_1 is therefore stored at the peers that are responsible for these three keys. This process is illustrated in Fig. 2. Now consider document d_3 with reference pairs (R_4, R_6), (R_4, R_0), and (R_6, R_0). The reference pair (R_4, R_0) will map an index of d_3 at the same peer where d_1's reference pair (R_4, R_0) mapped to. Hence d_1 and d_3, which are similar with respect to their reference lists, will be mapped to the same peer.

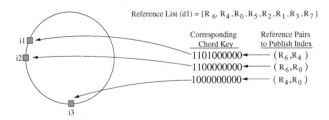

Fig. 2. Publishing a document index at multiple locations on the Chord ring

Note that if we use 7 reference vectors instead of 8, then no key with '111' prefix will be generated and a portion of the Chord ring will remain unused. Therefore the number of references should be a power of 2 for better utilization of the Chord ring.

3.3   Query Lookup

When a query is issued, its feature vector is computed and reduced into the LSI space. Similar to the distribution of document indices, the reference list of the query is calculated and the reference pairs are selected to lookup the query. The key for each lookup is calculated from the corresponding reference pair in the same way as the document index keys are calculated. The query is then routed to multiple locations on the Chord ring using these keys. Increasing the number of lookups for a query, i.e., *queryPerm*, results in more accurate answers but also causes extra network traffic and processing load.

Each lookup request contains the query vector. After the lookup message is delivered, the destination peer checks the local indices and identifies the documents similar to the query. The results are then sent back to the peer that initiated the query. The initiator peer collects the results of all lookup requests and returns the top results.

A peer can also choose to perform a progressive lookup so that the query answer is incrementally refined at each step. In this case, the querying peer generates only one lookup request for the query. If the results returned by this lookup are not satisfactory, then another lookup request corresponding to some other reference pair is generated and the query answer is refined using the results of this lookup. The querying peer continues the progressive lookup process until the cumulative results returned are satisfactory.

4   Load Balancing in the System

The basic model developed in the previous section may lead to an imbalanced load distribution among the peers. Some peers in the system may store more index information or answer more query lookups than others. We propose two enhancements to the basic model for solving this problem.

4.1   Multi-level Reference Sets

In the basic model, pairs of references are used to generate the Chord keys for the document indices. If there are 2^r reference vectors, then the document indices are distributed to $2^r * 2^r = 2^{2r}$ distinct locations on the Chord ring. For example, in a system with $2^5 = 32$ references, only 2^{10} Chord locations are utilized for storing indices. If the number of peers in the system exceeds 2^{10}, some of the peers will not be responsible for any of these locations and thus will not store any document indices. Although the basic key generation schema is enough when the number of participating peers is less than 2^{2r} for a system with r references, the model should be able to support more peers. Therefore a new schema is needed that provides finer distribution of the indices, i.e., maps the document indices to more locations on the ring.

We propose to use multiple levels of references to further refine the mapping of document indices to the Chord ring. Instead of one reference set, multiple reference sets are maintained. Each document has a reference list associated with each reference set. One reference pair from each reference list is then used to construct different portions of the key. Assuming that 2 reference sets with 2^r references each are used, the leftmost $2r$ bits of the Chord key can be constructed according to the reference pair from the first set, whereas the next $2r$ bits are determined by the reference pair from the second set. With this approach, $2^{2r} * 2^{2r} = 2^{4r}$ locations can be addressed using 2 reference sets of 2^r reference vectors. Note that if we choose to use the basic schema with two times $(2^r + 2^r = 2^{r+1})$ the reference vectors rather than using the 2-level schema, we can only address $2^{r+1} * 2^{r+1} = 2^{2r+2}$ locations. For example, increasing the the number of reference vectors from 32 to 64 in the basic schema increases the address space from 2^{10} to 2^{12}, whereas it can be increased to 2^{20} with 2 sets of 32 reference vectors. Note that the same reference sets and the order are used by every peer, however the number of reference pairs and the pairs themselves for publishing documents and looking up queries are chosen locally by the individual peers.

A nice property of the multi-level schema is that the documents that have the same first level pair and different higher level pairs are assigned to closer locations on the ring since the first level reference pair is used to construct the most significant bits of the key. When the number of peers in the system is small, these documents are likely to be stored at the same peer. Hence the higher level reference vectors will be effective as the number of peers in the system increases.

4.2   Load Aware Peer Joins

Some documents can be very popular and shared by many peers. All replicas of a popular document or a large group of very similar documents will be hashed to the same locations on the Chord ring, causing *hot spots* in the system. As a result, the peers that are responsible for those *hot spots* will have a higher load in terms of both the number of indices stored and the queries received.

To alleviate this problem, we propose *Load Aware Peer Joins* so that when a new peer joins the system, the join request is forwarded toward a heavily loaded peer, allowing it to reduce its load by transferring some of its indices to the new peer. In order to enable this forwarding, each peer in the system keeps load information about its neighbors in its routing table. The peers piggyback their load information on the refresh messages they exchange with their neighbors. Whenever a peer receives a join request, it checks its routing table to find the neighbor with the highest load. If the load on that neighbor is greater than this peer's load, the join request is forwarded to that neighbor. The join request is forwarded until it reaches a peer whose load is higher than the load of every peer in its routing table. This peer then divides the key range it maintains into two and assigns one half to the new peer.

In our experiments we only consider the number of indices stored at a peer as its load, however other information, such as the number of messages processed or the number of lookup requests received, can easily be incorporated into the load value. When a peer needs to divide its key range, it sorts the stored indices by their keys and uses the key of the median index as the split point. Thus the load, i.e., the number of indices stored, is divided evenly between this peer and the new peer. Note that peer failures are handled by the underlying Chord layer.

5 Experimental Results

We have evaluated the performance of our approach using a simulator implemented on top of the Chord Simulator[2].

5.1 Experimental Setup

All collections were indexed with the SMART[3] system [26]. The default stop list and stemmer of SMART were enabled and *atc* term weighting was used during the runs. We used LAS2 from SVDPACKC[4] for computing the SVD of the term-document matrix. All experiments were performed on a machine with dual Intel Xeon 2GHz processors and 1GB of main memory, running Linux RedHat 8.0.

Data Sets
We used three data sets for the experiments (Table 1 summarizes the information about these data sets):
MED[5] : Contains 1033 medical abstracts and 30 queries.
Ohsumed[6] : Consists of 348,566 documents from the online medical information database (Medline) over a period of five years (1987-1991) [27]. It was used for the TREC-9 Filtering Track [28]. It includes 63 queries.
Test10k: Created by randomly choosing 10000 documents from the Ohsumed collection. 63 queries from the Ohsumed collection were used as queries. This data set was used for calibrating the system and as an intermediate step for our scalability experiments.

Table 1. Data sets used in the experiments

Data Set	Doc. No	Term No	Doc-Term Assoc No	Query No	Query Term No
MED	1033	7996	54,478	30	9.93
Test10k	10,000	39,567	624,512	63	4.87
Ohsumed	348,542	108,697	14,294,276	63	4.89

When indexing Ohsumed, we randomly sampled 20% of the documents and discarded the terms that appear in only one sampled document. The term-

---

[2] Available at http://www.pdos.lcs.mit.edu/chord/.
[3] We used SMART version 11.0 from Cornell University, which is available at ftp://ftp.cs.cornell.edu/pub/smart.
[4] Available at http://www.netlib.org/svdpack/.
[5] Available at ftp://ftp.cs.cornell.edu/pub/smart.
[6] Available at http://trec.nist.gov/data.html.

document matrix had 69903 documents, 59428 terms and 14,245,007 nonzero entries. Indexing the sample set with SMART took around 5 minutes. Computing the SVD of the term-document matrix and folding-in the remaining documents took around 25 minutes. For the other two data sets, no sampling was used and no terms were discarded. All the documents were indexed using the abstract field. The queries were indexed based on the description field.

Evaluation Metrics

In the experiments, we measured the recall rate, the number of peers contacted for a query, and the distribution of indices among the peers. Our main focus was to determine the efficiency of our system for retrieving a fixed number, k, of documents that are most similar to given queries. We compared our system against centralized LSI. For each query, the top k documents obtained by running LSI on the whole data set, set A, were considered as the actual results. Then we used our system to retrieve k documents, set B, and computed the percentage of the actual results included in B. The recall rate for a query is computed as follows: $Recall = \frac{|A \cap B|}{|A|} \times 100\%$. We set k to 15. This is a reasonable value since most users only view the top 10 results when searching the Web [14]. Each lookup for a query returned the top 15 local results from the destination peers and these results were merged at the querying peer to compute the final result. Note that in this case, since we are interested in the top k documents and $|A| = |B|$, precision and recall values are the same.

Selecting Reference Pairs

The reference pairs for publishing indices and looking up queries were selected from the top 5 reference vectors. To determine the reference pair order, we executed sample queries over the sample set when computing the initial *global information*. The document indices were published and then queried for all possible pairs. The reference pair order is determined by the retrieval rate of each reference pair. We ran a set of queries over the Test10k data set and determined the return effectiveness of different reference pairs. Based on these experiments, we determined the following ordered list of 21 possible reference pairs for publishing documents: $\{1,1\}$, $\{1,2\}$, $\{2,3\}$, $\{3,2\}$, $\{2,1\}$, $\{4,3\}$, $\{5,2\}$, $\{1,3\}$, $\{1,4\}$, $\{1,5\}$, $\{2,4\}$, $\{2,5\}$, $\{3,4\}$, $\{3,5\}$, $\{3,1\}$, $\{4,2\}$, $\{4,5\}$, $\{4,1\}$, $\{5,3\}$, $\{5,4\}$, $\{5,1\}$. Thus the reference pairs for publishing a document are determined according to this order based on the value of *docPerm*. For example, if *docPerm*=3, d_1 from Example 1 is published for the reference pairs (R_6, R_6), (R_6, R_4), and (R_4, R_0). The identity pair, $\{1,1\}$, is used for a more uniform index distribution over the Chord ring. If we did not use the identity pair, a more complex algorithm would be needed for creating the Chord keys corresponding to the reference pairs, because the keys in certain portions of the Chord ring would never be utilized. The identity pair is used only once to avoid the overloading of the peers responsible for these pairs.

Setting *docPerm* to a big value is usually affordable because it only requires limited additional storage for storing the replicas of the index. However, increasing *queryPerm* is more costly as it increases the number of visited peers and the bandwidth consumed for processing a query. To reduce the query reference pairs, if the pair {i,j} is used, we ignored the inverse of the pair, i.e., {j,i}. Hence the 21 possible pairs reduce to the following: {1,1}, {1,2}, {2,3}, {1,3}, {2,5}, {1,4}, {1,5}, {3,4}, {2,4}, {4,5}, {3,5}.

5.2   Results Without Load Balancing

For the experiments, three different scenarios were used: *1)* MED data set over 100 peers, *2)* Test10k data set over 1000 peers, and *3)* Ohsumed data set over 10000 peers. The documents in the data sets were evenly assigned to peers and the peers joined an initially empty system. The queries were issued after all peers joined the system and initiated at randomly chosen peers. The reported results are the average values over all the queries.

We first ran the system without implementing the load balancing schemes discussed in Sect. 4. We used 32 randomly selected reference vectors. Figure 3 shows the corresponding recall rates for different values of *docPerm* (1 to 21) and *queryPerm* (1 to 11) for each scenario. The best results are obtained from MED data set (Figure 3(a)). Even with *docPerm*=1 and *queryPerm*=1, 48.2% of the actual results are retrieved. It goes up to 94.9% with increasing *docPerm* and *queryPerm*. As the data set and system size increase, the recall rates decrease but they are still quite good. This shows that the system is scalable because the recall rates do not degrade much when there are big increases in system size and data set size. For Test10k data set (Figure 3(b)), the recall rate starts from 38.8% and goes up to 94.7%, while varying between 47.6% and 89.4% for Ohsumed data set (Figure 3(c)). The recall improvements gained by increasing the values of *queryPerm* and *docPerm* diminish as their values increase. Setting the value of *queryPerm* between 4-8 results in good recall. When *queryPerm*=8 and *docPerm*=15, the recall rates are 93.1, 86.5, and 81.6 respectively for each scenario.

As seen in Figs. 3(b) and 3(c), when *queryPerm* is 1, the recall rate remains constant. That is because the query only goes to the peer corresponding to the identity pair, and thus increasing *docPerm*, i.e., publishing document indices for reference pairs other than the identity pair, does not improve the result. For the MED data set, however, the results do improve because there are very few peers in the system and the document indices published for other pairs are also likely to be assigned to the peer that is queried. The graphs for Test10k and Ohsumed data sets demonstrate very similar behavior, showing that the idea of selecting the reference pair order according to the sample set works.

Table 2 shows the average number of peers contacted to answer a query for different values of *queryPerm* for each scenario. The path length increases linearly with *queryPerm* as expected. More importantly, it scales well in terms of the number of peers. A single lookup visits 3.16 peers (0.32%) in a 1000 peer system, whereas it visits 7.02 peers (0.07%) when the peer number is increased to 10000. Thus our system delivers high recall by visiting very few peers.

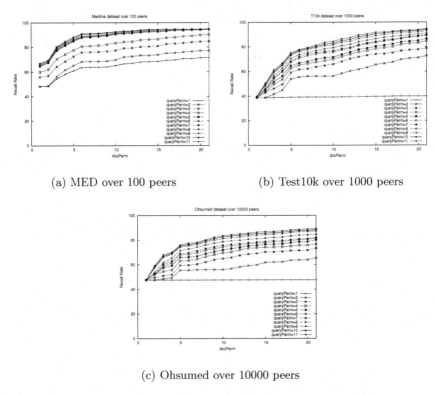

(a) MED over 100 peers   (b) Test10k over 1000 peers

(c) Ohsumed over 10000 peers

Fig. 3. Recall rates before implementing Load Balancing schemes

5.3   Results with Load Balancing

We also ran the system after incorporating the load balancing strategies. We used
two levels of reference sets with 32 randomly selected references at each level.
When constructing the keys, only one reference pair was selected from the second
level and combined with the pairs selected from the first level. Figure 4 shows
the corresponding recall rates. Load balancing reduces recall rates because the
documents are now distributed at a finer granularity with more reference vectors.
The amount of decrease is proportional to the number of peers: It is very little
for MED data set (Figure 4(a)) and much larger for Ohsumed (Figure 4(c)).
The recall now changes from 19.37% to 54.71% for Ohsumed data set. As seen
from Table 2, the number of visited peers for processing a query does not change
much after implementing load balancing.

Although the recall rates are high with the basic design, the distribution
of indices can be very skewed. Figure 5 shows the index distribution for each
scenario before and after the load balancing schemes are implemented. The peers
in the system are sorted in decreasing order of the number of indices they are
assigned. The *X axis* shows the percentage of peers, and the corresponding values
are the percentage of indices assigned to these peers. In the figure, *Optimal* shows

Table 2. Average number of peers visited to answer a query

query Perm	MED over 100 peers		Test10k over 1000 peers		Ohsumed over 10000 peers	
	Before LB	After LB	Before LB	After LB	Before LB	After LB
1	1.43	1.50	3.16	3.21	7.02	7.50
2	2.87	2.93	6.44	6.67	14.10	14.33
4	5.93	5.70	12.91	13.37	27.65	28.59
8	11.93	11.47	26.00	26.49	55.86	57.81
11	16.50	15.57	35.81	36.57	76.11	79.02

the result for the ideal case where every peer in the system is assigned the same number of indices. Without load balancing, the index distribution is very skewed for Ohsumed data set. All the indices are stored at only 10% of the peers. This shows that the distribution of indices becomes very imbalanced in the basic design when the number of peers in the system is large. Our load balancing strategies, greatly improved the index distributions in all three cases, however at the expense of inferior recall.

Reference Vector Selection

Finally, we evaluated the effect of the number and selection criteria of reference vectors on the system performance. We measured the recall rates using the Ohsumed data set over 10000 peers with load balancing implemented. For reference vector selection, we used two methods: *1)* Selecting randomly, *2)* Clustering the sample set and using the cluster representatives as references. For clustering, k-Means clustering was used. Figure 6 shows the recall rates for different number of references with random selection and cluster selection when *queryPerm* is 8. The graph validates our two predictions:

1) When the number of references is fixed, cluster selection provides better results. For 32+32 references (two levels), recall rates go up to 58.84% for cluster selection and 51.64% for random selection. **2)** Using more references decreases the recall rates. For example, when 64+64 clustered references are used, the highest recall is 56.93, while it is 58.84% when 32+32 clustered references are used. We also note that the index distribution gets better as the number of references increases, and random selection provides better distribution than cluster selection.

5.4   Discussion

The proposed architecture demonstrated efficient and scalable retrieval performance. The experiments suggest that setting the value of *queryPerm* between 4-8 and *docPerm* between 11-21 returns good recall rates. For the Ohsumed data set over 10000 peers with *queryPerm*=8 and *docPerm*=18, 83.4% recall is achieved by visiting 55.86 peers (0.56%) when there is no load balancing, and 50.4% recall is achieved by visiting 57.81 peers (0.58%) when load balancing is implemented. Thus the system can be configured for high recall (if the load imbalance among the peers is tolerable) or for more balanced load distribution

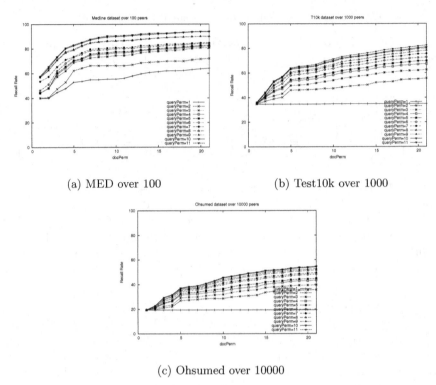

(a) MED over 100   (b) Test10k over 1000

(c) Ohsumed over 10000

Fig. 4. Recall rates after implementing Load Balancing schemes

with moderate recall. A similar tradeoff is posed by the reference selection criteria. Clustered references provide better recall rates than random references, but with a more skewed index distribution.

The storage and bandwidth requirements of the system is reasonable. A document index contains a 100-dimensional vector (100x4B) and some additional information (~100B). The size of an index is around 0.5KB. The amount of storage needed to store 10000 indices is only 5MB. Thus it is usually affordable to have a greater *docPerm*. For example, publishing a document with *docPerm*=21 takes 10.5KB. The data transferred to process a single query lookup, L, can be computed as: $L = p \cdot Q + k \cdot I$, where p is the average path length in the system, Q is the query message size, k is the number of results returned, and I is the size of an index. The total amount of data transferred to process a query, B, is:

$$B = queryPerm \cdot L = queryPerm \cdot (p \cdot Q + k \cdot I)$$

Both Q and I are 0.5KB. p is independent of the number of documents, query length, and document length, and increases logarithmically with the number of peers. Using the data from Table 2 for the 10000 peer system, the total amount of data transferred to answer a query with *queryPerm*=11 is $= 11 \cdot (7 \cdot 0.5 + 15 \cdot 0.5) = 121$KB.

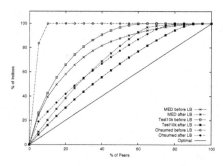

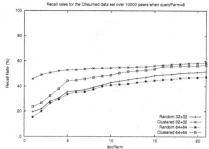

Fig. 5. Effect of Load Balancing (LB) on the index distribution

Fig. 6. Effect of reference vector selection

6   Conclusion

In this paper, we presented an architecture for efficient content-based document search over peer-to-peer systems. Our design is built on top of a structured P2P system, i.e., Chord [3]. We introduced a model for distributing and retrieving the index information for documents over a Chord ring using the feature vectors.

Due to properties inherited from the underlying P2P layer, the system is robust against peer joins and failures. When a new peer joins, it immediately starts serving by obtaining the assigned indices from an existing peer. Upon the departure or failure of a peer, the indices previously assigned to that peer are dynamically assigned to another peer.

The experiments demonstrate that our approach is both scalable and efficient for real data sets. Compared to prior work, our approach is based on solid IR techniques and results in good recall and precision performance.

References

1. Napster: (http://www.napster.com/)
2. Gnutella: (http://www.gnutella.com/)
3. Stoica, I., Morris, R., Karger, D., Kaashoek, M.F., Balakrishnan, H.: Chord: A scalable peer-to-peer lookup service for internet applications. In: Proceedings of the ACM SIGCOMM. (2001) 149–160
4. Ratnasamy, S., Francis, P., Handley, M., Karp, R., Schenker, S.: A scalable content-addressable network. In: Proceedings of the ACM SIGCOMM. (2001) 161–172
5. Rowstron, A., Druschel, P.: Pastry: Scalable, distributed object location and routing for large-scale peer-to-peer systems. In: Proceedings of the Middleware. (2001)
6. Zhao, B.Y., Huang, L., Stribling, J., Rhea, S.C., Joseph, A.D., Kubiatowicz, J.: Tapestry: A resilient global-scale overlay for service deployment. IEEE Journal on Selected Areas in Communications **22** (2004) 41–53
7. Crespo, A., Garcia-Molina, H.: Routing indices for peer-to-peer systems. In: Proceedings of the ICDCS. (2002) 23–32
8. Yang, B., Garcia-Molina, H.: Improving search in peer-to-peer networks. In: Proceedings of the ICDCS. (2002) 5–14

9. Cuenca-Acuna, F.M., Peery, C., Martin, R.P., Nguyen, T.D.: Planetp: Using gossiping to build content addressable peer-to-peer information sharing communities. In: Symposium on High Performance Distributed Computing (HPDC). (2003)
10. Bawa, M., Manku, G.S., Raghavan, P.: Sets: search enhanced by topic segmentation. In: Proceedings of the ACM SIGIR. (2003) 306–313
11. Reynolds, P., Vahdat, A.: Efficient peer-to-peer keyword searching. In: Proceedings of the Middleware. (2003) 21–40
12. Gnawali, O.D.: A keyword-set search system for peer-to-peer networks. Master's thesis, Massachusetts Institute of Technology (2002)
13. Harren, M., Hellerstein, J.M., Huebsch, R., Loo, B.T., Shenker, S., Stoica, I.: Complex queries in DHT-based peer-to-peer networks. In: Proceedings of the first International Workshop on Peer-to-Peer Systems. (2002)
14. Tang, C., Xu, Z., Dwarkadas, S.: Peer-to-peer information retrieval using self-organizing semantic overlay networks. In: Proceedings of the ACM SIGCOMM. (2003) 175–186
15. Deerwester, S., Dumais, S.T., Furnas, G.W., Landauer, T.K., Harshman, R.: Indexing by latent semantic analysis. Journal of the American Society for Information Science **41** (1990) 391–407
16. Zhu, Y., Wang, H., Hu, Y.: Integrating semantics-based access mechanisms with peer-to-peer file systems. In: Proceedings of the 3rd International Conference on Peer-to-Peer Computing (P2P2003). (2003) 118–125
17. Koloniari, G., Pitoura, E.: Content-based routing of path queries in peer-to-peer systems. In: Proceedings the EDBT. (2004) 29–47
18. Suel, T., Mathur, C., Wu, J.W., Zhang, J., Delis, A., Kharrazi, M., Long, X., Shanmugasundaram, K.: Odissea: A peer-to-peer architecture for scalable web search and information retrieval. In: Proceedings of the WebDB. (2003) 67–72
19. Li, J., Loo, B.T., Hellerstein, J., Kaashoek, F., Karger, D.R., Morris, R.: On the feasibility of peer-to-peer web indexing and search. In: Proceedings of the second International Workshop on Peer-to-Peer Systems. (2003)
20. Salton, G., Wong, A., Yang, C.S.: A vector space model for automatic indexing. Communications of the ACM **18** (1975) 613–620
21. Berry, M.W., Drmac, Z., Jessup, E.R.: Matrices, vector spaces, and information retrieval. SIAM Review **41** (1999) 335–362
22. Dumais, S.T.: Latent semantic indexing (lsi): Trec-3 report. In: Proceedings of the Third Text REtrieval Conference (TREC-3). (1995) 219–230
23. Papadimitriou, C.H., Raghavan, P., Tamaki, H., Vempala, S.: Latent semantic indexing: A probabilistic analysis. Journal of Computer and System Sciences **61** (2000) 217–235
24. Jiang, F., Kannan, R., Littman, M.L., Vempala, S.: Efficient singular value decomposition via improved document sampling. Technical Report CS-99-5, Duke University (1999)
25. El-Ansary, S., Alima, L.O., Brand, P., Haridi, S.: Efficient broadcast in structured p2p networks. In: Proceedings of the second International Workshop on Peer-to-Peer Systems. (2003)
26. Buckley, C.: Implementation of the SMART information retrieval system. Technical Report 85-686, Cornell University (1985)
27. Hersh, W.R., Buckley, C., J.Leone, T., Hickam, D.H.: Ohsumed: An interactive retrieval evaluation and new large test collection for research. In: Proceedings of the ACM SIGIR. (1994) 192–201
28. Robertson, S., Hull, D.A.: The TREC-9 filtering track final report. In: Proceedings of the 9th Text REtrieval Conference (TREC-9). (2001) 25–40

A Scalable Nearest Neighbor Search
in P2P Systems

Michal Batko[1], Claudio Gennaro[2], and Pavel Zezula[1]

[1] Masaryk University, Brno, Czech Republic
{xbatko, zezula}@fi.muni.cz
[2] ISTI-CNR, Pisa, Italy
gennaro@isti.cnr.it

Abstract. Similarity search in metric spaces represents an important paradigm for content-based retrieval in many applications. Existing centralized search structures can speed-up retrieval, but they do not scale up to large volume of data because the response time is linearly increasing with the size of the searched file. In this article, we study the problem of executing the nearest neighbor(s) queries in a distributed metric structure, which is based on the P2P communication paradigm and the generalized hyperplane partitioning. By exploiting parallelism in a dynamic network of computers, the query execution scales up very well considering both the number of distance computations and the hop count between the peers. Results are verified by experiments on real-life data sets.

1 Introduction

Peer-to-peer (P2P) communication has become a prospective concept for publishing and finding information on the ubiquitous computer networks today. Most P2P systems so far support only simple lookup queries, i.e. queries that retrieve all objects with a particular key value, for example [1] and [2]. Some recent work has extended this functionality to support *range queries* over a single attribute [3]. However, an increasing amount of data today can only be effectively searched through specific (relative) measures of similarity.

For example, consider a P2P photo-sharing application where each user publishes photographs tagged with color histograms as its metadata. A typical query in such a system would contain similarity predicates asking for photographs with color histograms which are not very different from the color histogram of the query photo sample.

The problem of retrieving elements from a set of objects that are close to a given query reference (using specific similarity criterion), has a lot of applications ranging from the pattern recognition to the textual and multimedia information retrieval. The most general abstraction of the similarity concept, which is still indexable, uses the mathematical notion of the *metric space*.

The advantage of the metric space approach to the data searching is its "extensibility", because in this way, we are able to perform the *exact match*, *range*,

W.S. Ng et al. (Eds.): DBISP2P 2004, LNCS 3367, pp. 79–92, 2005.

and *similarity* queries on any collection of metric objects. Since any *vector space* is covered by a metric space with a proper distance function (for example the Euclidean distance), even the n-dimensional vector spaces are easily handled. Furthermore, there are numerous metric functions able to quantify similarity between complex objects, such as free text or multi-media object features, which are very difficult to manage otherwise. For example, consider the *edit distance* defined for sequences and trees, the *Hausdorff distance* applied for comparing shapes, or the *Jacard coefficient*, which is often used to assess similarity of sets. Recently, the problem has attracted a lot of researchers with the goal of developing techniques able to structure collections of metric objects in such a way so that the search requests are performed efficiently – see the recent surveys [4] and [5].

Though metric indexes on single computers are able to speedup query execution, the processing time is not negligible and it grows linearly with the size of the searched collection. Such property has recently been confirmed by numerous experiments in [6]. The evaluation of metric distance functions can also take a considerable amount of computational time. To search the partitioned space, we usually have to compute distances (using the metric function) between many objects. The time to compute a distance can also depend on the size of compared objects. For example, the *edit distance* of two strings has the computational complexity $O(n \cdot m)$, where n and m represent the number of characters in the compared strings.

The distributed computer environment of present days is a suitable framework for parallel execution of the queries. With such infrastructure, parallel distance computations would enhance the search response time considerably. Modern computer networks have a large enough bandwidth, so it is becoming more expensive for an application to access a local disk than to access the RAM of another computer on the network. In this paper, we try to apply current approaches to the distributed data processing – *Scalable and Distributed Data Structures* (SDDS) and *Peer to Peer* (P2P) communication – to the metric space indexing. The motivation and the basic concepts of our proposal have been published in [7] considering only the *similarity range* queries. In this paper we show how such idea can be extended to the important case of similarity predicates, specifically the *nearest neighbors* queries.

The rest of the paper is organized as follows. In Section 2, we summarize the principles of metric queries, while in Section 3 we introduce a formal definition of the distributed metric index. Section 4 describes the strategies for the nearest neighbor search, which are experimentally evaluated in Section 5. Section 6 concludes the paper.

2   Metric Space and Similarity Queries

The mathematical metric space is a pair $(\mathcal{D}, d)$, where $\mathcal{D}$ is the *domain* of objects and d is the *distance function* able to compute distances between any pair of objects from $\mathcal{D}$. It is typically assumed that the smaller the distance, the closer or more *similar* are the objects. For any distinct objects $x, y, z \in \mathcal{D}$, the distance function d must satisfy the following properties:

$$
\begin{array}{ll}
d(x,x) = 0 & \text{\textit{reflexivity,}} \\
d(x,y) > 0 & \text{\textit{strict positiveness,}} \\
d(x,y) = d(y,x) & \text{\textit{symmetry,}} \\
d(x,y) \leq d(x,z) + d(z,y) & \text{\textit{triangle inequality.}}
\end{array}
$$

Let $\mathcal{F} \subseteq \mathcal{D}$ be the data-set. There are two basic types of similarity queries. The **range** query retrieves all objects which have a distance from the query object $q \in \mathcal{D}$ at most the specified threshold (range or radius) ρ:

$$
\{x \in \mathcal{F} \mid d(q,x) \leq \rho\}.
$$

The **nearest neighbor** query returns the object that is the nearest (having the shortest distance) to the query object q. We can extend this type of query to return k nearest objects that form a set $\mathcal{K} \subset \mathcal{F}$ defined as follows:

$$
|\mathcal{K}| = k \wedge \forall x \in \mathcal{K}, y \in \mathcal{F} - \mathcal{K} : d(q,x) \leq d(q,y).
$$

Other forms of similarity queries concern the **similarity joins** and the **reverse nearest neighbor** queries. In this article, we concentrate on the most frequent (the most natural) form of similarity queries – the nearest neighbors queries.

3 Principles of GHT*

The GHT* structure was proposed in [7] as a distributed metric index for similarity range queries. In this paper, we provide a new formalization of this approach and extend the capabilities of the GHT* with methods for processing the nearest neighbors queries.

3.1 Architecture of GHT*

In general, the scalable and distributed data structure GHT* consists of network nodes, peers, that can insert, store, and retrieve objects using similarity queries. The GHT* architecture assumes that:

- Peers communicate through the *message passing* paradigm. For consistency reasons, each *request message* expects a confirmation by a proper *acknowledgment message*.
- Each peer participating in the network has a unique *Network Node IDentifier* (NNID).
- Each peer maintains data objects in a set of *buckets*. Within a peer, the *Bucket IDentifier* (BID) is used to address a bucket.
- Each object is stored exactly in one bucket.

An essential part of the GHT* structure is the *Address Search Tree* (AST). In principle, it is a structure based on the Generalized Hyperplane Tree (GHT) [8], which is one of the centralized metric space indexing structures. In the GHT*, the AST is used to actually navigate to the (distributed) buckets when data objects are stored and retrieved.

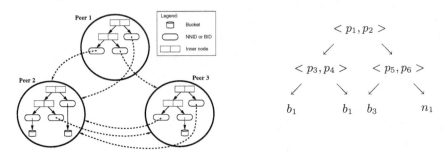

Fig. 1. The GHT* network (a) and an example of Address Search Tree (b)

3.2   Address Search Tree

The AST is a binary search tree, whose inner nodes hold routing information and the leaf nodes represent pointers to the data. Specifically, the inner nodes always store a pair of pivots – these are some representative metric objects from the data-set – and respective pointers to the left and the right subtrees. An example of AST can be seen in Figure 1b. When searching for a place where to store a new object, we start in the root and compute distances between the inserted object and the pivots. If the distance to the first pivot is smaller than the distance to the second pivot, we navigate to the left subtree of that inner node, otherwise, the right subtree is considered. This process is recursively repeated until a leaf node is reached.

The data objects are stored in buckets that are held either locally (thus we can address the bucket by its BID) or on another peer, which can be identified by a proper NNID. Therefore, the AST has always one of those two types of pointers in leaf nodes. Whenever the navigation procedure reaches the leaf node of the AST, the inserted object is stored either locally in the respective bucket (if a BID identifier is found) or on a remote peer (if an NNID identifier is encountered).

In order to avoid hot-spots caused by the existence of a centralized node accessed by every request, a form of the AST structure is present in every peer. Due to the autonomous update policy, the AST structures in individual peers may not be identical – with respect to the complete tree view, some sub-trees may be missing. However, the GHT* provides a mechanism for updating the AST automatically during the insertion or search operations.

Figure 1a illustrates the AST structure in a network of three peers. The dashed arrows from the leaves indicate the NNID pointers while the solid arrows represent the BID pointers. In case of identical ASTs on all peers, each peer knows all the other peers and the proper routing is done just in one step. However, the growth of replication is linear. The GTH* is also able to use the so called *logarithmic replication scheme* where the replicated data grows in a logarithmic way. In this case, each peer knows only few neighbor peers by keeping complete AST paths only to its local buckets. With such scheme, the routing is logarithmic in the worst case. The full explanation of the replication can be found in [7]. In the following, we introduce a notation and operators, which will help us define the insertion and search algorithms more precisely.

Address Search Tree Notation

Definition 1. *Suppose that* $\mathbb{L}_{BID}$ *is the set of all possible BIDs and* $\mathbb{L}_{NNID}$ *is the set of all possible NNIDs. The set of all possible ASTs* $\mathbb{T}_{AST}$ *of the data-set* $\mathcal{F}$ *is formed by the following rules:*

- $\mathbb{L}_{BID} \subset \mathbb{T}_{AST}$; *i.e., every BID pointer is a legal AST.*
- $\mathbb{L}_{NNID} \subset \mathbb{T}_{AST}$; *i.e., every NNID pointer is a legal AST.*
- *Let* $\langle p_1, p_2 \rangle \in \mathcal{F} \times \mathcal{F}$. *Let* $T_l \in \mathbb{T}_{AST}$ *and* $T_r \in \mathbb{T}_{AST}$. *Then the triple* $\langle \langle p_1, p_2 \rangle, T_l, T_r \rangle \in \mathbb{T}_{AST}$.
- *The set* $\mathbb{T}_{AST}$ *contains nothing else.*

Observe that every $T \in \mathbb{T}_{AST}$ is a rooted binary tree, where *leaf nodes* are elements of $\mathbb{L}_{BID}$ or $\mathbb{L}_{NNID}$ and the *inner nodes* are the pairs $\langle p_1, p_2 \rangle$. Every inner node contains two pointers: one to the *left subtree* (T_l) and one to the *right subtree* (T_r). For example, given the metric objects $p_1, p_2, p_3, p_4, p_5, p_6$, the BIDs b_1, b_2, b_3, and the NNID n_1, a possible address search tree $T \in \mathbb{T}_{AST}$ of three levels could be: $\langle \langle p_1, p_2 \rangle, \langle \langle p_3, p_4 \rangle, b_1, b_2 \rangle, \langle \langle p_5, p_6 \rangle, b_3, n_1 \rangle \rangle$, as Figure 1b illustrates.

Definition 2. *Let* $r(T)$ *be the function that returns the root node of the tree* $T \in \mathbb{T}_{AST}$. *In particular, the node returned by* $r(T)$ *is a pair* $\langle p_1, p_2 \rangle$, *a BID pointer, or an NNID pointer.*

Definition 3. *We represent a path of a generic tree* $T \in \mathbb{T}_{AST}$, *called* BPATH, *with a string of n binary elements* $\{0, 1\}$: $p = (b_1, b_2, \ldots, b_n)$. *Given a BPATH* p, *the function* $S(T, p)$ *returns the subtree reached by* p *on the tree* T, *as in the following:*

$$S(T, ()) = T$$

$$S(\langle \langle p_1, p_2 \rangle, T_l, T_r \rangle, (b_1, \ldots, b_n)) = \begin{cases} S(T_l, (b_2, \ldots, b_n)) & \text{if } b_1 = 0 \\ S(T_r, (b_2, \ldots, b_n)) & \text{if } b_1 = 1 \end{cases}$$

Let $p = (p_1, \ldots, p_n)$ *and* $s = (s_1, \ldots, s_m)$ *be two BPATHs, the concatenation operator* $+$ *is defined as* $p + s = (p_1, p_2, \ldots, p_n, s_1, s_2, \ldots, s_m)$. *The concatenation operator can be easily extended for sets of BPATHs. Let* $Q = \{q_1, q_2, \ldots, q_n\}$ *be the set of BPATHs, then* $p + Q = \{p + q_1, p + q_2, \ldots, p + q_n\}$.

Pruning mechanism. In order to search in an AST T, we need an algorithm able to execute a query in the tree. For this purpose we define the traversing operator Ψ. In principle, the operator examines every inner node (i.e. nodes with pairs of two pivots $\langle p_1, p_2 \rangle$) and it decides which subtree to follow. Such pruning is based on the well known generalized hyperplane principles from [8].

Definition 4. *Given an AST T, a metric object q, and a non negative real number ρ, the traversing operator $\Psi(T, q, \rho)$ returns a set of BPATHs as follows:*

$$\Psi(l_{bid}, q, \rho) = \{()\},$$
$$\Psi(l_{nnid}, q, \rho) = \{()\},$$

$$\Psi(\langle\langle p_1, p_2\rangle, T_l, T_r\rangle, q, \rho) = \begin{cases} (0) + \Psi(T_l, q, \rho) & \text{if } d(p_1, q) - \rho \le d(p_2, q) + \rho \\ (1) + \Psi(T_r, q, \rho) & \text{if } d(p_1, q) + \rho > d(p_2, q) - \rho \\ (0) + \Psi(T_l, q, \rho) \\ \qquad\qquad \cup & \text{if both conditions qualify} \\ (1) + \Psi(T_r, q, \rho) \end{cases}$$

The algorithm Ψ works as follows. If T is only composed of a leaf node n (the first two cases of the definition), then $\Psi(T, q, \rho)$ corresponds to a single empty BPATH (). For the other cases, the algorithm recursively traverses T, on the basis of the query range (q, ρ), as in the search algorithm of the GHT. If for the root node $\langle p_1, p_2\rangle$ the condition $d(p_1, q) - \rho \le d(p_2, q) + \rho$ holds, we concatenate all the BPATHs of the $\Psi(T_l, q, \rho)$ to the simple BPATH (0). Whenever $d(p_1, q) + \rho > d(p_2, q) - \rho$, we concatenate all the BPATHs of the $\Psi(T_r, q, \rho)$ to the BPATH (1). Note, that the conditions can be met simultaneously. When the radius $\rho = 0$, which corresponds either to the exact match query or to the process of insertion, a single BPATH is returned.

3.3   Insert and Range Search Algorithms

Insertion of an object starts at the peer, which is asking for insertion, by traversing its AST from the root to a leaf using the function Ψ with $\rho = 0$. If a BID pointer is found, the inserted object is stored in this bucket. Otherwise, the found NNID pointer is applied to forward the request to the proper peer where the insertion continues recursively until an AST leaf with the BID pointer is reached.

Algorithm 1
procedure *Insert(x, p)*
    $S_p = S(T, p);$
    $\{p_1\} = \Psi(S_p, x, 0);$
    $n = r(S(S_p, p_1));$
    if $n \in \mathbb{L}_{NNID}$ **then**
        send a request for *Insert(x,p_1)* to peer with NNID n;
    if $n \in \mathbb{L}_{BID}$ **then**
        insert x in local bucket with BID n;

Algorithm 1 formalizes this insertion procedure, where x is the inserted object and p represents the path in the AST traversed so far (using the BPATH notation), which is initially empty, i.e. $p = ()$. If the search is forwarded to another peer, the p parameter contains the BPATH already traversed by the sending peer.

Algorithm 2
procedure *RangeSearch(q,ρ,p)*
    $S_p = S(T,p)$;
    $P = \Psi(S_p, q, \rho)$;
    for each $p_i \in P$
        $n = r(S(S_p, p_i))$;
        if $n \in \mathbb{L}_{NNID}$ **then**
            send a request for RangeSearch(q,ρ,p_i) to peer with NNID n;
        if $n \in \mathbb{L}_{BID}$ **then**
            search (q, ρ) in local bucket with BID n;
    end for each

By analogy to insertion, the *range search* also starts by traversing the local AST of the querying peer. The AST is traversed by using the operator Ψ with the query object q and the search radius ρ. As already explained, the function Ψ can assign both the sub-trees as qualifying. For all qualifying paths having an NNID pointer in their leaves, the query request is recursively forwarded (including its known BPATHs) to the respective peers until a BID pointer occurs in every leaf. The buckets (with the respective BIDs) are then searched for matching objects.

4   Searching for Nearest Neighbors

Whenever we want to search for similar objects using the range search, we must specify the maximal distance of objects that qualify. However, it can be very difficult to specify the radius without some knowledge about the data and the used metric space. For example, the range $\rho = 3$ of the edit distance metric represents less than four edit operations between the two strings, which has a clear semantic meaning. However, a distance of two color-histogram vectors of images is a real number, which cannot be so easily quantified. When a too small query radius is specified, the result set can even be empty and a new search with a larger radius is needed to get a result. On the other hand, queries with too large query radii might be computationally expensive, and the response sets might contain many not significant objects.

An alternative way to search for similar objects is to use the nearest neighbors queries. Such queries guarantee the retrieval of k most relevant objects, that is the set of k objects with the shortest distances to the query object q. Though the problem of executing k nearest neighbors (kNN) queries is not new and many algorithms have been proposed in the literature, see for example [9] for many references and additional readings, the distributed kNN query processing have not been systematically studied.

4.1   kNN Search in GHT*

In principle, there are two basic strategies how the kNN queries can be evaluated. The first strategy starts with a very large query radius, covering all the data in a given data-set, to identify a degree to which specific regions might contain searched neighbors. Such information is stored in a priority stack (queue) so that the most promising regions are accessed first. As objects are found, the search radius is reduced and the stack adjusted accordingly. Though this strategy never accesses regions not intersecting the query region that is bound by the distance to the k-th nearest neighbor of the query, the processing of regions is strictly serial. On a single computer, the approach is optimum [9], but not convenient for distributed environments aiming at exploiting parallelism. The second strategy starts with the zero radius to locate the first region to explore and then extends the radius to locate other candidate regions, if the result set is still not correct. In this article, we adopt the second approach.

4.2   kNN Algorithm

In our algorithm, we first search for the bucket with a high probability of the occurrence of the nearest neighbors. In particular, we access the bucket in which the query object would be stored using the insert operation. In the accessed bucket, we sort its objects according to their distances with respect to q. Assume that there are at least k objects in the bucket, so the first k objects, i.e. the objects with the shortest distances to q, are the candidates for the result. However, there may be other objects in different buckets that are closer to the query than some of the candidates. In order to check it out, we issue a similarity range search with the radius equal to the distance of the k-th candidate. In this way, we get a set of objects of the cardinality always greater than or equal to k. If we sort all the retrieved objects and retain the first k with the shortest distances, we get the exact answer to the query.

If less than k objects are found in the first accessed bucket, other strategy must be applied because we do not know the upper bound on the distance to the k-th nearest neighbor. We again execute the range search operation, but we have to estimate the radius. If we get enough objects from the range query (at least k), we are done – the result is again the first k objects from the sorted result of the range search. Otherwise, we have to expand the radius and try again (i.e. iterate) until enough objects are received. There are two possible strategies how to estimate the radius.

Optimistic strategy. The objective is to minimize the costs, i.e. the number of accessed buckets and distance computations, by using a not very large radius, at the risk that more iterations are needed if not enough objects are found. In the first iteration we use the bounding radius of the candidates, i.e. the distance to the last candidate, despite of the fact that we have less than k candidates. The optimistic strategy hopes that there are enough objects in the other buckets within this radius. Let x be the number of objects returned from the last range query. If $x \geq k$, we are done, otherwise, we expand the radius to $\rho + \rho\frac{k-x}{k}$ and iterate again.

Pessimistic strategy. The estimated radius is chosen rather large so that the probability of next iteration is minimum, risking excessive (though parallel) bucket accesses and distance computations. To estimate the radius, we use the distance between pivots of the inner nodes, because the pivot selection algorithm (described in [7]) chooses pivots as the most distant pair of objects available. More specifically, the pessimistic strategy traverses the AST from the leaf with the pointer to the bucket up to the tree root and applies the distance between pivots as the range radius. Every iteration climbs one level up in the AST until the search terminates or the root is encountered. If there are still not enough retrieved objects, the maximum distance of the metric is used and all the objects in the structure are evaluated.

Algorithm 3
procedure $kNN(q,k,p)$
  $S_p = S(T,p);$
  $\{p_1\} = \Psi(S_p, x, 0);$
  $n = r(S(S_p, p_1));$
  if $n \in \mathbb{L}_{NNID}$ *then*
      send a request for $kNN(q,p_1)$ *to peer with NNID* $n;$
  if $n \in \mathbb{L}_{BID}$ *then*
      compute distances to all objects in local bucket with BID $n;$
      A = *sort object using the distances, smallest first;*
      do
          ρ = *EstimateRadius(); // Using some strategy*
          O = *RangeSearch(q, ρ, ());*
          insert sort objects O *into* A *using distances computed by the range search;*
      repeat until $|A| < k$
  end if

4.3   Implementation Issues

As an extension of the algorithms above, several optimization strategies have been implemented. To avoid multiple accesses to the same buckets, the so called BPATH sets are used during the range searches in the kNN iterations. In particular, if the distances to all objects in a bucket are evaluated during a range search, this bucket is never accessed again in the following iterations. Naturally, the first bucket (the one with candidate objects) is never searched twice.

If objects are sent to other peer during the query evaluation, the distances computed so far are always present in the message. Therefore the peer, which is sorting the result set, never repeats distance computations and only performs a rather quick merge sort of the distances. Unless necessary, we send only the object identities between peers and not the whole objects, which can be large. Recall that a range search can return more than k objects. In this way, the peer which initiated the query, only receives the matching objects and not all the intermediate results.

5   Performance Evaluation

In this section, we present results of performance experiments that assess different aspects of our GHT* prototype implemented in Java. We have conducted
our experiments on two real-life data-sets. First, we have used a data-set of
45-dimensional vectors of color image features with the L_2 (Euclidian) metric
distance function (*VEC*). This data-set have a normal distribution of distances
and every object has the same size (45 numbers). The second data-set is formed
by sentences of the Czech national corpus with the *edit distance* function as the
metric (*TXT*). The distribution of distances in this data-set is rather skewed –
most of the distances are within a very small range of values. Moreover, the size
of sentences varies significantly. There are sentences with only a few words, but
also quite long sentences with tenths of words.

For the experimental purposes, we have used 100 independent computers
(peers) connected by a high-speed network. Essentially, every peer provides some
computation capacity, which is used during the object insertion and the query
evaluation. We have used some of the peers to insert the data and the others
to execute queries. The number of peers storing the data was automatically
determined by the size of the data-set, because the number and capacity of
buckets on individual peers was constant.

Notice that our prototype uses the simplest bucket structure – a linked list of
objects – which needs to examine every object in a bucket in order to solve the
query. By applying a metric index on individual peers, the performance would
significantly improve.

5.1   Performance Characteristics

In our experiments, we have measured different performance related characteristics of the query evaluation. In order to quantify the CPU costs, we have counted
the number of distance computations necessary to evaluate a nearest neighbor
query. The number is the sum of the computations incurred during the navigation (i.e. while searching in the AST) and the computations necessary to evaluate
the query in the accessed buckets. The total number of distance computations
corresponds to the number of distance computations that would be needed in
a centralized environment. The parallel cost is the maximal number of distance
computations evaluated on a peer or a set of peers accessed serially. As we have
already explained, the evaluation algorithm for a kNN query consists of sequential steps. At the beginning we have to find the first bucket and examine its
objects (see Section 4.2), then, we iterate using the range search with the estimated radii. Naturally, the distance computations evaluated during these steps
must be considered serial.

We also measured the number of accessed buckets, which are of a limited
capacity. In our experiments, we have used a maximum of 2,000 objects per
bucket and maximally 5 buckets per a peer. The average bucket occupation was
about 50%. We have measured the total number of buckets accessed during a
query and the number of buckets accessed per a peer.

Finally, we have measured the number of messages exchanged between peers. The total number of messages can be seen as a representation of the network load. However, most of the messages are sent in parallel, because one peer can send a message to multiple peers. In specific situations, a peer must forward a message to a more appropriate peer. The number of those forwardings is usually called the *hop count*. In our experiments, we have measured the maximal hop count to execute a query. The hop count represents the sequential part of the message passing process, i.e. its parallel cost.

We do not use the execution time of the query evaluation as the relevant measure, because there are many factors (such as the speed of peer processors, the congestion of the network, the load of peers, etc.) that can directly influence the execution time of a query.

For comparison reasons, we also provide the costs of a range search for every experiment. The radius ρ is adjusted so that it represents the minimal bounding radius of the set of objects returned by the corresponding kNN query.

Every value in the graphs represents the average obtained from execution of 50 queries with different query objects and fixed k. We only show results for the pessimistic strategy, but with 1,000 objects per bucket on average, the strategy was only applied for evaluating queries with $k > 1,000$. In such situation, nearly all the objects in the data-set had to be accessed to solve the query. Therefore, the performance of the optimistic strategy was practically the same.

5.2   kNN Search Performance

In this set of experiments, we have analyzed the performance of the kNN search with respect to different k on data-sets of 10,000 objects. Results are summarized as graphs in Figure 2 for the VEC and Figure 3 for the TXT data-sets. Our experiments show that the parallel costs of our kNN queries remain quite stable for the increasing k while the total costs (note that graph values are divided by 10 and the x axis has a logarithmic scale) grow very quickly with the number of neighbors k. Note, that for k values greater than 100 for VEC (and values over 10 for TXT) almost all the objects had to be accessed and the distances to the query objects computed. However, this is not a general observation and it is strictly dependent on the distance distribution in the processed data. In the figures, we also show the costs of the corresponding range search, that is the range search with the radius equal to the distance of the k-th nearest neighbor. Naturally, the performance is better, but the overhead incurred by the kNN algorithm seems to be constant, not dependent on the value of k.

5.3   kNN Search Scalability

The effect of growing data-sets on the performance of queries (i.e. the scalability) is usually the worst problem with the centralized metric indices. For example, experiments with the D-Index [6] structure using the same TXT data-set have shown that a kNN query takes around 4 seconds for the data-set size of 10,000 and about 40 seconds for the size of 100,000 objects (sentences) – the increase

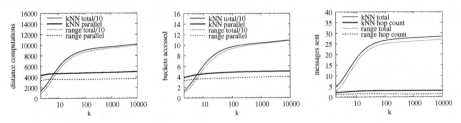

Fig. 2. Dependence of different costs on k for the VEC data-set

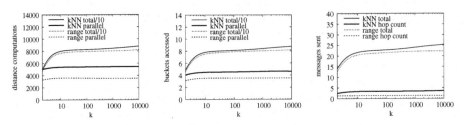

Fig. 3. Dependence of different costs on k for the TXT data-set

of the search costs in a centralized structure is linear with respect to the size of the data-set. Our experiments with the GHT* exhibit nearly constant parallel costs even when the data-set grows. Contrary to the D-Index, we have always achieved the response time around 2 seconds.

The leftmost graphs in Figures 4 and 5 confirm the scalability of the GHT* considering the number of distance computations – the cost around 4,000 computations remains stable even for the full data-set of 100,000 objects. The middle graphs show the number of forwarded messages, which in fact represent the number of peers actually addressed. This number is increasing, because more peers are used to store the data, therefore more peers have to be accessed in order to solve the query. The hop count, shown in the last graph, is slowly rising with the growing data-set. Compared to the range search, the values for the kNN are higher, because there is always the overhead with locating the first bucket. The observed increase of the number of hops seems to be logarithmic.

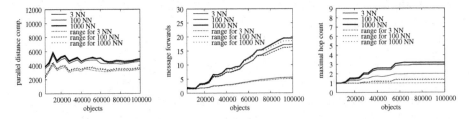

Fig. 4. The scalability of GHT* while resizing the VEC data-set

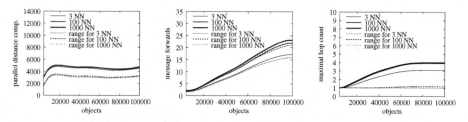

Fig. 5. The scalability of GHT* while resizing the TXT data-set

6   Conclusions

To the best of our knowledge, the problem of distributed index structures supporting the execution of the nearest neighbors queries on metric data sets has not been studied yet. The GHT* structure stores and retrieves data from domains of arbitrary metric spaces and satisfies all the necessary conditions of the scalable and distributed data structures. It is scalable in that it distributes the structure over more and more independent peer computers. The parallel search time for kNN queries becomes practically constant for arbitrary data volume, and the hop count grows logarithmically. It has no hot spots – all clients and servers use as precise addressing scheme as possible and they all incrementally learn from misaddressing during insertion or search. Finally, node splits are performed locally without sending multiple messages to many other peers.

Our future work will concentrate on strategies for updates (object deletion), pre-splitting policies, and more sophisticated strategies for organizing buckets. An interesting research challenge is to consider other metric space partitioning schemes (not only the generalized hyperplane) and study their suitability for implementation in distributed environments.

References

1. Litwin, W., Neimat, M.A., Schneider, D.A.: LH* - a scalable, distributed data structure. ACM TODS **21** (1996) 480–525
2. Ratnasamy, S., Francis, P., Handley, M., Karp, R., Schenker, S.: A scalable content-addressable network. In: Proc. of the 2001 conference on Applications, technologies, architectures, and protocols for computer communications. (2001) 161–172
3. Li, X., Kim, Y.J., Govindan, R., Hong, W.: Multi-dimensional range queries in sensor networks. In: Proceedings of the First International Conference on Embedded Networked Sensor Systems. (2003) 63–75
4. Chávez, E., Navarro, G., Baeza-Yates, R., Marroquín, J.L.: Searching in metric spaces. ACM Computing Surveys **33** (2001) 273–321
5. Hjaltason, G.R., Samet, H.: Index-driven similarity search in metric spaces. ACM Trans. Database Syst. **28** (2003) 517–580
6. Dohnal, V., Gennaro, C., Savino, P., Zezula, P.: D-index: Distance searching index for metric data sets. Multimedia Tools and Applications **21** (2003) 9–13

7. Batko, M., Gennaro, C., Savino, P., Zezula, P.: Scalable similarity search in metric spaces. In: Digital Library Architectures: Peer-to-Peer, Grid, and Service-Orientation, Pre-proceedings of the Sixth Thematic Workshop of the EU Network of Excellence DELOS, S. Margherita di Pula, Cagliari, Italy, 24-25 June, 2004, Edizioni Libreria Progetto, Padova (2004) 213–224
8. Uhlmann: Satisfying general proximity / similarity queries with metric trees. IPL: Information Processing Letters **40** (1991) 175–179
9. Hjaltason, G.R., Samet, H.: Distance browsing in spatial databases. ACM Trans. Database Syst. **24** (1999) 265–318

Efficient Range Queries and Fast Lookup Services for Scalable P2P Networks

Chu Yee Liau[1], Wee Siong Ng[2], Yanfeng Shu[1], Kian-Lee Tan[1], and Stéphane Bressan[1]

[1] Department of Computer Science,
National University of Singapore, Singapore
{liaucy, shuyanfe, tankl, steph}@comp.nus.edu.sg
[2] Singapore-MIT Alliance, 4 Engineering Drive 3,
National University of Singapore, Singapore
smangws@nus.edu.sg

Abstract. In this paper we propose a Peer-To-Peer (P2P) architecture using a tree based indexing scheme which allows for efficient lookup and range query services on documents in the network. We also present a basic load balancing technique by assigning a new node that joins the network to a heavily loaded area to take on some of load of its peers. Given a query, we need to search only a small number of nodes to locate matching documents hence making the architecture scalable. We also take into account the fact that nodes in a P2P environment need not have the same capability. We implemented a simulator and performed experiments to study to the performance of our proposed architecture. The results show that our proposed architecture is scalable and highly efficient when handling range queries.

1 Introduction

Peer-to-Peer (P2P) systems [1, 2, 3, 4] have presented an alternative to existing web resource sharing. The simplicity and efficiency of the P2P concept has made it an attractive choice for a platform for sharing data. Web sharing till recently has been mainly based on the client-server model with a small number of nodes handling very concentrated resources which require sophisticated techniques such as load balancing as well as large network bandwidth.

Search and Resource discovery mechanisms in recent years have grown in importance with the advent of various file sharing applications like Napster [2] and Gnutella [4]. As a result it has generated great interest in research as well as industrial community [5, 6, 7, 8, 9, 10, 11, 12, 13]. Search in a P2P system can be broken down into three major categories. In the *centralized* indexing architecture [2] a centralized server stores the index (a unique identifier) of all the peers. This centralized server is also responsible for handling all queries issued by the various peer nodes. Although implementation is easy, scalability issues harm its cause. Concentrating all the indexing and location information on a single node allows for a single point of failure and making it a potential target for Denial of Service (DOS) attacks. Furthermore centralization violates the very essence of P2P. On the other hand, in a *decentralized* indexing architecture as described in [14, 3], search usually involves broadcasting or multicasting the query across the

W.S. Ng et al. (Eds.): DBISP2P 2004, LNCS 3367, pp. 93–106, 2005.

network. These systems too suffer from scalability and performance issues caused by the flooding mechanism. A user is not guaranteed to retrieve queried data even though it exists in the network. [14, 15, 16] give us a third kind of search in P2P systems which is a distributed index that makes use of a hashing technique. Such a method guarantees that data will be retrieved if it exists in the network. The number of messages required to locate the data is usually in the scale of $\log(N)$ as opposed to N in the completely decentralized scheme where N is the number of nodes in the network. Although this scheme alleviates the scalability problem faced in the previous two schemes, it struggles when faced with a critical requirement of any retrieval system : a *range* query. A range query is useful when finding resources with an approximate attribute value and we might want to locate all resources with attribute values smaller or larger than a certain value.

We propose a P2P architecture that distributes the indexing information among a subset of nodes of the P2P network. We distribute the index which is built up from a group of nodes to resemble a tree structure. Each node in the tree maintains minimal information about its sub-tree such as local information (IP address etc.) of its immediate parent,children,siblings and neighbours. Their definitions are explained later in Section 3. In addition a node also maintains the range information of all its children, i.e. highest attribute value for each child. All this information can be easily obtained when a node joins the index tree and when data is inserted into the network.

Since a node needs only to maintain very minimal information and the amount of information is almost constant as opposed to those proposed by distributed hashing techniques[14, 15, 16], which grow with the number of participant nodes in the network, our proposed architecture proves to be more scalable.

This paper describes our contribution in terms of

- Capability Awareness: each peer node decides for itself the number of records and number of children it can handle. This value need not be the same for all peer nodes in the network.
- Fast Lookup of Information : given a keyword, the cost of the finding the peer node hosting the record is proportional to $\log(N)$ where N is the number of nodes in the network. Refer Section 4
- Efficient Range Query : The performance of range queries in our proposed architecture is comparable to the costs incurred for information lookup in the order of $\log(N)$.
- Load Balancing : New peer nodes are assigned to areas where the load is heavier and thus take some of the load off the heavily loaded nodes.

Section 2 presents some of the related work in the area. Section 3 describes our model and related algorithms in some detail. Section 4 presents our results derived from performance analysis experiments conducted on our system and finally we conclude with a summary of our findings as well as possible future work on the proposed architecture in Section 5.

2   Related Work

The first generation of P2P systems were mainly file sharing applications such as Napster, Gnutella and Freenet. Napster was one of the earliest applications to take the concept of

P2P technology to the people. Napster uses a number of centralized servers to maintain the index of files being shared by all participating peers. A peer issuing a query will send the query to an assigned server which searches through the database and returns the search result back to the querying peer. The returned results are used by the querying peer to establish contact with those peers sharing the necessary information.

Another technique is the distributed hash table (DHT) [14, 15, 16, 17] In this technique, documents are associated with a key, produced from mapping attributes of the document such as file name through technique like consistent hashing. Each node in the system is assigned a set of keys and is responsible for storing the keys. To locate a document in the network, a node issues a lookup operation and the request is routed to the node responsible for the key. The responsible node returns the record(s) found in the storage to the querying node. DHT supports fast lookup and provides assurance that if a document exists in the network, it will be found. However, most of the DHT techniques failed to support range query due to the use of hashing techniques. In addition, most of the systems assumes all the nodes to have equal capability which is not the case most of the time.

The problem of efficient queries on a range of keys is described in [18] which comes up with a solution based on CAN [15]. These newer P2P systems not only provide a more deterministic structure and performance guarantees in terms of logical hops but also take advantage of network proximity.

Some work has been done on storage in distributed systems in a manner allowing for fast lookups. [19] introduces a distributed data structure called RP* which provides for ordered and dynamic files on multicomputers and thus for more efficient processing of range queries and of ordered traversals of files. This allows them to support fast lookup and range queries. The authors mainly focus on an organization scale and assume the availability of multicast.

3   System Architecture

As mentioned earlier the indexing scheme is based on a rooted tree structure as shown in Figure 1. Each node in the tree is maintained by a peer in the network. However there are exceptional cases where peers can host more than one node. Each node n in the tree is connected to a parent node (if not the root), a sibling node (if any), a neigbour node (if any) and a set of m children where $m \geq 0$. The tree can be broken down into levels as shown in Figure 1. Each node on a particular level is connected to the node on its left and to the node on its right. If the nodes share the same immediate parent node, they are known as siblings. This is the case for node 112 and 113. If the connected nodes do not share the same immediate parent, they are known as neighbours. This is the case for 113 and 121. A node a is known to be the ancestor of a node n if there is a downward direct path from a to n. 12 is the ancestor of 1212. Similarly a node d is the descendant of a node n if there is a direct upward path from d to n. In the figure, 1211 is the descendant of 1.

Each of these connections is used to route a message to the next level or towards the destination when inserting or querying a document. Our routing mechanism is similar to searching in search tree. In order to achieve this, each node in the tree is responsible

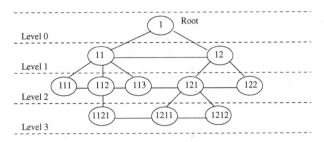

Fig. 1. Tree Index Architecture

for a range of values. In addition, each node will be required to store the minimum and maximum value of each of the sub-trees rooted at its children. This information can be obtained when documents are being inserted into the network, since all the documents to be inserted into the descendants of n will have to pass through node n.

The tree index structure is a dynamic structure where nodes can join or leave at any point of time. The tree grows as peers join the network. Although a tree structure is being used, operations such as insertion and deletion can originate from any node in the network, rather than only from the root of the tree. This mechanism prevents a particular node from overloading and avoids a single point of failure in the network. However, being a P2P system, the peers are autonomous and very often unpredictable. A peer can leave the network or even fail without giving any prior warning to its connected peers. For instance, when a node leave the network, the descendants of the node will be disconnected from the parent of the departing node. In order for the network to continue efficient and correct operation some kind of a recovery mechanism needs to be in place to fix the network.

3.1   Join

A peer intending to join the P2P network would need to connect with at least one of the peers already in the network. We present two methods by which a peer can join the network namely random join and preventive join.

Random Join. Assuming a peer p, which intends to join the network, contacts a node n in the network, p will send a join request message, JOIN-REQ, to n. Three possibilities may occur. If n does not have any children, it will add p as its child. If n has child nodes but can still take on more, it will then assign p to its vacant child node slot. On the other hand, if n is full and cannot support any more children, it sends n's JOIN-REQ message to one of its children c, and c continues the process until p is being assigned to a node. After being assigned to a node, p establishes a connection with its siblings and direct neighbours by querying its parent for their location information. This usually results in splitting of set of records stored in the exisiting neighbor nodes. The splitting algorithm is explained in detail in Section 3.3.

Preventive Join. In the preventive join scheme , after the peer p contacts n, it sends a JOIN-REQ message to n. Instead of directly accepting p as its descendant, n first

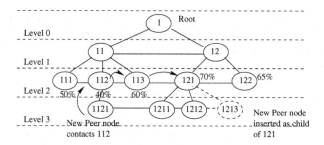

Fig. 2. Preventive Join

compares its load with that of its neighbouring peers. If any of the peers has a higher load, n forwards the join request message sent by p to the highest load peer for further processing. This is done so that the new node can hopefully take on some of the load of its new neighbour thus balancing the load distribution to an extent. This is done for a preset TTL or until n's load is the highest among the neighbours. When n's load is higher, it accepts p as its descendant. The process is similar to random join except that n checks the load of its children and forwards the JOIN-REQ message to a peer with the highest load.

Figure 2 shows us an example of how a new node wishing to join the network under the preventive join scheme gets inserted into the network. A new peer node, $newP$, establishes a connection with node 112 and sends a join request message. At this point in time node 112 compares its load (40%) with its siblings, node 111 (50%) and node 113 (60%). Since node 113 has a heavier load than node 112, node 112 forwards the join request message to node 113. Node 113 repeats the process, only this time node 113 has a neighbour, node 121 with a heavier load (70%). Node 113 now forwards the join request message to node 121. Node 121 checks the load of its only sibling node 122 and find out it cannot forward the join request message any further. Node 121 still has the capability to take on one more child node and the new peer node, $newP$ is accepted here as the new child, 1213.

3.2   Leave

The peers in the network can leave at any point of time. When a peer leaves, it can leave by informing its 'connected' peers, and arrange for an alternative peer to take over its position and stored information. On the other hand, if a peer leaves without giving any notification to the rest of the peers, the directly connected peers will have to figure out themselves in order to mend the broken link. A peer that has left the network must be fixed in order for the structure to continue working. This section looks at different scenarios under which a node 'leaves' the network and various approaches to handle a peer's departure.

Depart. A simple scenario is when a peer informs its direct connected peers before departing. The departing peer has enough time to pass the necessary information to the other peers. The departing peer transfers its responsibility for the node to either its parent or one of its children. The successor inherits all the information currently hosted by the peer and creates a virtual node to handle the responsibility. This is done by sending a *leave* message to its parent and children. Upon receiving the message, the parent and its children return a message indicating their current load (i.e., how many nodes it is responsible for) and the duration they have stayed in the network. We assume the longer a peer stays in the network, the more reliable it is. Based on this information, the peer will assign its current responsibility to the lower load and more reliable peer.

Failure. When a node fails, things get a little complicated. In this case, a node leaves the network without informing any of other peers, leaving a broken link among the peers. The broken link must be fixed to prevent complication of other operations such as searching for documents or inserting documents into the network. There are two strategies a node can employ to restablish a broken link, each with its own advantages and disadvantages.

The first strategy is to take proactive action. When a peer detects a parent failure it will immediately try to recover the parent node. This is possible if either the communication protocol is a connection oriented protocol or each node periodically sends 'heartbeats' to its connected nodes. This proactive strategy fixes a connection immediately after detecting failure hence ensuring that the network is always functioning properly and very likely will prevent further complication in the process of the network recovery caused by multiple node failure. The drawback of this strategy is that it might cause unnecessary effort in cases where the failure is temporary. For instance, if a peer is down for a very short period of time due to some network failure or power surge, there is a very high possibility the peer will reconnect with its peers when it comes back alive.

On the other hand, a peer can choose to be lazy, i.e. to fix the link only when required. This strategy solves the problem of fixing a link in the case of a temporary failure described earlier. However, fixing the connection only when required might result in increased response times when carrying out tasks such as node-join, query or insertion. Furthermore, multiple node failure in the vicinity complicates the situation a great deal.

When a peer detects a broken link it tries to establish a functioning direct ancestor. In Figure 3, node 121 suddenly fails without informing any of its connected peers. Suppose at some point in time node 1211 detects this failure when it tries to access its parent.

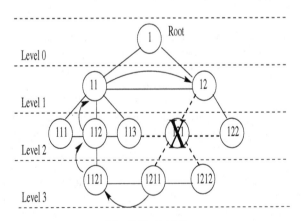

Fig. 3. Node Failure

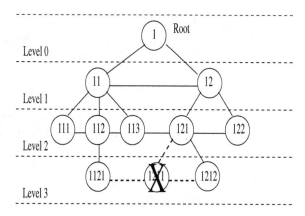

Fig. 4. Node Failure

Since the parent has failed, there is no point in asking the siblings for information of the failed node. The best bet is to ask the nearest neighbour to find an ancestor which is either the neighbour or a sibling of an ancestor of the failed parent node. In this case, node 1211 contacts node 1121 which forwards the request all the way up to node 11 which is the sibling of node 12, the parent of the failed node and the grandparent of node 1211. Node 12 has some information about the range information of its children and this can be used to recreate the failed node thus fixing the broken links.

On the other hand if a node with no children fails, its sibling or parent tries to fix the broken link by simply taking over the range the failed node was responsible for. In Figure 4, when node 1211 fails, if the parent node 121 discovers this failure it can simply use the information is has about the range of node 1211 and take over responsibility. But if a sibling, node 1212 discovers the broken link it contacts its parent, node 121 and obtains the range information of the failed node and takes over responsibililty.

3.3 Insertion

When a peer decides to share a document, it will advertise the attributes of the document (filename etc) in the network. In this discussion, we refer the act of advertising the attribute of the document as insertion. Insertion is the process of determining where the record will be hosted. To insert a document into the network, a peer will create a message INSERT-REQ with a record describing the document in the following format

$$< attribute, document\_id, document\_source >$$

where *attribute* is the searchable feature of the document, *document_id* is the identifier to be used when retrieving the document and *document_source* is the location where the document is being stored (IP address,URL etc).

The insertion process can be broken down into two steps. The first is to determine the insertion start point. Insertion start point is the node where as the name suggests an insertion starts. The insertion point will be the root of the insertion tree. The second step is the actual document record insertion procedure.

The first step of the insertion begins with the peer sending the INSERT-REQ message to itself. When the INSERT-REQ message is received , a node checks the attribute to see if it falls in its sub-tree's range. This process is rather straightforward. If the attribute does not fall within the range or the range is undefined (i.e. the node and its descendants are not hosting any document record), the node forwards the INSERT-REQ message to its parent. On the other hand, if the attribute falls within the range or the node does not have a parent (i.e. the node is the root of the tree), the node will be the insertion start point.

The second step in the insertion process involves the placement of the document record. The process starts at the insertion start point determined in the previous step. One of the descendants of the insert start point will be chosen to host the record. The decision process is as follows. At this stage we know that the attribute mentioned falls in the range of the sub-tree. When examined against the range values of the node, two possibilities arise: the range falls within the node's range or it falls within the range of sub-trees rooted at one of the children.

In the first scenario, the node stores the document record and hence is responsible for the record. In the second scenario, the node checks to see if the record falls in the range of one of its children and forwards the INSERT-REQ message to the child which is responsible for the record for further processing until a node is found where the record can be inserted. Once the record is stored, the node sends an INSERT-ACK message to the machine where the document is stored, as an acknowledgment of the completion of the insertion process.

After inserting the record at the chosen node, the node checks its load against its storage capacity. If it is overloaded, it splits into half and passes the upper half (higher value) to either its neighbour on its immediate right or one of its children. The splitting algorithm is shown in Figure 5.

3.4   Deletion

When a peer decides to unshare or remove a document from its storage, it will have to inform the node that hosts the record of the document. If the node has the INSERT-ACK message, it can simply send a DELETE-REQ message together with the document record to the node responsible for hosting the record. If the INSERT-ACK is not implemented, the process of deleting a document will be very similar to the process of inserting document. It has the two steps which is analogous to the insertion process i.e. determine deletion start point and removing the document record.

The first step in the deleting process is exactly the same as the insertion process. A node that receives a DELETE-REQ will check if the attribute falls within its range. If not, it will forward the request to its parent. The process continues until a node that responsible for the attribute is found. When this root node for the sub-tree is found, the next step will be to determine the actual node that will host the record. Starting from the sub-tree's root, the node checks if it hosts the record. If it does host the record, it will remove the record from its database and return a DELETE-ACK message to the initiating node and the delete process will end here. If it doesn't, the node will forward the DELETE-REQ to the child for which the attribute is within range and when this child is found, the record is deleted.

Algorithm *Split*
Input: PeerNode peer
3.   if(peer.right.parent = peer.parent)
4.   Split peer's stored records into *half*
5.   if(peer.right.range=null OR | peer.children |=0)
6.   Transfer *higher* half to peer.right
7.   Update peer.parent range information
8.   else
9.   Transfer *higher* half to peer.firstChild
10. else /*different parent*/
11.   splitNode = FindSplitNode(peer)
12.   if(!splitNode)
13.   Split peer's stored records into *half*
14.   Transfer *higher* half to splitNode
15.   Propagate range information change
                  till splitNode.parent
16.   else
17.   No Splitting Possible

Fig. 5. Split Algorithm

3.5   Search Query

Two types of search are allowed in the system: exact-match and selective range. The search mechanisms are discussed below.

Exact Match. Exact-Match search starts with node creating a query message,SEARCH-EXACT, together with a record

　　　<search_location, keyword>

where search_location is the location information (e.g. IP address) for the node that issues the search and keyword is the search attribute. We first determine the starting point for the search. It starts with a node sending the SEARCH-EXACT message to itself. When a node receives the message, it checks the search keyword against its sub-tree range. For keywords that fall outside the range, the SEARCH-EXACT message will be routed to the node's parent. If the node is the root of the whole tree or the keyword falls within the node's sub-tree range, it compares the search keyword with its range values.The possibilities are: keyword falls outside the sub-tree range, keyword falls within the range, keyword is greater than the range. For the first case, the node will send an empty result to the querying node indicating that the keyword being sought for does not match any value. For the second case, if the records exist, they should be within the range. The node checks its records and return the result to the querying node. The searching process ends there. For the last case, the keyword being search is within the node's sub-tree range but greater than its range. The node searches the index containing its children's sub-tree range and forwards the SEARCH-EXACT message to the child node that has a sub-tree range that matches the keyword to continue the process.

Algorithm *FindSplitNode*
Input: PeerNode peer
Output: PeerNode splitNode
1.   if(peer.parent = null AND
2.   peer.right = null AND
3.   peer.right.parent!=peer.parent)
4..   FindSplitNode(peer.parent)
5.   else
6.   if(!peer.right)
7.   /* cant find a peer node to split */
8.   return null
9.   else
10.   return peer.right

Fig. 6. FindSplitNode Algorithm

Range. Range search creates SEARCH-RANGE message together with the record <search_location, operator, keyword1,[keyword2]>. Search_location is as described in the exact-match search. Operator is the search operator and for this work we will only consider two of them: "start with" and "between". The keyword1 and keyword2 are the search keyword. Depending on the operator used, keyword2 is optional.

After creating SEARCH-RANGE message, the peer first sends the query message to itself. Similar to the first step of exact-match search, the SEARCH-RANGE message is forwarded to a node that has a sub-tree range that contains the keywords. However, the difference is when the operator value is between, both the keyword1 and keyword2 must falls within the sub-tree range.

Instead of only one node returning results to the querying peer, a range search might have more than one node returning results to the querying peer because the query range might span over more than one node. Apart from this, the selective range search is very similar to exact-match query.

4   Performance Analysis

We conducted detailed simulation to study the proposed architecture and the effect of different joining mechanisms discussed in previous section. In this section we discuss the experiment setting and the finding of the experiments. Firstly, we show the load of the root node, in terms of messages processed, as compared to the number of messages in the network. Secondly we show the cost of joining the network for the two different joining mechanisms. Thirdly, we present the effect of the joining mechanisms on the number of records stored in nodes. Finally, we present performance of the proposed architecture for exact-match and range query.

4.1   Performance Measure

We use *path length* as a measure of performance. Path length (PL) is defined as the number of hops a node takes to answer its query. Throughout the experimental study we recorded

- Maximum path length (Max) : the maximum value of the number of hops an operation takes in the entire experiment. This gives us an idea of the worst case scenario.
- Average path length (Ave) : the total number of hops for the entire experiment over the total number of operations performed.

4.2   Experimental Setting

We vary the number of nodes in the network, N, each being set a maximum capacity of 20. For each of these settings, we insert 10 x N number of records where N = 4000, 8000, 12000, 16000 and 20000. The experiment is conducted 10 times and the result is averaged to get the final result. For every new node that joins the network, 10 new records are inserted and 50 new search queries are performed.

Figure 7 shows the number of messages in the network for every simulation steps. The number of messages processed by root node of the tree architecture is significantly less than the amount of messages in the network. The messages processed by an arbitrary

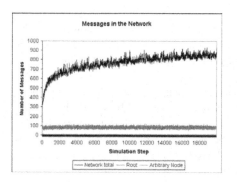

Fig. 7. Messages in network

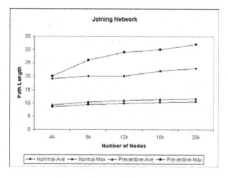

Fig. 8. PL for joining network

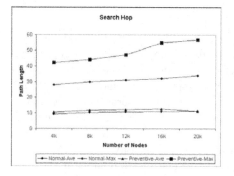

Fig. 9. PL for exact-match query

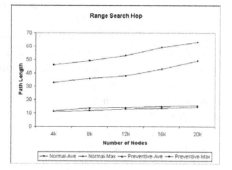

Fig. 10. PL for range query

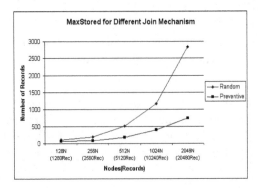

Fig. 11. Maximum records stored

node is only about 15% of those by root node. Despite of this, the load at the root node are constant even when the messages in the network increases, this suggest the scalability of the architecture. In addition, the high load at the root node does not represent possibly single point of failure as the processed of messages could be easily taken over by immediate children node of the root.

4.3   Joining Mechanism

We study the effect of different joining mechanisms discussed in Section 3.1 on the maximum record a node has to store and the results are presented in Figure 11. We infer that the preventive join mechanism, refer Section 3.1, evenly distributes the records across the peer nodes in the network.

In the random join scheme when a new peer node contacts one of the existing nodes in the network it has already been decided that this new node will become a descendant of the contacted node. This scheme does not take into account the load factor of its new parent and neighbors. On the other hand in the preventive join scheme the new peer node is led to the area of nodes which is more heavily loaded and helps to an extent in alleviating the load of its new neighbors or siblings.

In addition, we study the effect of these joining mechanisms on the path length for joining process. The results are presented in Figure 12. We can see that the path length for preventive join mechanism is greater than the random join mechanism due to the extra work required for load balancing.

Next, we study the performance of exact query and range query operations in the proposed architecture. For each set of experiment, we record the average path length and the maximum path length needed to resolve a query. We use the same set of records as those inserted in exact query experiment to study the performance of a range query. However, when searching, we randomly choose two keys in the set of records and devise range queries for values that fall within the range. The results are plotted in Figure 9 and 10.

While the number of node in the network increases, the increase of the path length for searching processes is very minimal. This suggest the scalability of the architecture. Furthermore, the architecture is able to support range query with minimal increase in the maximum path length as compared to exact matched query. We also noticed that the

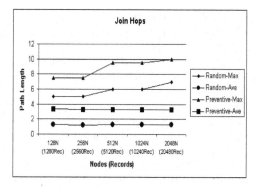

Fig. 12. PL for joining network

path length for searching with the preventive join mechanism is greater than with random join mechanism. This could be the effect of more balanced architecture in random join mechanism. The preventive join mechanism tend to increase the height of the tree and causes the maximum path length to increase. However, on the average path length, the differences are insignificant.

5   Conclusion and Future Work

We proposed an architecture for a P2P network that is able to scale up to a large number of nodes. Despite of being a tree architecture, we have shown in the experiment that the number of messages processed by root node is significantly lesser than total number of messages in the network. We also show that the performance of joining network as well as searching process is proportional to $log(N)$. We have also introduced a preventive joining mechanism where nodes joining the network are assigned to heavily loaded areas in the network to alleviate some of the load in the nodes there. In addition, our proposed architecture allows peers to define their capability and decide what is the maximum number of records it can store. This is an important achievement as peers in a P2P network are not required to have the same capability.

We are currently working on node replication issues in order to make the architecture more resilient and caching techniques to further enhance the search performance. In addition, we are also devising more efficient ways to further reduce messages handled by top level nodes by utilizing sibling/neighboring link.

Acknowledgement

This research is supported by a grant from Agency of Science and Technology (ASTAR) Singapore.

References

1. Bestpeer. In *http://xena1.ddns.comp.nus.edu.sg/p2p/*.
2. NAPSTER. http://www.napster.com.

3. B. Wiley I. Clarke, O. Sandberg and T. W. Hong. Freenet: A distributed anonymous information storage and retrieval system. In *Lecture Notes in Computer Science*, 2001.
4. GNUTELLA. http://gnutella.wego.com.
5. B. C. Ooi D. Papadias P. Kalnis, W. S. Ng and K. L. Tan. An adaptive peer-to-peer network for distributed caching of olap results. In *ACM SIGMOD 2002*, pages 25–36, Madison , Wisconsin, USA, 2002.
6. JXTA Project Home Page. In *http://www.jxta.org*.
7. Microsft .NET Home Page. In *http://www.microsoft.com/net*.
8. B. Yang and H. Garcia-Molina. Comparing hybrid peer-to-peer systems. In *Proc. of The Conf. on Very Large Data Bases (VLDB)*, 2001.
9. S.Saroiu, P.K.Gummadi, and S.D.Gribble. A measurement study of peer-to-peer file sharing systems. In *Technical Report UW-CSE-01-06-02*, Department of Computer Science and Engineering University of Washinton Seattle WA, July 2001.
10. J. Kubiatowicz et al. Oceanstore: An architecture for global-scale persistent storage. In *Proceedings of the Ninth international Conference on Architectural Support for Programming Languages and Operating Systems (ASPLOS)*, Boston, MA, November 2000.
11. A. Halevy, Z. Ives, D. Suciu, and I. Tatarinov. Schema mediation in peer data management systems. In *Proceedings of the 19th International Conference on Data Engineering*, Bangalore, India, March 2003.
12. S. Gribble, A. Halevy, Z. Ives, M. Rodrig, and D. Suciu. What can databases do for peer-to-peer. In *ACM SIGMOD Workshop on the Web and Databases(WebDB)*, 2001.
13. R. Dingledine, D. Molnar, and M. J. Freedman. The free haven project: Distributed anonymous storage service. In *Proceedings of the Workshop on Design Issues in Anonymity and Unobservability*, 2000.
14. D. Karger F. Kaashoek I. Stoica, R. Morris and H. Balakrishnan. Chord: A scalable Peer-To-Peer lookup service for internet applications. In *Proceedings of the 2001 ACM SIGCOMM Conference*, pages 149–160, 2001.
15. M. Handley R. Karp S. Ratnasamy, P. Francis and S. Shenker. A scalable content addressable network. In *Proceedings of the 2001 ACM SIGCOMM Conference*, 2001.
16. P. Druschel and A. Rowstron. Past: A large-scale, persistent peer-to-peer storage utility. In *Proceedings of the Eighth Workshop on Hot Topics in Operating Systems (HotOS-VIII)*, 2001.
17. J. D. Kubiatowicz B. Y. Zhao and A. D. Joseph. Tapestry: An infrastructure for fault-tolerant wide-area location and routing. Technical report, Technical Report UCB/CSD-01-1141, Computer Science Division, U. C. Berkeley, April 2001.
18. A. Andrzejak and X. Zichen. Scalable, efficient range queries for grid information services. Technical report, Technical Report HPL-2002-209, Internet Systems and Storage Laboratory, HP Laboratories Palo Alto, July 2002.
19. M. A. Neimat W. Litwin and D. Schneider. Rp: A family of order-preserving scalable distributed data structures. In *Proc. of The Conf. on Very Large Data Bases (VLDB)*, 1994.

The Design of PIRS, a Peer-to-Peer Information Retrieval System

Wai Gen Yee and Ophir Frieder

Database and Information Retrieval Laboratory,
Department of Computer Science,
Illinois Institute of Technology,
Chicago, IL 60616
yee@iit.edu, ophir@ir.iit.edu

Abstract. We describe the design of PIRS, a peer-to-peer information retrieval system. Unlike some other proposed approaches, PIRS does not require the centralization of data onto specially designated peers. It is therefore applicable to a larger environment. We explain our design decisions, analyzing its benefits and potential shortcomings. We then show that PIRS significantly improves over search performance found in todays P2P file sharing systems.

1 Introduction

Many of today's peer-to-peer (P2P) file sharing systems were initially conceived as successors to Napster, which was used primarily for the exchange of music. As such, they are designed to allow simple annotation of files, including the artist and song title.

As long as a file's metadata are well-known, searches are simple. A query matches a file if its terms are substrings of the metadata's terms. For example, consider two instances of the same song, annotated by the terms "Smashing Pumpkins 1979," and "Pumpkins Greatest Hit 1979," respectively. A query for a query "Smashing Pumpkins Greatest Hits" (which likely refers to the song) will not return either instance.

This problem illustrates a limitation of P2P search: It requires the user to know the exact metadata associated with an instance of the file to perform a successful search. This is problematic for the naive user, who is unaware of annotation conventions, or for a user not looking for a particular song, but for a particular type of music (e.g., "songs from bands from Chicago"). This problem is exacerbated by the fact that many song files are automatically annotated using Web databases, such as freedb.org. Such annotation results in the identical annotation of all copies of a particular song, and gives users disincentives to make their own annotations.

The goal of this paper is to describe how information retrieval (IR) can help alleviate this problem in a P2P environment. In our analysis, we spend some time describing the characteristics of P2P systems, and the degree to which existing

W.S. Ng et al. (Eds.): DBISP2P 2004, LNCS 3367, pp. 107–121, 2005.

P2P systems possess them in Section 2. In Section 3, we informally describe the P2P file sharing model. We describe the design of PIRS, our **P2P IR System**, in Section 4, and present some experimental results in Section 5. In Section 6, we discuss PIRS's compatibility with other work, as well as the future of P2P IR. We make concluding remarks and discuss future work Section 7.

2   Limits of Current Work in P2P Information Retrieval

2.1   Characteristics of P2P Systems

As described in [1], P2P systems are characterized by low maintenance overhead, improved scalability and reliability, synergistic performance, increased autonomy, privacy, and dynamism. P2P systems are inexpensive to maintain and have good scalability because they use the full resources of all participants, who function as both clients and servers. They are more reliable, because the failure of any one peer does not disable the entire system. They offer synergistic performance because peers can utilize resources (e.g., data, CPU cycles, disk space) that are underutilized by others. They are dynamic, allowing peers to autonomously join and leave the system, and thereby changing the types of resources offered. They offer privacy because P2P networks lack central authentication servers. P2P systems are therefore ideal in environments populated by many autonomous users with dynamic needs and surplus resources.

These characteristics distinguish P2P systems from previous technologies, such as distributed computing, and ad-hoc communication. Distributed computing refers to computing on a platform where resources are located on many physically distinct locales. Unlike P2P systems, these resources may be highly integrated and interdependent. Ad-hoc communication refers to a communication platform in which a client can automatically join an existing network. Ad-hoc networking deals with the lower-level communication infrastructure on which P2P systems can be built. P2P computing is therefore a unique paradigm that creates new possibilities for information technologies.

2.2   The Limits of Information Retrieval Using Web Search Engines

The Internet offers a medium by which everyone can easily gather, and share information. Today, the dominant paradigm for sharing information is via the Web. Organizations set up Web servers that host Web sites where they can publish information. Individuals also have a chance to publish information through personal Web pages or *blog* pages. To access this information, users simply type in the appropriate URL into a Web browser.

There is a gap, however, in bringing together information publishers and consumers–how exactly does one find the appropriate URL that points to desired information? Today, this gap is bridged by Web search engines, such as Google. A consumer enters some relevant terms into Google, which returns heuristically-defined best matches.

The problem with relying on Google to find published data is that publishers must wait for Google to *crawl* their Web pages before they appear in any search results. Because crawling occurs only periodically, material published today will not be found for some time. Another problem is that Google caches indexed content. Once this happens, publishers lose control over the dissemination of their material [2]. Furthermore, the results returned by search engines can be suspect. For example, rankings can be influenced by commercial interests [3]. Finally, centralizing query services limits the scalability and reliability of the search engine: A single server can only index so much content (Google claims to index slightly more than 4 billion Web pages, which is considered only a small fraction of those available), and also is a single point of failure. A more relevant example is Napster, whose centralized architecture made it easy prey for legal attacks.

Recent P2P file sharing systems that focus on file transfer, such as BitTorrent [4] suffer from the same problems as Web search engines. BitTorrent is different from Gnutella in that the former focuses on download performance, whereas the latter focuses on search. BitTorrent allows a client to download a single file from multiple sources simultaneously, thereby improving performance, and distributing load. However, it relies on Web search engines to provide search capabilities for shared content, and therefore has all the problems discussed above.

P2P systems solve many of these problems. Because queries are sent directly to data sources, results are up-to-date and reflect the currently available data. Upon receipt of results, the peer can use custom algorithms to rank them. This eases their perusal as users have more trust in their rankings. Finally, there is no single point of failure with P2P systems. A query likely returns results even with the failures of multiple nodes [5].

2.3   Current Peer-to-Peer Information Retrieval Systems and Their Limits

Work on P2P information systems has focused on either bandwidth efficiency, or the development of unifying data models. The PeerSearch system [6] is built on top of the CAN routing infrastructure [7]. CAN places content in a P2P network based on its hash value. PeerSearch proposes to create a distributed index, which is partitioned and similarly placed on a network. This deterministic placement of content improves bandwidth efficiency by constraining the way a query is routed. (The original version of Gnutella, in contrast, floods queries over the network [8].) In [9], the authors take a similar approach. They assume a hybrid networking architecture where some the peers that are deemed more reliable and capable act as servers. These servers, besides routing queries, also store metadata statistics, such as term frequencies, that are used by traditional IR algorithms.

Other systems, such as Edutella [10] and PeerDB [11] propose data models that standardize the way data and services are published and queried.

While these systems have much potential, they are limited due to the constraints that they put on the infrastructure and applications. The PeerSearch system works best in an environment where peers are reliably connected to the Internet. This is necessary because shared content is centralized in certain peers based on their hash values. The loss of a peer results in the loss of all its associated content or the transfer of massive quantities of data. Furthermore, it takes control of data placement out of the users' hands. These characteristics violate the principles of P2P systems that are described in Section 2.1. A solution to this problem is to replicate content by applying multiple hash functions on content. This is problematic as well, because it increases both the amount of data every peer must maintain and network traffic as well. Notably, no work we know of has been done on P2P information retrieval in highly dynamic environments where peers frequently join and leave the network.

Edutella and PeerDB focus more on standards than on information retrieval. Standardization, however, tends to raise the bar for entry into a network because it forces users to do more work to publish content. This has the effect of limiting the amount of data that are published, thereby reducing the network's overall usefulness [12].

Note that it is not our goal to be purists in P2P system design. The popularity of Napster (in terms of market impact and user satisfaction) demonstrates that, under certain conditions, there is no need. At the same time, pure P2P systems were shown to have scalability problems [13], which can be alleviated by the use of a hybrid architecture [14]. However, the fact that a system works without being purely P2P does not mean that it might not work better if it were so.

3   Model

In a typical file sharing model, each peer (which we may refer to as a client or a server, depending on the context) maintains a set of shared files (or *data objects*). Each file is annotated with a set of metadata *terms*, contained in a *descriptor*. The particular terms contained in a descriptor of an *instance* of a file is user-tunable.

Users create *queries* to find files in the P2P system. A query is a metadata set that a user thinks best describe a file. These queries are routed to reachable peers. (Queries generally do not reach all peers due to network conditions or details of the routing protocol.) Returned are pointers to instances of files that match the query, and the file's metadata set. The *matching criterion* is for all the query terms to be substrings of some term of the file's metadata set.

Users study the returned metadata sets to decide on the file to download. Once the user makes her selection, she downloads the file by selecting its associated file pointer. The client follows the pointer, downloads the file, and then becomes a server for an instance of that file.

Note that although our discussion uses music file sharing as an application, it also applies to other applications. For example, an HTML document is also a file that can analogously be annotated with metadata in the form of META tags. The terms in the META tags can be tuned independent of the "content" of the HTML document.

4   The Design of PIRS

4.1   Goals

Our goal is to design a P2P IR system that focuses on client behavior and is fully distributed. The system must make little or no assumptions about the underlying communication infrastructure and the behavior of servers (i.e., other peers). For example, CAN routing and PeerSearch (mentioned above in Section 2) tacitly assumes that the network is stable and servers are reliable. Consequently, although these systems have potentially excellent performance, violating either of these assumptions results in the loss of either queries or data. In this light, these systems tend to fall somewhat between the categories of distributed and P2P systems.

A system that does not make assumptions about the communication infrastructure and behavior of peers avoids these problems. The obvious questions to ask therefore are:

1. How well would such a P2P IR system work? For example, IR requires global statistics about the available data for effective ranking. In a highly dynamic environment, such statistics are hard to yield. Furthermore, even if such data were available, would it be possible to implement IR ranking functions in a P2P application? The question here is about performance in terms of query result quality as well as computational complexity.
2. Could such a system adapt to changes in system conditions? Making no assumptions in designing a P2P system may be too conservative an approach. In some cases, the network and peers are capable and reliable. Can the P2P system take advantage of this condition, if available? Gnutella's Ultrapeer architecture demonstrates adaptability; it conserves bandwidth given a stable environment, but also works (albeit less efficiently) in an unstable one [14].

Our goal is to answer these two questions. To do this, we describe the design of PIRS. In doing this, we highlight the complexities of applying IR techniques to a P2P environment.

4.2   Overview

PIRS is designed to combine the search capabilities of information retrieval systems with the dynamic network management of P2P systems. It works by managing metadata in such a way as to *gradually increase the variety* of queries that can be answered for a given file. This is done by adapting the annotation of a particular file to match query patterns. PIRS accomplishes its goals in three ways:

1. Metadata collection (Section 4.3) - Collect as much metadata as possible for a shared file, using various means. Increasing the amount of metadata increases the likelihood that a query will find matches. For simplicity, the size of the metadata set is generally limited in size, thus a decision must be made as to which metadata to maintain.

2. Metadata distribution (Section 4.4) - Heuristically replicate metadata from other peers when downloading a file. By sharing metadata from multiple peers, the variety of queries that can be matched for a given file increases. Again, the client must decide on a limited set of metadata to maintain.
3. Metadata use (Section 4.5) - Utilize IR techniques to rank results, disambiguating them, and thereby improving the likelihood of a correct download.

The processes of metadata collection, distribution, and use work together to improve the search capabilities of PIRS. Ostensibly, they can work independently to improve search, but with diminished benefits. For example, IR ranking functions alone can be incorporated into Gnutella, without PIRS's metadata distribution techniques.

By design, PIRS is simple to incorporate into many existing P2P protocols. This is a consequence of its functionality being concentrated on client behavior, and its independence from networking infrastructure. Many existing P2P protocols focus on aspects of query routing, which is independent of PIRS's functionality. Consequently, PIRS can be built on top of many of today's popular P2P file sharing applications, such as Gnutella and FastTrack. We discuss this in more detail in Section 6.

PIRS Versus Other P2P IR Systems. The major difference between PIRS and other P2P IR systems is that PIRS treats metadata as a dynamic resource that should be managed collectively by all peers. Effective management of metadata improves query result quality. The inspiration of this work stems from the notion that, from a client's perspective, the P2P network is a repository of files, each of which is described collectively by a *body of metadata*. The better a file's body of metadata describes the file, the easier the file should be to find.

Current P2P IR systems do not have this perspective. They treat each download as an individual transaction, without regard to how it (the download) affects the file's body of metadata. The download of a file generally also results in the replication of that file's metadata from a particular server. The downloading client becomes an additional server for the file, but with marginal benefit, because the clients it serves are exactly those which the original server serves. The additional server's role in the network is largely redundant.

4.3   Metadata Collection

Metadata collection is the process by which a file is annotated with identifying terms. We now describe how metadata collection is typically done in commercial P2P systems. We also describe a unit of metadata that PIRS exploits for good performance.

Metadata terms are directly used for query matching. It is therefore important to build into PIRS effective means of annotating files. One of these means includes creating an easy to use user interface, which encourages users to add metadata. Other means include automatic annotation via metadata *foraging* and the use of *intrinsic* file characteristics.

Recent versions of P2P file sharing systems offer templates that help a user annotate certain types of files, such as audio files, using special application-specific fields [15]. These templates structure metadata, potentially increasing the query matching possibilities.

Much metadata are also automatically foraged from Internet sources. For example, when *wav* files are *ripped* from commercial compact disks, the ripping software automatically collects ID3 metadata (e.g., title, artist) [16] for it from Web sites such as freedb.org. Other metadata are *intrinsic* to the file. Such metadata include the size of the file, its filename, and the last time it was accessed. Making these metadata available for querying requires some simple programming.

Finally, some systems automatically derive useful metadata from the intrinsic characteristics of the file. BitTorrent, for example, generates a unique *hash key* (e.g., an SHA-1 hash [17]) for each file, which can simplify its search and be a means of validating the file's contents [4]. A hash key can also be used to group files that are returned by queries.

PIRS uses a file's hash key for validating and grouping files. Such use of the hash key has not been universally adopted. LimeWire's Gnutella groups by filename, file type, and file size [18]. BearShare and eDonkey only use hash keys to authenticate files.

One problem with requiring all files to be annotated with a hash key is its computational cost. This problem has been acknowledged by BearShare, which claims that computing keys in a background process takes only 25% of a CPU's cycles [19]. Hash keys can also be computed while a file is being downloaded, extracted (if it is compressed), or ripped. Piggybacking these processes amortizes the cost of computing the hash key.

Maintaining a hash key for files also does not hurt PIRS's compatibility with existing P2P file sharing systems. It would be treated as another generic unit of metadata by a peer that did not realize its significance.

4.4   Metadata Distribution

Metadata distribution is the process by which peers exchange metadata with each other in order to describe a file. In this process, each peer does just a little work to better collectively describe shared data. This process complements metadata collection in building an effective body of metadata for each shared file.

Metadata distribution is crucial for two reasons. First, if metadata are not distributed among multiple nodes, then the system may become vulnerable. If all metadata were concentrated on a single node (e.g., as with Napster), the system becomes unusable if that node becomes unreachable. This vulnerability violates a basic principle of P2P systems.

Second, data that are not distributed *properly* could leave correlations in term occurrences, which limit the degree of query matching. For example, assume there are two metadata ripping systems for song files: one extracts the album name (denoted t_1) and the song's track number (t_2), and the other extracts the album's label (t_3) and year (t_4). If files were only annotated using these two rippers, then a query, $\{t_1, t_3\}$ would not return any results due to the matching criterion.

PIRS distributes metadata in a way that avoids this problem. During a query, it groups all metadata for each unique file in the results. When a user selects a file, metadata are heuristically replicated from the file's group onto the client. Grouping of unique files is straightforward, as each result is assumed to contain the file's hash key. The heuristics we consider for metadata replication include:

- Server terms (**server**) - The client selects the metadata that exist on the single server from which it downloads. This is the solution that is commonly used in today's P2P file sharing systems. It is notable for its simplicity.
- Most frequent terms in the group (**mfreq**) - The client selects the terms that occur most frequently in the group. The justification for this approach stems from the assumption that, because these terms appear so much, they are strongly associated with the file, and therefore most likely to occur in queries.
- Least frequent terms (**lfreq**) - The client selects the terms that occur least frequently in the group. The usefulness of this approach is that these terms help distinguish this file from others. It also balances out the term distribution.
- Random terms (**rand**) - The client randomly selects terms from the group, maximizing the number of term combinations.
- Random terms based on freq (**wrand**) - The client randomly selects terms from the group weighting more frequently occurring terms proportionately higher. Like **rand**, this technique also increases the number of term combinations, but gives preference to more commonly occurring terms.

In the last four techniques, **mfreq**, **lfreq**, **rand**, and **wrand**, the client selects metadata terms until it reaches a system defined limit.

These metadata distribution techniques are an improvement over the current technique of replicating metadata from a single server. They increase the variety and sizes of metadata sets, and thereby should improve their ability to accurately describe a file. The effects they have on the states of bodies of metadata vary, however, and a goal of the PIRS project is to examine their effects of query results quality.

4.5   Metadata Use

IR style ranking in P2P systems is difficult, due to certain characteristics of P2P systems. For example queries are short and peers are unreliable. PIRS acts a testbed for both traditional and P2P-specific ranking functions. Specifically, we use PIRS to determine the dependence of ranking functions on metadata distribution techniques.

We consider five ranking functions. Some of these techniques are classical IR techniques, and some are unique to P2P file sharing:

- Group size (**gsize**) - The number of results in a group. A large GS indicates that either a particular file has large support for satisfying a query, or that the file is generally popular, and is therefore something desirable anyway.
- Term frequency (**tf**) - Counting the number of times query terms appear in a file's metadata. Terms that occur frequently in metadata sets likely represent the contents of the file.
- Precision (**prec**) - Dividing TF by the total number of terms in the group. Precision adjusts for problems with TF caused by large metadata sets.
- Cosine similarity (**cos**) - Cosine similarity maps group descriptors and the query to vectors. It ranks highest the groups with the descriptor vectors that have the highest cosine similarity to the query vector.

We implemented other ranking functions, such as term frequency with inverse document frequency (**tf/idf** from [20]). **Tf/idf**, however, requires some modification, because global information on the number of documents in which each term appears, required by **tf/idf**, does not exist in P2P systems. We instead approximate *document frequency* by the number of query results in which a term appears. Since **tf/idf** is another variation of vector space model ranking, of which **cos** is a representative, and its performance is not much different, we do not further discuss it.

4.6   Implementation Issues

Due to the distributed nature of a P2P system, query results arrive at clients asynchronously, over a period of time. The client must be able to display these results and update their rankings in real-time.

PIRS groups each of the N results in $O(\log N)$ time using the hash key. It also updates rankings for all results within $O(N^2)$ time, depending on the ranking function. While this complexity is a current upper bound, it is within the $O(N^2 \log (N) KM)$ complexity of grouping of Limewire's Gnutella [18], where K and M are grouping similarity metrics. More details about the implementation of grouping and ranking in PIRS are posted on the authors' Web sites.

5   Experimental Results

We now demonstrate the effect that metadata distribution and ranking have on query result quality via simulation. We measure performance by the number *successful* queries (i.e., those that lead to the download of the desired data object) that the clients perform. We do not consider traditional IR metrics, such as *precision* and *recall*. Precision measures the percentage of correct results to a query, and is irrelevant because, in our model, the user requests a specific data object, and any replica of the desired data object will satisfy her. For the same reason, recall, the percentage of possible results returned, is also irrelevant in our model.

5.1   The Simulator

The design of our simulator is based on observations and analyses of P2P file sharing systems. In the event that relevant design parameters are unavailable, we borrow from work on done on Web information systems and IR.

The major objects in our simulator are terms, data objects, peers, and queries. The **universal set** of terms T that can describe a data object is finite, and each term is assigned a relative access probability based on the accepted Zipf distribution [21]. A random number of terms from T are assigned to each data object's (F_i) universal term **subset** (T_i) based on the initial Zipf distribution. The terms of each data object's universal term subset are then reassigned probabilities according to a Zipf distribution to diversify term usage, as described in [22]. For example, a term that is rarely associated with one data object need not be so for another. We call the set of probabilities that terms will be associated with a data object the data object's **natural (term) distribution**.

We also make the generally unrealistic assumption that terms are independent. For example, the occurrence of "Britney" in a descriptor is independent of the occurrence of "Spears". This is incorrect in general, but is common practice, as it simplifies the simulation environment without making it trivial. Note, however, that this term independence assumption is not unique to our work. Such an assumption is heavily relied upon in the probabilistic information retrieval model in IR.

Each data object is also associated with an access probability, according to a Zipf distribution. This conforms to the access patterns observed for Web objects that were described in [23]. Observations of data object frequency in a P2P system also suggest a high access skew [24].

Initially, a random number of copies of each data object are instantiated, each with a subset of its universal term subset in its descriptor. These copies are assigned to random clients.

There are a fixed number of peers and a fixed number of data objects in the system. At each iteration of the simulation, a random peer is chosen to download a random data object based on the data object' access probability distribution. To do this, the peer generates a query of random length containing a subset of the data object's universal term subset. We assume that length distributions follow those of Web search engines, and use the empirical distribution described in [25]. Personal observations of queries in LimeWire's query monitor window seems to corroborate this assumption. Each term in the query is randomly chosen based on the data object's natural term distribution.

The query is routed to a random subset of servers. We do not send the query to all servers because, in practice, only a subset of them is reachable at any time [24]. The servers return results that fulfill the matching criterion (Section 3) to the client.

Client Behavior. If more than one group forms in response to a query, then the client ranks the groups. The highest ranked group is selected for download. Although, in general, the user may be equally likely to select any one out of the first few highest ranked groups, all else being equal, we can generally assume that she will select the one that is highest ranked.

We say that the query is **successful** if the desired data object is ranked first and downloaded. In an unsuccessful query, either the incorrect group is ranked first and downloaded, or there are no results.

Once the data object is downloaded, the user has a probability of manually annotating the data object with some personally chosen terms. These terms are randomly chosen from the data object's universal term subset, based on the natural term distribution. This is the only way that the variety of terms that exists in the system for a data object can increase beyond what exists at initialization. If the user downloads the incorrect data object, then she may mis-annotate it in this step, leading to incorrect metadata for the data object.

After this is done, the client heuristically copies some of the chosen group's metadata into the replica's descriptor, with the constraint that only a limited number of terms may be copied. The data object is then available for other peers to find in subsequent iterations of the simulation.

We do not model freeriders or malicious users. Freeriders are users who download, but do not upload data objects. Since they do not contribute any metadata to the system, they do not affect the results. Malicious users are those who may contribute misleading metadata for data objects to the system. These users may affect the rankings, but only marginally. Rankings are based on the aggregate metadata of a group of users, not on the metadata of an individual.

Table 1. Parameters Used in the Simulation

Parameter	Value or Range
Number of peers	1000
Number of data objects	1000
Number of terms in universal set	10000
Number of terms in the universal set of a data object	100-150
Maximum descriptor size for a data object on a peer (terms)	20
Number of terms in initial descriptors	3-10
Number of replicas of each data object at initialization	3
Probability that a peer is reachable	0.5
Probability of client adding metadata	0.05
Number of Terms Added by client	1-5
Query length	1-8, dist from [25]
Number of queries	10000
Number of trials	50

The parameters we use in the experiments are shown in Table 1. The size of the simulation is scaled down to reveal any convergences in the results more quickly. More significant than the scale of the simulation are the relative values of each parameter, such as the total number of possible terms for a data object, versus the number of terms with which each data object is initially annotated.

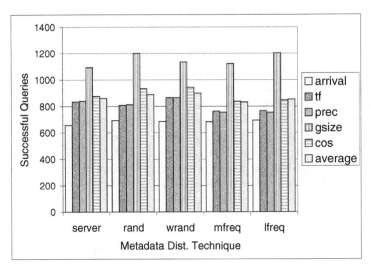

Fig. 1. Number of Successful Queries vs. Metadata Distribution Technique for Multiple Ranking Functions

These numbers are based on observations from other studies [26, 24], as well as personal observations. For example, song data objects that appear on Gnutella networks typically have about three or more types of information associated with them from ID3 data: artist, song name, album name, track number, etc. This is reflected in the *Number of terms in initial descriptors* parameter.

We performed fifty trials with each set of parameters and report the average results. The 95% confidence intervals generally were well within 4% of the reported mean–the results are statistically significant. However, to simplify the presentation of the main results, we do not present them.

5.2   Results for Various Combinations of Metadata Distribution and Ranking

We see that **gsize** is the best ranking function regardless of metadata distribution technique in 1. This is somewhat surprising, considering its simplicity. **Gsize** works relatively well because only the correct data object will likely contain *all* query terms, and thereby satisfy the matching criterion. Other data objects' descriptors may be near-misses. **Cos** does a distant second best. It does poorly because the matching criterion does not return an unbiased sample of results; all results contain all query terms. It therefore cannot discriminate between relevant and irrelevant very well. Finally, **prec** and **tf** are subject to the same problems they have in traditional IR; they are highly influenced by large metadata sets or by noise.

We also see that the metadata distribution techniques that randomize the metadata (**rand** and **wrand**) do best on average. Furthermore, the combination of **rand** and **gsize** do the best. However, no ranking function in combination with **wrand** outperforms **gsize** with **lfreq**. The reason that **lfreq** does better than **wrand** in this case is that **lfreq** is better at increasing the total number of terms in the body of metadata for a data object. **Wrand** replicates common terms, introducing a skew. Descriptor space is therefore occupied by repetitions of common terms. **Lfreq**, in general, replicates terms that do not occur frequently. It therefore has the effect of replicating every term in the long run. This larger body of metadata is in this sense more descriptive, resulting in more relevant results for a query. Besides **gsize**, the best performing ranking function using **wrand** is **cos**. This is expected, because **cos** requires term frequencies to be skewed in order to work correctly. **Lfreq**, by comparison, does worse with **cos**, because it results in uniform distributions of terms in bodies of metadata.

Server and **mfreq** do poorly because they fail to mix the metadata during distribution. **Server** simply replicates a single server's descriptor. **Mfreq** replicates terms that have already been frequently replicated. This does little to increase the variety of descriptors that describe a data object.

6 Discussion

6.1 Compatibility with Existing Technologies

A feature of PIRS is that it is compatible with Gnutella. A PIRS peer interacts with others via message passing. These messages are in standard Gnutella format, and no special messages are required. Furthermore, no special architectures are required by PIRS. PIRS simply allows peers to create and respond to queries in a way that is transparent to standard Gnutella peers. A PIRS peer can therefore readily integrate itself into an established P2P file-sharing system.

In a similar vein, PIRS can also take advantage of optimizations designed for Gnutella-like P2P systems. Routing optimizations, such as *shortcuts* [27] and Ultrapeers [14] are available. Search optimizations, such as specially designated index nodes are also possible [9]. In the latter case, although special index nodes improve the quality of search results, they do not obviate the need for metadata distribution and client-side ranking of results.

6.2 The Outlook for Peer-to-Peer Information Retrieval

P2P file sharing system vendors have been actively pursuing new markets. Kazaa, for example, has adapted its networks for content distribution for media companies, online dating with MatchNet, and voice-over-IP telephony with Snype [28]. These new applications will surely bring new users into the area.

Other industry trends seem to indicate that P2P information retrieval will be a strategic technology in the near future. Google is currently working on Puffin, a desktop search tool that helps users find information stored on their desktops [29]. Whether this is a counterattack to Microsoft's Longhorn [30] strategy or not, it signals a new focus on harnessing the information stored on desktops.

P2P file sharing has been a consistently active Internet activity for the last several years. This condition shows no sign of weakening, despite recent legal actions by the recording industries [31]. As the user base and variety of P2P applications grows, PIRS and other P2P search tools will only gain in significance.

7   Conclusion

P2P file sharing is a popular activity among Internet users, and shows little signs of slowing down. As volumes of data grow, so does the need for good IR to sort through the results. PIRS, our P2P IR system is one solution. It is compatible with current P2P file sharing systems, but more powerful.

PIRS is flexible, as P2P systems should be. Unlike other work in P2P IR, it allows for unpredictable user behavior, and makes no assumptions about the underlying network. As a dynamic system, it also escapes some of the problems that exist when using centralized systems, such as Web search engines; data can be made available much quicker.

PIRS is unique in that it allows users to tune the ways in which a client distributes metadata. It treats the metadata that exist in all instances of a data object in the system as a collective description of the data object. With improved descriptiveness, query results improve in quality.

PIRS also includes various ranking functions. Our simulation results show that the effectiveness of ranking somewhat depends on the metadata distribution, and that the correct combination can improve performance from 15% up to 90%.

We are currently considering the relationship between the matching criterion and ranking functions. The current matching criterion is based on conjunctive queries. Although this economizes on bandwidth consumption, it may reduce the quality of queries results. We are considering the effect of alternatives, such as disjunction. We will focus on server-side responses to queries.

References

1. Milojicic, D.S., Kalogeraki, V., Lukose, R., Nagaraja, K., Pruyne, J., Richard, B.: Peer-to-peer computing. Technical Report HPL-2002-57, Hewlett-Packard Laboratories, Palo Alto (2002)
2. Noguchi, Y.: Online search engines help lift cover of privacy. Washington Post (2004) Feb. 9, 2004.
3. Hansell, S.: Yahoo to charge for guaranteeing a spot on its index. New York Times (2004) Mar. 2, 2004.
4. Cohen, B.: Bittorrent home page. (Web Document) bitconjurer.org/BitTorrent.
5. Watts, D.J., Strogatz, S.H.: Collective dynamics of small-world networks. Nature **393** (1998)
6. Tang, C., Xu, Z., Dwarkadas, S.: Peer-to-peer information retrieval using self-organizing semantic overlay networks. In: Proc. ACM SIGCOMM. (2003)
7. Ratnasamy, S., Francis, P., Handley, M., Karp, R., Shenker, S.: A scalable content-addressable network. In: Proc. ACM SIGCOMM. (2001)
8. LimeWire, LLC: Gnutella protocol 0.4. Web Document (2004) www9.limewire.com/developer/gnutella_protocol_0.4.pdf.

9. Lu, J., Callan, J.: Content-based retrieval in hybrid peer-to-peer networks. In: Proc. ACM Conf. on Information and Knowledge Mgt. (CIKM). (2003) 199–206

10. Nejdl, W., Wolf, B., Qu, C., Decker, S., Sintek, M., Naeve, A., Nilsson, M., Palmr, M., Risch, T.: Edutella: A p2p networking infrastructure based on rdf. In: Proc. World Wide Web Conf. (2002)

11. Ng, W., Ooi, B.C., Tan, K., Zhou, A.: Peerdb: A p2p-based system for distributed data sharing. In: Proc. IEEE Intl. Conf. on Data Eng. (ICDE). (2003)

12. Google, I.: Simplicity and enterprise search. Technical report, Google, Inc. (2003)

13. Ritter, J.: Why gnutella can't scale. no, really. Web Document (2001) www. darkridge.com/~jpr5/doc/gnutella.html.

14. Singla, A., Rohrs, C.: Ultrapeers: Another step towards gnutella scalability. Technical report, Limewire, LLC (2002) rfc-gnutella.sourceforge.net/src/ Ultrapeers_1.0.html.

15. Thadani, S.: Meta information searches on the gnutella network. (Web document) www.bearguru.com/kb/articles/metainfo_searches.htm.

16. Nilsson, M.: Id3v2 web site. Web Document (2004) www.id3.org.

17. of Standards, N.I., Technology: Sha1 version 1.0. Web Document (1995) www.itl.nist.gov/fipspubs/fip180-1.htm.

18. Rohrs, C.: Search result grouping {in gnutella}. Technical report, LimeWire (2001) www.limewire.org/project/www/result_grouping.htm.

19. Free Peers, Inc.: Bearshare technical faq. Web document (2004) www.bearshare. com/help/faqtechnical.htm.

20. Grossman, D., Frieder, O.: Information Retrieval: Algorithms and Heuristics. Number ISBN 0-7923-8271-4. Kluwer Academic Publishers (1998)

21. Knuth, D.E.: The Art Of Computer Programming. Second edn. Volume 3:Sorting and Searching. Addison-Wesley Publishing Company (1975)

22. Schlosser, M.T., Condie, T.E., Kamvar, S.D.: Simulating a file-sharing p2p network. In: Proc. Wkshp. Semantics in Peer-to-Peer and Grid Comp. (2003)

23. Crovella, M., Bestavros, A.: Self-similarity in world wide web traffic: evidence and possible causes. IEEE/ACM Trans. Networking **5** (1997) 835–846

24. Saroiu, S., Gummadi, P.K., Gribble, S.D.: A measurement study of peer-to-peer file sharing systems. In: Proc. Multimedia Computing and Networking (MMCN). (2002)

25. Reynolds, P., Vahdat, A.: Efficient peer-to-peer keyword searching. In: Proc. ACM Conf. Middlware. (2003)

26. Ripeanu, M., Foster, I.: Mapping the gnutella network: Properties of large-scale peer-to-peer systems and implications for system design. In: Intl. Wkshp. on P2P Sys. (IPTPS). Number 2429 in LNCS (2002)

27. Sripanidkulchai, K., Maggs, B., Zhang, H.: Efficient content location using interest-based locality in peer-to-peer systems. In: Proc. IEEE INFOCOM. (2003)

28. CBC: The future. CBC/Radio-Canada (2004) www.cbc.ca/disclosure/archives/ 040309_swap/future.html.

29. Markoff, J.: Google moves toward clash with microsoft. New York Times (2004) May 19.

30. Microsoft, Inc.: Longhorn development center. Web Document (2004) msdn. microsoft.com/longhorn/.

31. Reardon, M.: Oops! they're swapping again. CNET News (2004)

Adapting the Content Native Space for Load Balanced Indexing

Yanfeng Shu[1], Kian-Lee Tan[1], and Aoying Zhou[2]

[1] School of Computing,
National University of Singapore, Singapore
{shuyanfe, tankl}@comp.nus.edu.sg
[2] Department of Computer Science,
Fudan University, China
ayzhou@comp.nus.edu.sg

Abstract. Today, there is an increasing demand to share data with complex data types (e.g., multi-dimensional) over large numbers of data sources. One of the key challenges is sharing these data in a scalable and efficient way. This paper presents the design of ZNet, a P2P network for supporting multi-dimensional data. ZNet directly operates on the native data space, which is partitioned dynamically and mapped to nodes within the network. Particular attention is given to reduce load imbalance among nodes due to skewed data distribution. Results from an extensive simulation study show that ZNet is efficient in routing and processing range queries, and provides good load balancing.

1   Introduction

Today, there is an increasing demand to share complex data types (e.g., multi-dimensional) and to support complex queries (e.g., range queries). For example, in grid information services, computing resources are typically characterized by multiple attributes like the type of operating systems, CPU speed and memory size. It is not uncommon for such a system to search for resources that meet multiple attribute requirements, e.g, a resource with LINUX operating system and CPU speed of 1-2 GFlop/sec. As another example, in sensor networks, data or events are also characterized by a set of attributes. For a sensor network that monitors the weather, a typical query may be like this, to find regions whose temperature falls between [0,10] degrees, wind speed in [30,40] nautical miles, and so on.

One of the key challenges for these systems is to share these multi-dimensional data in a scalable and efficient way. Due to a large number of data sources, a centralized approach is always not desirable, sometimes, it may not even be feasible (e.g., in sensor networks). Though P2P technology, as an emerging paradigm for building large-scale distributed systems, could be used for sharing data in a scalable way, today's P2P systems are unable to cope well with complex queries (range queries) on multi-dimensional data. Early P2P systems, such as Gnutella[6], mainly depend on flooding techniques for searching, thus they offer no search guarantee; moreover, data availability could not be ensured unless all nodes in the network are visited. While more recent systems, such as Chord[13] and

W.S. Ng et al. (Eds.): DBISP2P 2004, LNCS 3367, pp. 122–135, 2005.

CAN[9], can guarantee data availability and search efficiency, they are mainly designed for *exact* key lookup; range queries cannot be supported in most cases.

In this paper, as one of the initial attempts to address the above challenges, we present the design of ZNet. ZNet directly operates on the native data space, which is partitioned and then mapped to nodes within the network. ZNet focuses on addressing two important issues. The one is load balancing. We want to make sure that each node contains nearly the same amount of the data. Since data distribution in multi-dimensional data space may not be uniform, if the space is partitioned and assigned to nodes evenly, some nodes may contain more data than others. In ZNet, this issue is addressed by dynamically choosing subspaces which may be densely populated to be split further, so that space could be partitioned in a way that follows the data distribution.

The second issue is to facilitate efficient indexing and searching. Our basic idea is to partition the space in a quad-tree-like manner with some subspaces being recursively partitioned. To facilitate searching, all subspaces resulted from one partitioning are ordered by a first order Space Filling Curve (SFC). As such, the whole data space(multi-dimensional) is mapped to 1-dimensional index space by SFCs at different orders. Two data that are close in their native space are mapped to the same index or indices that are close in the 1-dimensional index space, which are then mapped to the same node or nodes that are close together in the overlay network. Any SFC could be used for the mapping. In our current implementation, Z-ordering is chosen mainly due to its simplicity. Skip graph [2] is extended as the overlay network topology (nonuniform node distribution in ZNet makes DHT-based P2P networks (such as Chord) unsuitable). From an extensive simulation study, it shows that ZNet is good in load balancing when the data distribution changes little, and efficient in supporting range searches.

The rest of the paper is organized as follows: Section 2 discusses the related work; Section 3 presents the system design in space partitioning, searching and load balancing; The experimental results are presented in Section 4; And finally, section 5concludes the whole paper.

2 Related Work

Existing P2P systems can be generally classified as unstructured or structured. For unstructured systems (such as Gnutella [6]), there has no guarantee on data availability and search performance. Therefore, research on range query support in P2P is mainly focused on structured systems.

There are two kinds of structured P2P systems: DHT-based and skip-list based. DHT-based systems, like Chord [13], CAN [9], Pastry [10], and Tapestry [15], use a distributed hash table to distribute data uniformly over all nodes in the system. Though DHT systems can guarantee data availability and search efficiency on exact key lookup, they cannot support range searches efficiently, as hashing destroys data locality. Skip graph [2] and SkipNet [7] are two skip-list based systems, which can support range queries. However, they did not address how data are assigned to nodes. As such, there is no guarantee about data locality and load balancing in the whole system.

In [3], Chord and skip graph are combined into one system to support range searches. Chord is used to assign data to nodes, while skip graph is used to do range searches.

Though load balancing can be ensured in [3], searching is not efficient, which is at a cost of $O(\log m)$, where m is the number of data.

Most work supports range queries by drawing its inspiration from multi-dimensional indexing in the database research [5]. Specifically, locality-preserving mapping is used to map data that are close in their data space to nodes that are close in the overlay network. For example, in [1], the inverse Hilbert mapping was used to map one dimensional data space (single attribute domain) to CAN's d-dimensional Cartesian space; and in [12], the Hilbert mapping was used to map a multi-dimensional data space to Chord's one dimensional space. Though [12] can support multi-dimensional range queries, its performance is poor when the data is highly skewed as the node distribution (which follows data distribution) is not uniform any more. DIM [8] supports multi-dimensional range queries in sensor networks by using k-d trees to map multi-dimensional space to a 2-d geographic space. Load balancing, unfortunately, is not addressed in DIM.

Different from above work, MAAN [4] uses a uniform locality preserving hashing to map attribute values to the Chord identifier space, which is devised with the assumption that the data distribution could be known beforehand. Multi-attribute range queries were supported based on single-attribute resolution. In our work, we do not assume any a prior knowledge on the data distribution, and load balancing is achieved fully based on heuristics that partition dense subspaces.

Still, there are some other orthogonal work. pSearch[14], proposed for document retrieval in P2P networks by extending CAN, bears some similarity to our work in load balancing. However, its main focus is to retrieve some relevant documents, and not to support range searches. [11] proposed a framework based on CAN for caching range queries. By caching the answers of range queries over the network, future range queries can be efficiently evaluated.

3   ZNet

The whole system consists of a large number of nodes, each publishing its data objects (multi-dimensional) and sending queries for other data objects over the network. Range query is the kind of query ZNet is mainly interested in.

To support range queries efficiently, data that are close in their native space needs to be mapped to nodes that are close in the network. In ZNet, a kind of locality preserving mapping is used, and multi-dimensional data space is mapped to 1-dimensional index space by z-curves at different orders. And also, by extending skip graph as the overlay network, queries can be routed efficiently in ZNet, with each node maintaining $O(logN)$ neighbors (N is the number of nodes). Besides query processing, ZNet also addresses the load balancing issue. Two strategies are employed in ZNet to reduce load imbalance. All this will be described next in detail.

3.1   Space Partitioning and Mapping

In ZNet, data space is partitioned in a way as in the generalized quad-tree, that is, each partitioning halves the space in all dimensions. As such, for d dimensions, 2^d subspaces are generated from one partitioning. We call each of such subspaces a *zone*.

Partitioning always occurs when a new node joins and the joining destination (an existing node in the network) has only one zone; if the joining destination has more than one zone, it just passes part of its zones to the new node. Zones from one partitioning are at the same level, which is one level lower than the level of the zone where the partitioning occurs. For the first node (and also the node in the network), it covers the whole data space (at level 0).

By filling zones (from one partitioning) with a first order z-curve, each zone which is at a certain level (call z-level) corresponds to a z-value in $0..2^d - 1$ (for d-dimensional space), which can be computed in the following way: suppose the centroid before partitioning (at z-level i) is $(C_{i,0}, C_{i,1}, ..., C_{i,d-1})$ (for z-level 0, the centroid is (0.5, 0.5, ..., 0.5)), the centroid of a new zone (at z-level $i + 1$) generated from partitioning is $(C_{i+1,0}, C_{i+1,1}, ..., C_{i+1,d-1})$, then the new zone's z-value at z-level $i + 1$ is $(b_0 b_1..b_{d-1})_2$, where b_k is 0, if $C_{i+1,k}$ is less than $C_{i,k}$; otherwise it is 1 ($k = 0..d - 1$).

A zone in the space can be uniquely identified by its z-address. For a zone Z at lth z-level, its z-address will be like $z_1 z_2...z_l$, where z_i is the z-value's binary representation of a zone which is at i z-level and contains Z. Z's z-address can be recursively constructed: first, z_1 is decided in the same way as the above z-value computation by comparing Z's centroid with the centroid (0.5, 0.5, ..., 0.5) at z-level 0; then z_2 is decided by comparing Z's centroid with the centroid of the zone of z-value z_1, and so on, until the level is l.

The z-address of a point in the space is the same as the z-address of a zone which covers the point and is at the lowest z-level. Since the space is unevenly partitioned, z-addresses of two points may be of different lengths. When comparing two z-addresses of different lengths, only the prefix part of the longer one is compared to the shorter one.

Figure 1 illustrates the space partitioning process in a 2-dimensional data space. In the figure, (a) is the initial state of the data space (z-level 0). After the first partitioning (b), four zones are generated with z-values from 0 to 3 (corresponding z-addresses are from 00 to 11). The new zones are at z-level 1. In (c), zone 00 (the zone's z-address is 00) is further partitioned, forming the second level (z-level 2). Suppose zone 0010 is partitioned again, the third level (z-level 3) will be formed.

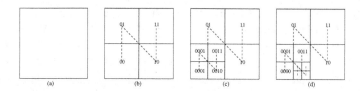

Fig. 1. Z-curves at different levels (0-3)

In sum, by z-curves at different levels (lower level z-curves correspond to higher order of z-curves), multi-dimensional data space is mapped to 1-dimensional index space. Meanwhile, this 1-dimensional space is mapped to nodes in the network. In ZNet, each node always contains continuous zones (zones are continuous in the sense that their z-addresses are continuous).

3.2   Query Routing and Resolving

Since routing in ZNet is based on skip graph[2], in this subsection, we will give a brief description of skip graph first, then we describe query routing and resolving in ZNet in detail.

Skip Graph. Skip graph generalizes skip list for distributed environments. Each node in a skip graph is a member of multiple linked lists at $\lceil logN \rceil$ skip-levels, where N is the number of nodes. The bottom skip-level is a doubly-linked list consisting of all nodes in increasing order by key. Which lists a node belongs to is controlled by its membership vector, which is generated randomly. Specifically, a node is in the list L_w at skip-level i, if and only if w is a prefix of its member vector of length i.

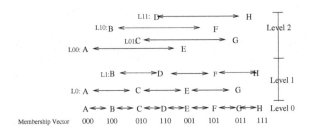

Fig. 2. A skip graph with 3 skip-levels

Figure 2 gives a example of a skip graph with 3 skip-levels. In the figure, there are 8 nodes (from A to H),each of which has one key (not shown in the figure). For simplicity, membership vectors of nodes are distinct, which are chosen from 000 to 111 (in implementation, the membership vectors are randomly generated, which could be same). At skip-level 0, all nodes are doubly-linked in sequence by their keys. At skip-level 1, there are two lists: L_0, L_1. Since the first bit of the membership vectors of nodes A, C, E, G is 0, these nodes belong to L_0. So are nodes for other lists.

Each node (except the first and the last node) in a list has two neighbors: left neighbor and right neighbor. For example, in Figure 2, node C has two neighbors B, D at skip-level 0. At skip-level 1, in L_0, it also has two neighbors A, E. At skip-level 2, it has only one neighbor G. All neighbors of a node form the node's routing table. When searching, a node will first check its neighbors at the highest skip-level. If there is a neighbor whose key is not past the search key, the query will be forwarded to the neighbor; otherwise, neighbors at a lower skip-level are checked. For example, in Figure 2, suppose node C receives a query, whose destination is F. C will first check its neighbor at skip-level 2, G. Since G's key is larger than F's key, searching will go down to skip-level 1. Among C's neighbors at skip-level 1 (A and E), E is qualified, whose key is between C's key and the search key F. The query will be forwarded to E, and so on. The search operation in a skip graph with N nodes takes expected O(log N) time. Note each node has only one key.

Query Routing in ZNet. Skip graph was proposed to handle range queries with one key per node, thus each node needs to maintain $O(logm)$ state, where m is the number

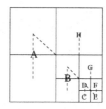

Fig. 3. A routing example

of keys. In addition, in skip graph, there is no description about how keys are assigned to nodes in the system, thus making no guarantee about system-wide load balancing.

In ZNet, since zones mapped to each node are continuous (each node covers continuous z-addresses), and also, load balancing is ensured among nodes, ZNet can extend skip graph for query routing while not having its problems. In ZNet, each node maintains only O(log N)state, where N is the number of nodes.

When given a search key (a point), a node will first transform the point to a z-address, which is then compared to z-addresses covered by the node's neighbors as defined in skip graph. Complexities for routing in ZNet rise in that the z-address of a search point may not be able to be fully resolved initially due to uneven space partitioning.

For example, in Figure 3, the space is partitioned among 8 nodes, $A(00,01)$(A contains z-addresses 00 and 01), $B(1000,1001)$, $C(101000)$, $D(101001)$, $E(101010)$, $F(101011)$, $G(1011)$, $J(11)$. The membership vector of each node is shown as in the figure 2, thus, A has 3 neighbors B, C, E; B has 4 neighbors, and so on. Suppose A receives a point query, whose destination is node D. Since A's zones are at z-level 1, it can only transform the point to z-address (10) according to z-address transformation process (A has no idea about the complete space partitioning status). For z-address (10), two of A's neighbors are qualified: C, E. At current implementation, we just randomly choose one. Suppose E is chosen, and the query will be forwarded to E. When the query arrives at E, another z-address transformation will be done again, and at this time, full z-address (101001) of the search point is obtained (since zones covered by both E and D are at same z-level). By choosing D from E's neighbors as the forwarding node, the query is finally resolved.

Therefore, given a search point, a node may only get a prefix of the point's full z-address, due to incomplete knowledge about space partitioning. With each routing step, however, the point's z-address will become more refined. The routing convergence can be ensured, since with each routing, the query is routed closer to the destination. However, the routing cost in ZNet may be a little worse than O(logN), where N is the number of nodes. In the worst case, the cost could be O(l*logN), where l is the deepest z-level in the space.

Range Query Resolving. In ZNet, range queries are resolved in a recursive way. The Algorithm is shown in Figure 5, including two parts(A and B).

For d-dimensional space, a range query QR will be like $([l_0, h_0], ..., [l_{d-1}, h_{d-1}])$. When a node receives such a query, it will first decide the routing z-level (l), whose space covers the query range (line 1 in A). For a node, besides its own space (it is responsible for), it also has knowledge about the spaces which cover its space. For example, figure 4

Fig. 4. Level Spaces

shows the network status for a 2-d space after 5 nodes joining. In the figure, nodes A, B are at z-level 2 (zones covered by them are at z-level 2). So are for nodes C, D. However, nodes A, B and nodes C, D have different knowledge about spaces. For node A, its own space, level 2 space, level 1 space are shown respectively in (a)'s, (b)'s, (c)'s shaded area. Node B's level 1 space and level 2 space are same as node A's.

Based on the z-level l, a node can compute the smallest and largest z-address of QR: the smallest z-address of QR (zL) is the z-address of point$(l_1, ..., l_d)$, and the largest z-address of QR (zH) is the z-address of point $(h_1, ..., h_d)$. (line 2-3 in A).

Then the query is routed at l, checking nodes whether their l level space overlaps with QR. If a node whose l level scope space does not overlap with QR, it needs to find a neighbor from its routing table which is closer than itself to the lowest z-address (line 1-3 in B); else the node checks whether it is at z-level l, if it is at l (this means that the node's own space overlaps with QR), it will send a message to the query initiator (line 5-6 in B); if it is not at l, the query will go down one lower z-level and repeat the whole process (line 8-10 in B).

Two methods are employed about how a query is routed at a certain z-level when a node's level space overlaps with the range. One is *one-way*, that is, the query is always routed from the smallest z-address to the largest z-address. For this method, unnecessary visits may be incurred. Another method is *two-way*, the query is partitioned into two parts which will be routed at a z-level along opposite directions to avoid unnecessary visits: in one direction, the query is always forwarded to nodes which contain larger z-addresses than the current node's at the z-level; in the other direction, the query is always forwarded to nodes which contain smaller z-addresses than the current node's at the z-level. Figure 5 only shows two-way method (line 11-18 in B).

3.3   Node Join and Leave

When a new node joins the network, it needs to find an existing node X in the network to get some space it is responsible for (How X is decided is described in next subsection). After X splits its space, the new node will build its routing table by selecting neighbors in the network, according to its membership vector which is generated randomly (maybe same as another node's membership vector). The join cost of a node is at $O(logN)$.

For example, in Figure 3, suppose node J joins the network and node B is chosen to split the space. J will first insert itself in skip-level 0 (in the skip graph). Suppose z-addresses covered by B are smaller than ones covered by J, J will choose B and C as its skip-level 0 neighbors. Neighbors at upper skip-levels are decided by J's membership vector. Suppose J's initial generated membership vector is 110 (which is the same as

Part A: N.RangeSearch(QR)

1. l=DecideRouteZLevel(QR);
   // decide the lowest and highest z-address of QR
2. zL = LowestZAddress (QR, l)
3. zH = HighestZAddress (QR, l)
4. RangeSearch1(QR, zL, zH, l)

Part B: N.RangeSearch1(QR,zL,zH,l)
   // QR is the query range;
   // zL and zH are the lowest and highest
   // z-addresses of QR at l;

1. If N at z-level scope space doesn't overlap $zL - zH$
2. M = FindCloserNode(zL)
3. M.RangeSearch1(QR, zL, zH, l)
4. else
5.   If N is at l
6.   send message to query initiator
7.   else
8. l=l+1;
9.   QR = QR $\cap$ N' l level space
10. N.RangeSearch(QR)
       // route at two-way;
11.   If $zL - zH$ contains the largest z-address covered by N at l
12.   reset zL
13. M = FindCloserNode(zL)
14. M.RangeSearch1(QR, zL, zH, l)
15.   If $zL - zH$ contains the smallest z-address covered by N at l
16.   reset zH
17. M = FindCloserNode(zH)
18. M.RangeSearch1(QR, zL, zH, l)

Fig. 5. Range Search in ZNet

D's), it will choose B as its neighbor at skip-level 1, D as its neighbor at both skip-level 2 and 1. At this time, a new skip-level (3) will be generated, D is its only neighbor at skip-level 3.

ZNet can route correctly as long as the bottom skip-level neighbors of each node are maintained, since all other neighbors contribute only to routing efficiency, not routing correctness. Thus, each node in ZNet maintains redundant neighbors (in the right neighbor-list and the left neighbor-list) which include the closest (right and left) neighbors along the bottom skip-level list to deal with node failure or departure. A background stabilization process runs periodically at each node to fix neighbors at upper skip-levels.

3.4   Load Balancing

In ZNet, we only consider load balancing from storage perspective, since routing load balance is achieved due to the symmetric nature of skip graphs.

If two nodes contain nearly the same number of indices, then loads on these two nodes will be nearly the same. We try to balance data distribution among nodes by choosing appropriate nodes and splitting their space when new nodes join the network. Currently, two strategies are employed in ZNet: In the first strategy, when a node joins the network, it randomly chooses one data object *which has already published to the network*, and uses the point which corresponds to the data object as the join destination. And then the join request is routed to the node whose space covers the point. In the second strategy, m such candidates are used, the one whose corresponding destination node has the heaviest load is chosen as the joining destination. The second strategy could achieve better load balancing than the first one, however, the join cost is m times higher.

With large number of nodes, nodes should be distributed in a way which is approximately proportional to the data distribution. A large number of nodes will be clustered in the space which is densely populated. Also, another benefit from this kind of joining is that the publishing cost of a new joining node could be saved (suppose that most data objects in a node are similar, they will be published into nearby nodes).

One problem with above load balancing is that it only considers static data distribution. Thus, when there is data evolution, the load will not be balanced anymore. As future work, we plan to use the following method to address this problem: a node first gets load information about other nodes either by enquiring its neighbors or by random walks on the overlay network, then the node which is less loaded (under a certain threshold) will leave the network and rejoin to the node which is more loaded (above a certain threshold).

4   Experimental Results

In this section, we evaluate our system via simulation. We first measure how index distribution are balanced in the network, followed by the test of average lookup cost of routing in ZNet; Then we focus on range queries.

The set of experiments are done on synthetic datasets of increasing dimensionality, which are generated based on normal distribution. By default, we use data sets with skewed 8-dimensional 300,000 data points, and 6,000 nodes in the network. The dimensionality of data in the experiments is varied from 4 to 20, and the number of nodes is varied from 2,000 to 10,000.

4.1   Load Balancing

We measure load balancing mainly in data distribution among the nodes in network. Two approaches are employed to balance the load: one is LB-1, the other is LB-x. In LB-1, when a node joins, a random point of a data object (published by the node) is chosen as a representative for the node to decide the join destination; In LB-m ($m > 1$), m such candidates are used and tried, the one whose corresponding destination has the heaviest load is finally chosen for node joining. In the experiment, we choose m to be 5. Larger m is also tried, however, no further improvement is observed.

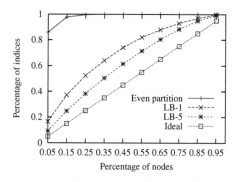

Fig. 6. Load Balance Measurement

Our approaches are compared with two cases: One is an ideal case, where each node contains the same amount of data; The other is an extreme case, where the data space is partitioned and assigned to nodes *evenly*.

In Figure 6, nodes are sorted in decreasing order according to the number of data contained by them. From the figure, we can see that, when space is assigned to nodes evenly, 80% of indies are inserted in 5% of nodes, the data distribution among nodes is severely unbalanced. Both LB-5 and LB-1 achieve good load balancing, with LB-5 close to the ideal case. LB-5 is better than LB-1, since it makes the decision according to the current load distribution in the network. This figure shows that our approaches, esp., LB-5, follow the data distribution well. All following experiments are done with LB-5 assumed.

4.2   Average Lookup Cost

In this set experiment, we measure average lookup cost for point queries in ZNet.

The lookup cost is measured by the number of hops between two random selected nodes, averaged over 10 times the network size. Figure 7 shows the effect of network size on lookup cost. As shown in the figure, the average lookup cost increases with the network size (which is a little more than $0.5 * logN$).

4.3   Range Search Cost

We focus on two metrics for measuring range searches:

- Processing Cost: The number of nodes whose spaces overlap the query range. These nodes are needed to search their virtual databases for query results;
- Routing Cost: The number of nodes for routing the query *only*. These nodes are visited for routing the query to nodes whose spaces overlap the query range;

Three factors are involved for range searches: network size, the dimensionality, and the query range size. Thus, to measure the cost for range queries, we vary these three factors respectively at each time. All range queries are generated according to the data

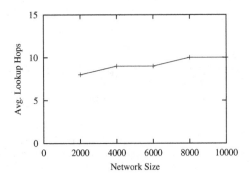

Fig. 7. Average Lookup Cost for point queries

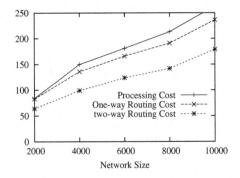

Fig. 8. The Effect Of Network Size On Range Queries

distribution: queries are clustered in dense data area, which can be initiated from any node in the network. For each measurement, results are averaged over 200 randomly generated range queries with fixed range size, each is initiated from 100 random nodes in the network.

Two methods (one-way and two-way) are compared in terms of the routing cost with the network size varied (same trends are observed with dimensionality and query range size varied).

Effect of Network Size. To measure the effect of network size over the cost, we fix query range size at each dimension to be 0.2. Data set is the same for all network sizes.

As shown in Figure 8, the processing cost increases with the network size, since more nodes are clustered in the dense data area according to our space partitioning method. For the routing cost, the routing costs of both one-way and two-way increase with the network size also, however, two-way method visits less nodes than one-way method.

High processing and routing costs in Figure 8 are mainly due to the relatively high dimensionality (8) we used in the experiments. With higher dimensionality, the clustering

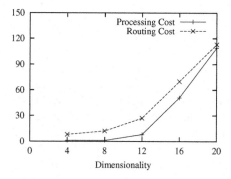

Fig. 9. The Effect Of Dimensionality On Range Queries

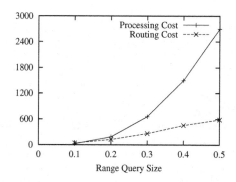

Fig. 10. The Effect Of Query Range Size On Range Queries

of z-ordering becomes worse. When the dimensionality is low, the cost is much lower. The effect of dimensionality on cost is tested next.

Effect of Dimensionality. The effect of dimensionality is measured by fixing query selectivity. Because of small selectivity we choose, range queries are covered by only one node when dimensionality is 4 and 8 (in Figure 9). However, even with a small query selectivity, we can see from the figure that the number of processing nodes increases quickly when dimensionality increases. This is because the range size of a query with the same selectivity increases rapidly with higher dimensionality. Consequently, much bigger data space has to be searched, more nodes have to be visited for routing.

Effect of Range Size. Finally, we test the effect of range size on costs. The query range size at each dimension is varied from 0.1 to 0.5. As shown in Figure 10, range size has much effect on the number of processing nodes and routing cost. With larger query range size, more nodes in ZNet need to be visited for processing or routing, since more nodes are clustered in dense data area and our queries are also clustered in the dense area.

5   Conclusion

In this paper, we described the design of ZNet, a distributed system for efficiently supporting multi-dimensional range searches. ZNet directly operates on the native data space, which are partitioned dynamically and assigned to nodes in the network. By choosing appropriate subspaces to be split further, load imbalance could be reduced. By ordering subspaces in Z-curves of different granularity levels, we could extend skip graph to support efficient routing and range searches. Results from a simulation study show that ZNet is efficient in supporting range searches, esp. when dimensionality is not very high. In future work, we plan to address the load balancing problem when the data distribution is dynamic, and the efficiency problem when the dimensionality is high.

Acknowledgements. The authors would like to thank Beng Chin Ooi and Yingguang Li for their helpful discussion.

References

1. A. Andrzejak, Z. Xu:Scalable, Efficient Range Queries for Grid Information Services. Proceedings fo the Second IEEE International Conference on Peer-to-Peer Computing(P2P2002)
2. J. Aspnes, G. Shah:Skip graphs. Proceedings of the 14th Annual ACM-SIAM Symposium on Discrete Algorithms (SODA 2003)
3. B.Awerbuch, C.Scheideler:Peer-to-Peer systems for Prefix Search. Proceedings of the Symposium on Principles of Distributed Computing(2003)
4. M. Cai, M. Frank, J. Chen, P.Szekely: MAAN: A Multi-Attribute Addressable Network for Grid Information Services. 4th International Workshop on Grid Computing (Grid2003)
5. V. Gaede, O. Günther: Multidimensional access methods. ACM Computing Surveys, Volume 30,Issue 2 (1998)
6. Gnutella Development Home Page: http://gnutella.wego.com/.
7. N. J. A. Harvey, M. B. Jones, S. Saroiu, M. Theimer, A. Wolman: SkipNet: A Scalable Overlay Network with Practical Locality Properties. Fourth USENIX Symposium on Internet Technologies and Systems (USITS 2003)
8. X. Li, Y. J. Kim, R. Govindan, W. Hong: Multi-dimensional range queries in sensor networks. Proceedings of the first international conference on Embedded networked sensor systems(2003)
9. S. Ratnasamy, P. Francis, M. Handley, R. Karp, S. Shenker: A scalable content-addressable network. Proceedings of the ACM Special Interest Group on Data Communication(SIGCOMM 2001).
10. A. Rowstron, P. Druschel: Pastry: Scalable, distributed object location and routing for large-scale peer-to-peer systems. IFIP/ACM International Conference on Distributed Systems Platforms (Middleware 2001)
11. O. D. Sahin, A. Gupta, D. Agrawal, A.El Abbadi:A Peer-to-peer Framework for Caching Range Queries. Proceedings of the 18th International Conference on Data Engineering (ICDE 2004)
12. C. Schmidt, M. Parashar: Flexible Information Discovery in Decentralized Distriubted Systems. 12th IEEE International Symposium on High Performance Distributed Computing (HPDC 2003)
13. I. Stoica, R. Morris, D. Karger, F. Kaashoek, H. Balakrishnan: Chord: A scalable peer-to-peer lookup service for internet applications. Proceedings of the ACM Special Interest Group on Data Communication(SIGCOMM 2001)

14. C. Tang, Z. Xu, S. Dwarkadas: Peer-to-Peer Information Retrieval Using Self-Organizing Semantic Overlay Networks. Proceedings of the ACM Special Interest Group on Data Communication(SIGCOMM 2003)
15. B. Y. Zhao, J. D. Kubiatowicz, A. D. Joseph: Tapestry: An Infrastructure for Fault-tolerant Wide-area Location and Routing. UC Berkeley Technical Report,UCB/CSD-01-1141 (2001)

On Constructing Internet-Scale P2P Information Retrieval Systems

D. Zeinalipour-Yazti, V. Kalogeraki, and D. Gunopulos

Department of Computer Science & Engineering,
University of California - Riverside,
Riverside CA 92521, USA
{csyiazti, vana, dg}@cs.ucr.edu

Abstract. We initiate a study on the effect of the network topology on the performance of Peer-to-Peer (P2P) information retrieval systems. The emerging P2P model has become a very powerful and attractive paradigm for developing Internet-scale systems for sharing resources, including files, or documents. We show that the performance of Information Retrieval algorithms can be significantly improved through the use of fully distributed topologically aware overlay network construction techniques. Our empirical results, using the Peerware middleware infrastructure, show that the approach we propose is both efficient and practical.

1 Introduction

In the last few years, the new emerging Peer-to-Peer (P2P) model has become a very powerful and attractive paradigm for developing Internet-scale file systems [20, 13, 22, 23, 25] and sharing resources (i.e., CPU cycles, memory, storage space, network bandwidth) [24, 10] over large scale geographical areas. This is achieved by constructing an overlay network of many nodes (peers) built on top of heterogeneous operating systems and networks. Overlays are flexible and deployable approaches that allow users to perform distributed operations such as information retrieval [9, 32] without modifying the underlying physical network.

The first wave of P2P systems implement *unstructured* P2P overlays [13] in which no global structure or knowledge is maintained. To search for data or resources, messages are sent over multiple hops from one peer to another with each peer responding to queries for information it has stored locally. *Structured* P2P overlays [22, 23, 25] implement a distributed hash table data structure in which every data item can be located within a small number of hops, at the expense of keeping some state information locally at the nodes. Recently more efficient query routing techniques based on routing indices [8], heuristics [30] and caching [32] were proposed.

However, an important problem that these systems have not fully considered is how the heterogeneity of the underlying infrastructure affects the performance of the information retrieval algorithms/systems. The P2P infrastructure can en-

W.S. Ng et al. (Eds.): DBISP2P 2004, LNCS 3367, pp. 136–150, 2005.

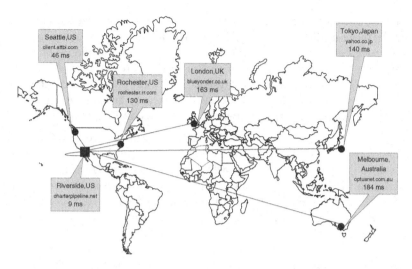

Fig. 1. Typical end-to-end delays from Riverside to sites around the world

compass resources with different processing and communication capabilities, located across different geographical areas. As a result, retrieving information over Internet-scale environments is subject to greater variations due to unpredictable communication latencies, excessive resource consumption and changing resource availability. Figure 1 shows typical end-to-end delays from Riverside to different sites around the world.

P2P systems are very effective mechanisms to share and store documents, because their decentralized nature allows easy additions, updates, large storage, and offers fault-tolerant properties through the use of replication and caching. However, a system for storing large amounts of data should also provide efficient search mechanisms, and the decentralized nature of the unstructured P2P networks hinders the use or the maintenance of the indexing structures traditionally used in Information Retrieval. So the effective use of P2P systems for document storage depends on new efficient and distributed solutions to the problem of finding the documents one is looking for.

In the paper we focus on *keyword search*, that is, we aim to find the documents that contain a given set of query terms. There is a lot of recent work on improving keyword search in unstructured P2P networks (section 2 provides an overview). A common theme in this work is the use of the number of messages as a metric of the performance of the technique. While this is justified when the algorithm is network-agnostic and does not use the characteristics of the network to improve the search, we believe that taking advantage of this knowledge can significantly improve the performance of Information Retrieval and allow us to design techniques that make the problem practical in Internet-scale systems.

Our Contribution: In this paper we initiate a study on the design of fully distributed P2P information retrieval techniques that are topologically aware and can take advantage of the network characteristics to optimize the efficiency of the search. We consider and evaluate the impact of the use of topologically aware overlay network constructions on the accuracy and the performance of currently proposed fully distributed P2P information retrieval techniques. Although the necessity of topologically-aware overlays has been widely addressed in the context of structured overlays [4, 21, 29, 33], it hasn't received the same attention in the context of unstructured overlay networks. More specifically:

(i) We discuss and evaluate the performance of information retrieval algorithms over topologically-aware Internet-scale overlays. We consider both *agnostic* techniques that do not maintain any knowledge of the data distribution in the network (BFS and RBFS), as well as techniques that collect past statistics (>RES, ISM). We describe the Random and BinSL overlay construction techniques and describe the advantages and disadvantages of the BinSL technique for the P2P Information Retrieval problem.

(ii) We study the impact of the overlay construction techniques on the information retrieval algorithms using our *Peerware* infrastructure. Our objective is to improve the latency, while maintaining the accuracy of the results. We note here that our results show that the use of topologically-aware overlays minimizes network delays while maintaining high recall rates and a low number of messages.

The remainder of the paper is organized as follows: In section 2 we outline search techniques that have been proposed for efficient information retrieval in unstructured P2P networks. In section 3 we describe the Random and BinSL overlay construction techniques and describe their advantages and disadvantages. Section 4 describes our experimental methodology and our middleware infrastructure. In section 5 we present our experimental evaluation and section 6 concludes the paper.

2   Search Techniques for Unstructured P2P Networks

In this section we provide a brief overview of techniques and algorithms that can be used to perform content-based searches in P2P system. The techniques do not use any global knowledge, thus they are completely decentralized and scale well with the size of the network. We consider a network of n nodes (peers). We assume that D_u is the set of documents that are stored in peer u. We assume that each document d is characterized by a sequence of keywords, and let $s(d)$ be the (unordered) set of keywords in d. Given a query q, itself a set of keywords, the result of the query should be the *answer set* $\{(d, u) | u$ is a peer and $q \subset s(d)$ and $d \in D_u\}$, that is, the documents in the network that include the keywords in q.

Agnostic Techniques: Breadth First Search (BFS) and Random BFS (RBFS): BFS is a technique widely used in P2P file sharing applications, such as Gnutella [13]. BFS sacrifices performance and network utilization for the sake of simplicity. It works as follows : A node v generates a `Query` message q when it wants to search for contents located on other peers. v propagates q to all its neighbor peers. When a peer u receives a `Query` request, it first propagates q further by again along its neighbors (except the sender), and then searches its local repository for relevant matches. If some node w has a match, w generates a `QueryHit` message to transmit the result. `QueryHit` messages are sent along the same path that carried the incoming `Query` messages. The disadvantage of BFS is that a query is consuming excessive network and processing resources because a query is propagated along all links. In order to avoid flooding the network with queries, as the network might be arbitrary large, each query is associated with a time-to-live (TTL) field which determines the maximum number of hops that a given query should be forwarded.

In [16] we propose and evaluate the *Random Breadth-First-Search (BFS)* technique (see figure 2a). RBFS improves over the naive BFS approach by allowing each node to forward the search request to only a fraction of its peers. This fraction can be selected at random and is a parameter to the mechanism (in our experiments we used a fraction of 0.5, so that a peer propagates the request to half its peers, selected at random). This technique uses fewer messages than BFS, however it may miss large segments of the network since it is random and may not choose a particular link that could propagate the query to such segments.

The Most Results in the Past Heuristic (>RES): In [30], Yang et al., present a technique where each node forwards a query to some of its peers based on some aggregated statistics. The authors compare a number of query routing heuristics and mention that the *Most Results in Past (>RES)* heuristic has the best satisfaction performance. A query is defined to be *satisfied* if Z, for some constant Z, or more results are returned. In >RES a peer u forwards a search message to the k peers which returned the most results for the last 10 queries.

The technique is similar to the Intelligent Search Mechanism we describe below, but uses simpler information about the peers, and is optimized to find Z documents efficiently (for a fixed Z) rather than finding as many documents as possible. The nature of >RES allows it to explore the larger network segments (which usually also contain the most results) and the most stable neighbors (the peers that have routed back many queryhits), but it doesn't manage to explore the nodes which contain content related to the query. We therefore characterize >RES a *quantitative* rather than *qualitative* approach.

The Intelligent Search Mechanism (ISM): In [16] we propose the Intelligent Search Mechanism (ISM) which is a fast and efficient mechanism for information retrieval in unstructured P2P networks (figure 2b).

Keys to improving the speed and efficiency of the information retrieval mechanism is to minimize the communication costs, that is, the number of messages sent between the peers, and to minimize the number of peers that are queried for each search request. To achieve this, a peer estimates for each query, which of its peers are more likely to reply to this query, and propagates the query message to those peers only.

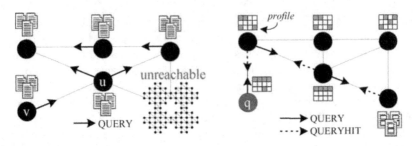

Fig. 2. Searching in a peer-to-peer network using **Random Breadth First Search (RBFS)** and the **Intelligent Search Mechanism (ISM)**

The Intelligent Search mechanism consists of two components that run locally in each peer:

The *Profile Mechanism* is used to maintain the T most recent queries and the corresponding queryhits along with the number of results. Once the repository is full, the node uses the Least Recently Used (LRU) replacement policy to keep the most recent queries.

The *RelevanceRank (RR)* function is used by a node P_l to perform an online ranking of its neighbors in order to determine to which ones to forward a query q. To compute the ranking of each peer P_i, P_l compares q to all queries in the profiling structure, for which there is a queryhit, and calculates $RR_{P_l}(P_i, q)$ as follows:
$$RR_{P_l}(P_i, q) = \sum_{j = "\text{Queries answered by } P_i"} Qsim(q_j, q)^\alpha * S(P_i, q_j)$$
The deployed distance metric $Qsim$ is the cosine similarity[1] and $S(P_i, q_j)$ is the number of results returned by P_i for query q_j. RR allows us to rank higher the peers that returned more results. α allows us to add more weight to the most similar queries. For example, when α is large then the query with the largest similarity $Qsim(q_j, q)$ dominates the formula. If we set $\alpha = 1$ all queries are equally counted, while setting $\alpha = 0$ allows us to count only the number of results returned by each peer (essentially, the >RES heuristic). In the experiments we forward the query to the half best neighbors, plus to a random neighbor to brake out of potential cycles.

ISM works well in environments which exhibit strong degrees of query locality and where peers hold some specialized knowledge. Our study on the Gnutella network shows that it exhibits a strong degree of query locality [31].

Other Distributed Techniques and Algorithms: In the following we describe other proposed distributed techniques; there is a lot of work on centralized systems however this is not directly relevant to our problem. In [8], Crespo et al., present a hybrid technique where each peer builds indices using aggregate information on the contents of the documents of its peers. In the *PlanetP* [9] system, participating nodes build a global inverted index which is partially constructed by each node. The framework is based on bloom filters, which capture the index of some node, and which are randomly gossiped across the community. In a different approach, the pSearch [26] system explores semantic spaces by using advanced techniques from the Information Retrieval field. It uses the Vector Space Model (VSM) and Latent Semantic Indexing (LSI) to generate a semantic space which is then distributed on top of a CAN [22] structured P2P overlay.

In the Random Walker model, which is presented in [19], each node forwards a query message by selecting a random neighbor and the query message is called a *walker*. This model however doesn't use any explicit technique to guide the query to the most relevant content. In *APS* [27] each node deploys a local index, which captures the relative probability of each neighbor to be chosen as the next hop for some future request. The main difference with Random Walkers is that in APS a node utilizes feedback from previous searches to probabilistically guide future walkers.

Distributed file indexing systems such as CAN[22] and Chord[25] allow peers to perform efficient searches using object identifiers rather than keywords. These systems, usually referred as *Structured Overlays* or *Distributed Hash Tables (DHT)*, use a specific structure with some hashing scheme that allows peers to perform object lookup operations getting in return the address of the node storing the object. A disadvantage of DHTs is that they consider only the problem of searching for keys, and thus cannot perform content-based retrieval. Recent work in [12] shows that content-based query resolution is feasible in DHT systems if these are using *Rendezvous Points (RP)*. More specifically the framework proposes the registration of the content (i.e. attribute-value pairs that describe the content) at *RP*s. Queries might then be routed, using Chord, to a predefined set of *RP*s which consequently resolve the query. Finally Freenet [7], is another distributed information storage and retrieval system that uses instead an intelligent *Depth-First-Search (DFS)* mechanism to locate the object keys in the system. The advantage of DFS search is that a small set of peers can be queried quickly and efficiently; however by its nature it can take a long time if we want to find all the results to a query.

3   Overlay Topologies for Efficient Network Utilization

In this section we discuss two distributed overlay construction techniques that can be deployed in the context of unstructured overlay networks. Let $G = (V, E)$ be an overlay topology, with a vertex set $V = \{1, 2, ..., n\}$ and an edge set E, which represents the overlay connections between the vertices in V. Assume that a user, is connected to some vertex v and that it uses one of the search techniques outlined in the previous section in order to search for content in G. Then his query is expected to form a spanning tree T which spans over the subgraph G' ($G' \subset G$). The main goal of an overlay construction technique is to minimize the **Aggregate Delay** (Δ_T) which is the sum of the delays w associated with each edge in the tree T, more formally defined as following: $\Delta_T = \sum_{\forall \epsilon \in T} w(\epsilon)$.

It is important to notice that the delay cost associated with each edge might be different for each direction between two nodes v_i and v_j (i.e. $delay(v_i \rightarrow v_j)$ $\neq delay(v_j \rightarrow v_i)$). This happens because packets on the Internet may follow different itineraries or because the upstream and downstream bandwidth of a node

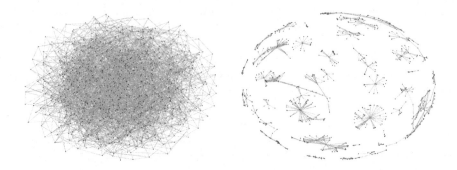

Fig. 3. Visualization of a Connected (Random) and Disconnected (SS) graph of 1000 peers (degree=6) using the Fruchterman-Reignold visualization model in Pajek [2]. Random and BinSL topologies have the advantage that they remain connected while *SS* topologies get disconnected because each node greedily selects other close-by nodes

might greatly vary (e.g. Cable/ADSL Modem Users). Another interesting point is that the construction of an optimal overlay is known to be NP-complete [11] therefore the following popular algorithms are based on heuristics.

Random Topology: In this algorithm, each vertex v_i selects its d neighbors by randomly choosing d other vertices. This is the algorithm deployed in most current P2P networks such as [13, 17] and its main advantages are that it is simple, does not require any knowledge on the distances, and leads to connected topologies if the degree $d > log_2 n$ [3].

BinSL Topology: In [21], Ratnasamy et al. propose the Short-Long (SL) overlay construction technique. SL alleviates the network unawareness of the Random Topology in the following way: Each vertex v_i, selects its d neighbors by picking the $d/2$ nodes in the system that have the shortest latency to itself (these connections are called *short links*) and then selects another $d/2$ vertices at random (these connections are called *long links*). Therefore *SL* requires the nxn IP-latency matrix in order to find the latencies between the various node pairs. The intuition behind this algorithm is that the $d/2$ connections to "close-by" nodes will result in well-connected clusters of nearby nodes, while the random links serve to keep the different clusters interconnected and the overall graph connected. It is important to mention that by only selecting the shortest latency nodes will in most cases result in disconnected graph topologies. This can be observed in the visualization of figure 3 where we visualize a random and a short (*SS*) topology of 1000 peers.

Although the *SL* construction technique works well in practice, it is limited by the fact that some node in the system needs to know the "physical" distances between all node pairs (i.e. an nxn IP-latency adjacency matrix). In practice such centralized architectures don't scale well, are expensive and are vulnerable to denial of service attacks. In order to overcome the global knowledge requirement of the SL algorithm, Ratnasamy et al. propose the *BinSL* topology construction technique [21], which is a distributed adaptation of the SL algorithm. Since the adjacency-matrix of IP latencies is not available in a distributed setting, *BinSL* deploys the notion of *distributed binning* in order to approximate these latencies. More specifically each node calculates the round-trip-time (RTT) from itself and k well-known *landmarks* $\{l_1 l_2 .. l_k\}$ on the Internet. The numeric ordering of the latencies represents the "bin" the node belongs to. Latencies are then further classified into *level* ranges. For instance if the latencies are divided into 3 levels then; *level 0* accounts for latencies in the range [0,100), *level 1* for the range [100,200) and *level 2* for all other latencies. The level vector is then augmented to the landmark ordering of a node yielding a string of the type "$l_2 l_3 l_1 : 012$". It is expected that nodes belonging to the same bin will be topologically close to each other although *false positives* are possible, that is, some nodes do belong to the same "bin" although they are not topologically close to each other. We will investigate the accuracy of the binning scheme in the experimental section.

Other Topologically-Aware Construction Techniques: Recently an approach to create resilient unstructured overlays with small diameters was proposed in [28]. In the proposed algorithm a node selects from a set of k nodes, r nodes at random ($r \subset k$) and then finds from the rest $f = k-r$ nodes the ones that have the largest degree. This algorithm results in networks with power-law distributions of node degrees differentiating from Random and BinSL in which we have a uniform distribution.

Topologically-aware overlays have also been addressed in the context of *Structured* P2P overlays in [4, 21, 29, 33]. These systems however rely on some hashing scheme which allows nodes to quickly send messages to some destination node. Although structured overlays are of particular importance in applications such as decentralized web caches [15], they are not appropriate for content-based retrieval systems [9, 32] and large-scale systems with transient user populations [5].

Application-layer multicast systems such as Narada [6] initially construct a richer connected graph (mesh) and then use some optimization algorithm to generate a mesh that has certain performance properties. As part of the mesh quality improvement algorithm, Narada nodes randomly probe each other and calculate the perceived gain in utility. BinSL is simpler and cheaper in terms of messages. It is furthermore designated for larger groups of members, which might leave and join in an ad-hoc manner.

4   Experimental Evaluation Methodology

Our experimental evaluation focuses on three parameters: (i) the **aggregate tree delay** (Δ_T) which is a metric of network efficiency for a given query that spans in the sub-graph G', (ii) the **recall rate**, that is, the fraction of documents each of the search mechanisms retrieves, and (iii) the **overhead** of the techniques, that is, the number of messages that are consumed in order to find the results. As the baseline of comparison we used the results retrieved by query-

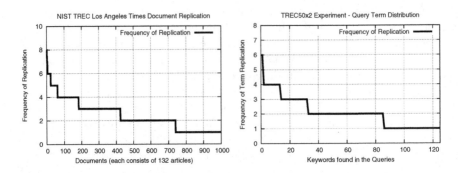

Fig. 4. a) Data Replication scheme for the TREC-LATimes dataset, **b) Query Term Frequency** distributions for the TREC50x2 queryset

ing the collection in a centralized setting (i.e. as a corpus of documents) which therefore returns all relevant documents. We chose to implement the algorithms that require only local knowledge (i.e. BFS, RBFS, >RES and ISM) over Random and BinSL topologies of the same size and degree.

The TREC Dataset: We use two series of experiments which are based on the *TREC-LATimes* dataset which is a document collection that consists of randomly selected articles that appeared on the LA Times newswire from 1989 to 1990. The size of this dataset is 470MB and it contains approximately 132,000 articles. These articles were horizontally partitioned into 1000 xml documents each of which was subsequently indexed using the Lucene [18] IR API. These indexes, which are disk-based, allow the efficient querying of text-based sources using many IR features. We then generate Random and BinSL topologies of 1000 peers in which each peer shares one or more of the 1000 documents (see figure 4a). We use this scheme in order to provide some degree of article replication. We don't use the *"qrels"* relevance judgments, since the compared algorithms don't attempt to address the issue of precise document retrieval. We will refer to these peers as the *TREC-LATimes Peerware*.

For the evaluation of the TREC-LATimes corpus we will use, as indicated by NIST, the TREC "topics" 300-450. One problem with the provided 150 queries is that the query term frequency is very low and most terms are presented only once. This is not a realistic assumption since studies on real P2P networks (e.g. [31]) indicate that there is a high locality of query terms. Therefore we used the 150 queries to derive the **TREC50x2** dataset, which consists of a set $a =$ "50 randomly sampled queries out of the initial 150 topics". We then generated a list b of another 50 queries which are randomly sampled out of a. *TREC50x2* is then the queries in a and b randomly shuffled and the distribution of query terms can be viewed in figure 4b.

Simulating Network Distances: Evaluating distances in network topologies requires a dataset in which the IP latencies are not synthetic. We didn't chose to use a real dataset of ≈300,000 IPs found in the Gnutella network [31], as obtaining the distances among the different hosts was practically not feasible. We therefore chose to base our experiments on the measurements of the *Active Measurement Project (AMP)* [14], at the *National Laboratory for Applied Network (NLAR)*. AMP deploys a number of monitors distributed along 130 sites to actively monitor the Internet topology. AMP monitors ping and traceroute each other at regular intervals and report the results back to the project servers. Most of the current 130 monitors currently reside in the U.S with a few exceptions of some other International sites.

In our experiments we use an AMP 1.8 GB snapshot of traces obtained on the 30th of January 2003. The set includes data from 117 monitors out of which we extracted the 89 monitors which could be reversed DNS (i.e. given their IP we obtained a DNS name). We then construct the nxn IP-latency matrix (for all n=89 physical nodes), that contains the latency among all monitors. Since all 89 hosts are located at different domains, we chose to incorporate some degree of host replication per domain. Our study in [31] shows that hosts in a real overlay network, such as Gnutella, exhibit this characteristic. More specifically we randomly replicate each host $[1..k]$ times. In our experiments we set $k = 24$ which generated distances for all 1000 nodes in the TREC-LATimes Peerware.

Peerware Simulation Infrastructure: In order to benchmark the efficiency of the information retrieval algorithms, we have implemented *Peerware*[1], a distributed middleware infrastructure which allows us to benchmark different query routing algorithms over large-scale P2P systems. We use Peerware to build a decentralized newspaper network which is organized as a network of 1000 nodes. Our experiments are performed on a network of 75 workstations (each hosting a number of nodes), each of which has an AMD Athlon 800MHz-1.4GHz processor with memories varying from 256MB-1GB RAM running Mandrake Linux 8.0 (kernel 2.4.3-20) all interconnected with a 10/100 LAN. Peerware is written entirely in Java and comes along with an extensive set of UNIX shell scripts that allow the easy deployment and administration of the system.

Peerware consists of three components: (i) *graphGen* which pre-compiles network topologies and configuration files for the various nodes participating in a given experiment, (ii) *dataPeer* which is a P2P client that is able to answer to boolean queries from its local xml repository using the Lucene IR Engine [18], and (iii) *searchPeer* which is a P2P client that performs queries and harvests answers back from a Peerware network. Launching a Peerware of 1000 nodes can be done in approximately 10-20 seconds while querying the same network can be performed in around 250ms-1500ms.

The Discarded Message Problem: We define the *DMP* problem in the following way: Node P_k receives some query q with TTL_1 at time t_1. P_k first checks if it has forwarded the same query (identified by GUID) in the past. If yes, it will immediately discard the message in order to avoid forwarding the

---

[1] Details about the Peerware infrastructure can be found in [32].

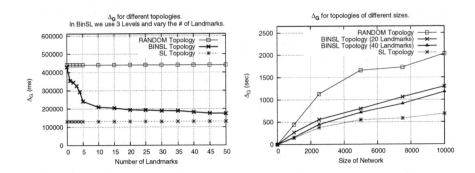

Fig. 5. a) The rate of *false positives* of the Binning scheme is a function of how many landmarks are used. b) Scalability of the Binning Scheme

message several times. If not, it will decrease $TTL_1=TTL_1$-1 and forward q to some of P_k's peers. Now what happens if node P_k receives the same query q with some TTL_2, where $TTL_2 > TTL_1$ at some time t_2, where $t_2 > t_1$? Most of the commercial P2P clients will discard q. The result is that a query reaches fewer nodes than expected. We fix the problem by allowing the TTL_2 message to proceed. Of course there is some redundancy which will add up in the "number of messages" graph (approximately 30% in the experiments).

5 Experiments

In this section we describe a series of experiments that attempt to investigate the effect of the Random and BinSL overlay topology structure on the recall rate and the messaging of the various information retrieval search techniques that were described in section 2. We are particularly interested in investigate if the BinSL topology can indeed minimize the aggregate network delay without sacrificing the recall rate.

Efficiency of Landmarks in BinSL: The first experiment, we attempt to find the right number of landmarks, as this plays an important role on how small the Δ_T becomes in a fixed size network. By using more landmarks, the number of *false positives* also decreases as we have fewer collisions in the landmark ordering codes of hosts that are not topologically close to each other. In figure 5a, we calculate the sum of the delays w associated with all edges in the respective graphs G (1000 peers each with an average degree of 6). This sum is more formally defined as $\Delta_G = \sum_{\forall e \in G} w(e)$ and we use this metric, instead of the Aggregate Delay Δ_T, as it is independent of the deployed search technique. In BinSL, we first randomly sample out of the original network the set of landmarks.[2] The

---

[2] In a real setting, peers would have a predefined list of well chosen landmarks (i.e. globally spread HTTP or DNS servers).

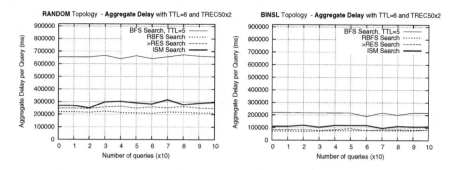

Fig. 6. Aggregate Delay for the evaluation of the TREC50x2 queryset using the Random (left) and BinSL (right) topology

figure indicates that by using no landmarks, the BinSL topology is essentially a Random topology. This happens because a node selects all its connections at random which makes Δ_G of the Random and BinSL topologies identical. By adding a few landmarks (i.e. 1-10), Δ_G decreases substantially, after which point Δ_G decreases at a lower rate. Therefore by selecting an arbitrary large number of landmarks may not be very efficient as each landmark probing comes with an additional network cost and because the Δ_G parameter of the network graph may not significantly drop.

Although figure 5a shows that by using 20 landmarks might be satisfactory for a network of 1000 nodes, in practice the network size might not be known a priori. In figure 5b, we plot the Δ_G parameter for networks of different sizes. The figure indicates that the Random Topology does not scale very well with respect to the Δ_G parameter. By using BinSL and 20 landmarks on the other hand, the Δ_G parameter decreases by 46% from what the Random topology uses, while using 40 landmarks drops Δ_G by 54%. We can see that although we doubled the number of landmarks the Δ_G parameter improved by only 8%. The picture also shows that the lower bound provided by SL is on average 66% less than what the random topology requires, but SL is not feasible in practice as it requires global knowledge. In the experiments presented in the subsequent subsections, we set the number of landmarks to 20.

Minimizing Network Delays: In our second experiment, we investigate if we can minimize the Aggregate Delay Δ_T of a query that spans in the subgraph G', while retaining high recall rates and low messaging. In the BFS case, we configure each query messages with a TTL parameter of five since this technique is consuming extraordinary amounts of messages. With this setting, query messages are able to reach 859 out of the 1000 nodes.[3] Therefore it was expected that BFS's recall rate would be less than the recall rate obtained by evaluating

---

[3] With a TTL of 6 and 7, we would be able to reach 998 and 1000 nodes at a cost of 8,500 messages/query and 10,500 messages/query respectively.

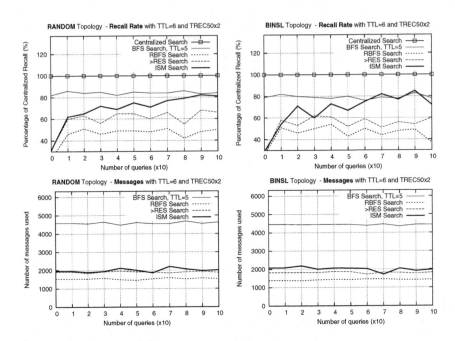

Fig. 7. a) Recall Rate (top) and **b) Messages (bottom)** for the evaluation of the TREC50x2 queryset using **Random (left)** and **BinSL (right)** topologies

the whole dataset in a centralized setting. The rest techniques (i.e. RBFS, ISM and >RES), use a TTL of 6 as they offer reduced messaging, which allows us to explore the network graph deeper while maintaining low messaging. Finally, the average time to perform a query for the BFS case is in the order of 1.5 seconds but results start streaming back to the query node within the first few milliseconds. In the first row of figure 7, we plot the Aggregate Delay Δ_T for the Random (left) and BinSL (right) topology. The two figures indicate that by using BinSL any of the presented search techniques, can reduce the Δ_T parameter by a factor of three.

Maintaining High Recall Rates and Low Messaging: So far we have seen that by using a BinSL topology we are able to reduce the Δ_T parameter. However this single parameter is not enough in the context of information retrieval applications, as these applications are required to return the most relevant documents. Furthermore, if some search technique always explored the shortest latency neighbors then the Δ_T parameter would be minimal but the query would with very high probability get locked in some region and would not explore the larger part of the network graph. This would consequently reduce the recall rate which is not desirable.

In figure 7, we plot the recall rate and the number of messages required by the different search algorithms using the Random and BinSL topologies presented in the previous subsection. The figures indicate that we can maintain the same levels of recall rate and messages while keeping the Δ_T parameter low. In the same figures we can also observe the effectiveness of each search technique. More specifically, BFS requires almost 2.5 times more messages than the other techniques. The ISM search technique on the other hand, learns from its profiling structure and guides the queries to the network segments that contain the most relevant documents. On the other hand both RBFS's and >RES's recall fluctuate, which indicates that >RES may behave as bad as RBFS if the queries don't follow some repetitive pattern.

6 Conclusions and Future Work

We considered and evaluated the impact of the use of topologically aware overlay network constructions on the accuracy and the performance of currently proposed fully distributed P2P information retrieval techniques.

Our empirical results show that the use of the topologically-aware BinSL overlay network construction technique significantly improves the latency times for all the information retrieval techniques we considered. These included both agnostic techniques (BFS, RBFS), and techniques that used past statistics (ISM, >RES), and we compared the performance of the BinSL overlay network with a random graph of the same average degree. In all cases, the accuracy remained approximately the same.

Our results clearly show the advantage of our approach. In our future work we plan to design new techniques that tightly integrate the construction of the overlay network with the actual information retrieval mechanism.

References

1. Baeza-Yates R.A. and Ribeiro-Neto B.A., "Modern Information Retrieval." ACM Press Series/Addison Wesley, New York, May 1999.
2. Batagelj V. and Mrvar A. "PAJEK - Program for large network analysis", Connections, 21:47–57, 1998.
3. Bollobás B. "Modern Graph Theory, Graduate Texts in Mathematics" vol. 184, Springer-Verlag, New York, 1998.
4. Castro M., Druschel P., Charlie Hu Y., Rowstron A. "Topology-aware routing in structured peer-to-peer overlay networks", *In IFIP/ACM Middleware'01.*
5. Chawathe Y., Ratnasamy S., Breslau L., Lanham N., Shenker S. "Making Gnutella-like P2P Systems Scalable", *In ACM SIGCOMM'03.*
6. Chu Y-H, Rao S.G., Zhang H. "A Case For End System Multicast", *In ACM SIGMETRICS'00*, Santa Clara, CA, June, 2000.
7. Clarke I., Sandberg O., Wiley B. and Hong T.W. "Freenet: A Distributed Anonymous Information Storage and Retrieval System". *Proc. of the ICSI Workshop on Design Issues in Anonymity and Unobservability*, Berkeley, CA, 2000.
8. Crespo A. and Garcia-Molina H. "Routing Indices For Peer-to-Peer Systems", *In ICDCS'02*, Vienna, Austria, 2002.
9. Cuenca-Acuna F.M. and Nguyen T.D. "Text-Based Content Search and Retrieval in ad hoc P2P Communities". Int. Workshop on Peer-to-Peer Computing, 2002

10. Entropia Home Page, "Entropia", http://www.entropia.com.
11. Garey M.R. and Johnson D.S. "Computers and Intractability: A Guide to the Theory of NP-Completeness", W.H. Freeman, 1979.
12. Gao J., and Steenkiste P. "Design and Evaluation of a Distributed Scalable Content Discovery System." *IEEE Journal on Selected Areas in Communications*, Special Issue on Recent Advances in Service Overlay Networks, 22(1):54-66.
13. Gnutella, http://gnutella.wego.com.
14. Hansen, T., Otero, J., McGregor, A., Braun, H-W., "Active measurement data analysis techniques", *In CIC'00*, Las Vegas, Nevada, June, 2000.
15. Iyer S., Rowstron A., Druschel P., "SQUIRREL: A decentralized, peer-to-peer web cache" *In PODC 2002*, Monterey, CA, 2002.
16. Kalogeraki V., Gunopulos D., and Zeinalipour-Yazti D. "A Local Search Mechanism for Peer-to-Peer Networks", *In ACM CIKM'02*, McLean, Virginia.
17. Kazaa, Sharman Networks Ltd. http://www.kazaa.com/
18. Lucene, The Apache Jakarta Project. http://jakarta.apache.org/lucene/
19. Lv Q., Cao P., Cohen E., Li K., and Shenker S. "Search and replication in unstructured peer-to-peer networks". ICS02, New York, USA, June 2002.
20. Napster, http://www.napster.com/.
21. Ratnasamy S., Handley M., Karp R., Shenker S. "Topologically-Aware Overlay Construction and Server Selection", *In IEEE INFOCOM'02*, NY, June 2002.
22. Ratnasamy S., Francis P., Handley M., Karp R., Shenker S. "A Scalable Content-Addressable Network", *In ACM SIGCOMM'01*, August 2001.
23. Rowstron A. and Druschel P., "Pastry: Scalable, distributed object location and routing for large-scale peer-to-peer systems", *In IFIP/ACM Middleware'01*.
24. SETI Project Home Page, "SETI@Home", http://setiathome.ssl.berkeley.edu.
25. Stoica I., Morris R., Karger D., Kaashoek M.F., Balakrishnan H. "Chord: A scalable peer-to-peer lookup service for Internet applications", *In ACM SIGCOMM'01*, San Diego CA, August 2001.
26. Tang C., Xu Z., and Dwarkadas S. "Peer-to-Peer Information Retrieval Using Self-Organizing Semantic Overlay Networks". *ACM SIGCOMM 2003*.
27. Tsoumakos D. and Roussopoulos N. "Adaptive Probabilistic Search for Peer-to-Peer Networks". *Proc. of the Third IEEE Int. Conf. on P2P Computing*, 2003.
28. Wouhaybi R. and Campbell A. "Phenix: Supporting Resilient Low-Diameter Peer-to-Peer Topologies" *In IEEE INFOCOM'04*, Hong Kong, to appear in 2004.
29. Xu Z., Tang C., Zhang Z. "Building Topology-Aware Overlays using Global Soft-State", *In ICDCS 2003*, Providence, Rhode Island, 2003.
30. Yang B., and Garcia-Molina H. "Efficient Search in Peer-to-Peer Networks", *In ICDCS'02*, Vienna, Austria, July 2002.
31. Zeinalipour-Yazti D. and Folias T., "Quantitative Analysis of the Gnutella Network Traffic", Technical Report UC-CS-89, University of California, Riverside.
32. Zeinalipour-Yazti D., Kalogeraki V., Gunopulos D. "Exploiting Locality for Scalable Information Retrieval in Peer-to-Peer Systems", Information Systems Journal, Elsevier Publications, to appear in 2004.
33. Zhao B.Y., Duan Y., Huang L., Joseph A.D., Kubiatowicz J.D. "Brocade: landmark routing on overlay networks" In IPTPS'02, Cambridge MA, March 2002.

AESOP: Altruism-Endowed Self-organizing Peers*

Nikos Ntarmos and Peter Triantafillou

R.A. Computer Technology Institute and
Computer Engineering and Informatics Dept.,
University of Patras, Rio, Greece
{ntarmos, peter}@ceid.upatras.gr

Abstract. We argue the case for a new paradigm for architecting structured P2P overlay networks, coined AESOP. AESOP consists of 3 layers: (i) an architecture, PLANES, that ensures significant performance speedups, assuming knowledge of altruistic peers; (ii) an accounting/auditing layer, AltSeAl, that identifies and validates altruistic peers; and (iii) SeAledPLANES, a layer that facilitates the coordination/collaboration of the previous two components. We briefly present these components along with experimental and analytical data of the promised significant performance gains and the related overhead. In light of these very encouraging results, we put this three-layer architecture paradigm forth as the way to structure the P2P overlay networks of the future.

1 Introduction

P2P networks have recently been receiving an everincreasing recognition and attention. Given the desirable characteristics and the inherent promises of the peer-to-peer computing paradigm, attention is likely to increase in the coming years. Within the related research a fundamental problem of "routing" (lookup) in P2P networks has received special attention; given a request arriving at a specific peer node, for a document id, route the request to the peer in the network, which stores the document.

Recent research in P2P networks has largely focused on structuring efforts for the network overlay so to ensure the fast routing of requests to the peers storing the requested objects. Most prominent in these efforts is a class of P2P network overlays based on Distributed Hash Tables (DHTs). DHT-based solutions [1, 2, 3, 4] can provide routing in the steady-state case in $O(logN)$ hops, in a network of N peers, providing routing efficiency and scalability. These performance characteristics constituted an important step forward, compared to the original, pioneering attempts for "unstructured" P2P networks [5, 6]. In unstructured networks related overheads are much higher and no guarantees can be given for the efficiency or the locating of the requested documents.

Currently, there are efforts underway for bridging this structure chasm: unstructured networks are being enriched with DHTs (e.g., Limewire[7] and Mnet[8] (ex-Mojonation[9]) with Chord[2]) and structured networks aim to deal effectively with the

---

* This work is partly supported by the 6th Framework Program of the EU through the Integrated Project DELIS (#001907) on Dynamically Evolving, Large-scale Information Systems.

W.S. Ng et al. (Eds.): DBISP2P 2004, LNCS 3367, pp. 151–165, 2005.

operational characteristics found in applications built on top of unstructured networks (e.g., Structella [10]).

1.1 Our Perspectives and Position

Real-World Perspective. Our starting position is that our world consists of altruists, selfish people, and of others with behavior ranging in between, with a non-negligible percentage of the last category showing altruistic behavior if given the incentives to do so. Within the world of P2P networks this fact has been clearly manifested and documented: take as example the 'free riders'[11] phenomenon, first measured in the Gnutella network.

The bad news is that the great majority of Gnutella peers were proven to be free riders (more than 70%). And this is indeed very bad news for DHT-style overlays, since the great majority of peers may be joining the network and leaving very soon thereafter – [12] have show that the median session duration in Gnutella and Napster is approximately 60 minutes! There also exist other independent reports offering evidence that half of the peer population is changing almost every half an hour[13].

The good news are that a non-negligible percentage of the peers were proven to be altruistic[1]. In Mojonation[9], more than 1-2% of all users, stayed connected almost all the time. In Gnutella, 1% (10%) of peers served about 40% (90%) of the total requests [11], while [12] have shown that the longer a node has been up, the more likely it is to remain up. Note that the routing algorithm in Gnutella acts as a counter-incentive to acting altruistically, flooding peers with requests. Also, the majority of Mojo Nation users were dissatisfied with it and that is why they permanently disconnected. Thus, we conjecture that, by giving incentives (to avoid the so-called tragedy of the commons) and taking away such counter-incentives, more network nodes will be willing to act altruistically.

Research Perspective. Looking at related research in DHT-structured P2P networks, one notices that given a highly-dynamic environment, routing performance degrades to $O(N)$ hops (that is, if the network remains connected). Fundamentally, this is due to the difficulty in keeping up with the required updates to routing state for special neighbors which ensure $O(logN)$ hops in the steady-state case. Much to their credit, the authors in [14] studied how to guarantee in highly-dynamic cases $O(logN)$ routing performance. To do this, $O(log^2N)$ so-called stabilization "rounds" need be ran by every node every half-life to update routing state (successors, predecessors, and fingers). However, this (i) transfers overhead from routing to the stabilization phases, (ii) this solution is expensive, yielding a total message overhead of $O(NlogN)$ per half life: e.g., each node in an one-million node network needs to run on the order of 400 stabilization rounds, say, every

---

[1] There is some disagreement whether this is true altruistic behaviour or a positive externality (i.e., a benefit to the community that results from peers acting in their own self- interest); Nonetheless, be it altruism or "altruism", the benefits to the community contributed by these peers are recognized by all!

For this reason and for brevity in the remaining discussion we refer to altruistic nodes implying both altruistic and powerful nodes.

half hour!, and (iii) detecting the presence/absence of low-bandwidth nodes (which are the great majority) during stabilization is time- consuming and highly error prone (think of nodes behind 56Kbits lines). Hence, given the huge scales and the highly- dynamic nature of the vast majority of peers, current architectures fail to ensure $O(logN)$ routing in the highly- dynamic case.

Furthermore, even $O(logN)$ hops, achieved in steady-state assuming 'good node behavior', may not be good enough; after all, these are overlay hops with each being translated into multiple physical network hops. In addition, even $O(logN)$ hops over peers with low bandwidth will definitely create performance problems. Finally, within the DHT world there is a complete lack of attention on exploiting powerful peers in order to improve performance.

But even when considering the unstructured P2P research efforts, one also notices a lack of considerable attention on research exploiting the heterogeneities among peer nodes [12]. As an exception, [15] talk about exploiting powerful nodes, which are thought of consisting of a number of smaller, "virtual" nodes. This transforms several hops among weaker nodes, into internal "virtual hops" within a powerful peer. [16] presents distributed algorithms to force-flow increased loads towards more capable nodes.

But still, heterogeneity means more than a mere distinction between powerful and weak nodes; there is also heterogeneity with respect to their behavior, being altruistic or selfish. For example, there will be powerful nodes that will not be acting altruistically. It is reasonable to expect that altruistic nodes will tend to have greater (processing, memory, and bandwidth) capabilities, willing to share them (when not in use) with others (practically at very small extra costs, given the flat-rate resource pricing) . This expectation has been validated in [13].

Despite this, the aforementioned related work has made some good progress, show-ing the way in exploiting powerful nodes. Similar to our work, they are criticizing DHTs and structured overlays in failing to cope with highly-dynamic environments, such as the ones expected in sharing P2P networks [17]. However, this led them to avoid using structured overlays, which unfortunately led to their inability to deliver definite perfor-mance guarantees, with respect to routing hop counts and robustness. Conversely, we follow a different path; we add further structure to DHTs, leveraging altruistic peers. In this way, we can deliver definite performance guarantees for the steady-case and, perhaps more importantly, for the highly-dynamic cases. Over and above any hop-count improvements, we ensure a more stable infrastructure, especially during high churn[18].

Fundamental Peer Characteristics and Implications. In general, in this work we define altruistic peers to be the peers having the following characteristics. They:

- stay connected for significantly longer periods of time, and
- are willing and possess the necessary capacity to accept greater loads.

With these altruists' characteristics in mind we revisit the "traditional" arguments about routing hot spots and about the overhead in dealing with the frequent topology changes inherent in P2P networks. Specifically:

- It is a good idea to concentrate most routing chores at altruistic peers; these peers are willing to carry extra load and have the required capabilities to do so. This results in more efficient routing than forcing weaker nodes to partake heavily in the routing tasks.

– The above decision will undoubtedly create greater routing tables at altruists. Traditionally, this causes greater reorganization overhead incurred when nodes enter and leave the network. However, the additional routing table entries of altruists will concern other altruistic peers. Because these stay connected for long periods of time, maintaining the freshness of this extra routing state does not result in prohibitively increased bandwidth overheads.

Our Position and Contributions. This paper intends to show how to leverage the coexistence of altruists and selfish peers found in real-life networks and harness them to improve routing performance. We will focus on structured networks, and in particular we will base our proposal on the desirable characteristics of Chord[2], which include its simplicity, its acceptability within the community (as evidenced by the systems utilizing it, which include Limewire, MNet, Sun's JXTA, and others) and its flexibility [19]. However, the proposed architecture can also be applied on other DHTs as well. More specifically, our position is:

1. Weaving into the structured P2P network architectures the behavior and capability differences of peers, much-needed, quantifiable, and significant further routing speedups can be attained.
2. Routing speedups should refer to hop counts, routing state size and maintenance requirements, and robustness, and they should not be achieved by transferring overhead to other system operation phases (e.g., stabilization).
3. Routing speedups should pertain to the steady-state and highly-dynamic cases.
4. Altruistic and powerful nodes can be harnessed to offer these significant efficiency gains, while requiring that only a very small percentage of peers be altruistic, being burdened with only small overheads.
5. A software layer responsible for identifying and managing altruistic and powerful nodes can go long ways in offering these significant efficiency gains, while requiring that only a very small percentage of peers be altruistic, being burdened with only small overheads.
6. As a result, a paradigm that facilitates the cooperation of an altruist-based architecture and an auditing/accounting layer identifying altruist nodes is needed in order to take the next step in structured P2P network architectures.

2   PLANES: Altruists to the Rescue

In PLANES, node and document IDs consist of m bits, allowing $N \leq 2^m$ nodes and documents. A small percentage of nodes (i.e. $A << N$) is altruistic.

2.1   Architecting Layered, Altruism-Based P2P Networks

The fundamentals of our approach are:

1. The N nodes are partitioned into DHT-structured clusters. For each cluster, a DHT-structured overlay network is created. (Note that any similar structure of choice

---

[2] Due to this, the log()-notation in the examples to follow refers to base-2 logarithms.

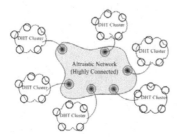

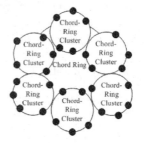

Fig. 1. An Example Network with $N=30$, $C=6$, $S=5$

Fig. 2. Forming Clusters in an Altruism-based P2P Network – A Chord Ring of Chord Rings

can be used instead of DHTs, such as [20, 21] yielding similar relative performance gains to that we show for DHTs). Given the desired cluster size, S, and the number of clusters, C, overall, $C = \frac{N}{S}$ clusters are formed.

2. Each node requires minimal overhead for associating node IDs with cluster IDs (e.g. by hashing node IDs to cluster IDs).
3. The vast majority of a cluster's peers are selfish. Within each cluster there exists at least one altruistic peer.
4. Altruistic peers maintain greater routing state, with an entry for all other altruists, creating a completely connected altruistic overlay network. Thus, communication between altruistic nodes (and thus between clusters) requires 1 hop[3]. Later, we will do away with the complete connectivity requirement.
5. Within every DHT cluster, all nodes maintain routing state for their neighbors, as required by the cluster's DHT. Thus, each node has $O(\log S)$ neighbors. Also, all nodes keep routing state pointing to the altruistic node(s) in their cluster.

Routing is performed in two levels:

1. Across clusters, from any node to a node in a different cluster: given the completely-connected altruistic overlay network, routing to reach any cluster from outside the cluster requires two overlay hops: one hop from a node to its altruist and another from this altruist to the altruist of the target cluster.
2. Within clusters, from any node (including an altruistic node) to another node in the same cluster: routing is performed by sending the message over the cluster DHT network.

Fig. 1 visualizes an example layered P2P network.

Forming Clusters Using Consistent Hashing. We present one possible alternative for cluster formation.

1. Clusters are assigned IDs as follows:
$$ID(c_i) = \frac{2^m}{C} \cdot (i-1), \quad i = 1, \ldots, C$$

---

[3] In practice, we talk about a "highly-connected" altruistic network, and $O(1)$ hops since complete connectivity is hard to achieve.

2. Using consistent hashing[22][4] each node ID is mapped to one of the C cluster IDs: node n_j is assigned to cluster c_i if $ID(c_i) < ID(n_j) < ID(c_{i+1})$. Thus, step 1 partitions a Chord ring into C subrings, onto which node IDs are assigned (see fig. 2).
3. Using consistent hashing once more each node ID is placed within its cluster (subring).

Figure 2 illustrates the clusters fomred for a network of eight clusters.

2.2   PLANES Algorithms

Routing. The routing algorithm is called at a node with srcNodeId, requesting docId, and produces the nodeId storing this document. In the algorithm, there are two functions used to send messages: send() and Route() (uses the cluster's DHT to route the message).

PLANESRouting (srcNodeId, docId): nodeId

1: srcNodeId.send (srcAltrNodeId, docId); /* send request to altruist within source cluster */
2: ClusterId := srcAltrNodeId.ConsistentHash(docId); /* id target cluster */
3: destAltrNodeId:=srcAltrNodeId.LookUp (ClusterId); /* get target cluster's altruistic node id */
4: srcAltrNodeId.send (destAltrNodeId, docId); /* send to target cluster's altruistic peer */
5: nodeId := destAltrNodeId.Route (ClusterId, docId); /* route to node in target cluster and return its id */

Addition and Deletion of Documents. The id of the document being added is hashed to, first, the proper cluster and then, using the cluster's DHT document addition protocol, to one of the cluster's nodes where it is stored. Deleting a document requires no extra state maintenance.

Addition and Deletion of Peer Nodes. A node (altruistic or not) n_i joins the network, as usual, by finding the address of any member node, say of cluster c_s. Communicating with it, finds the address of the altruistic node for c_s. Then the id of the cluster to which it will belong, c_d, is determined by hashing the id of n_i, as explained earlier in sec. 2.1 (discussing cluster formation using consistent hashing). The altruistic node of the target cluster c_d is then found using the altruist for c_s. Finally, n_i joins the DHT structure of the target cluster, using the DHT join protocol and including an entry in its routing table for the cluster's altruist.

Adding an altruist also involves communication within the altruist network to store the altruist network's routing table and update the other altruists' tables to include it. Further, all DHT-cluster nodes need add an entry for it.

A node leaving the network affects only the cluster's DHT structure, calling on the leave protocol of the DHT. Altruist deletion requires informing its cluster nodes and may

---

[4] Consistent hashing ensures that, with high probability, all clusters will have equal numbers of peer nodes (with negligible differences).

require finding a replacement for it, e.g., if it is the last altruist for its cluster. This can be done examining its local routing table and selecting another altruist (typically one that is associated with a small number of clusters).

2.3   Performance of Routing in PLANES

To illustrate the improved efficiency, we first present a simple "winning configuration" for PLANES. We set $C = \frac{N}{logN}$, yielding $S = logN$. Furthermore, we structure each cluster network using a DHT, as explained in sec. 2.1.

Routing Hop-Count Efficiency. This configuration will ensure routing in $O(logS) = O(log(logN))$ hops, in the steady-state case, within each cluster. This follows straightforwardly from the adoption of a DHT-cluster organization and the $O(1)$ hop-count routing between the altruistic nodes.

The "hard" case occurs when peers join and leave the network concurrently with such high rates that the DHT cannot maintain fresh routing states (i.e., information about neighbors of nodes). Depending on the adopted DHT organization, the probability of facing this "hard" case varies. However, in highly dynamic networks, as argued earlier, the performance of routing will degrade to $O(N)$. Since DHTs guarantee routing hop counts in this case in the order of the size of the DHT network, it follows that with our architecture, in this highly dynamic case, routing is ensured in $O(S) = O(logN)$ hops, given the $O(1)$ hops between the altruists.

The existence of $\frac{N}{logN}$ clusters implies requiring a number of at least $\frac{N}{logN}$ altruistic peers (one per cluster). However, note that as N increases, an increasingly smaller percentage of N is required: e.g., for 1000 nodes, 10% of the nodes need be altruistic; for one million nodes, only 5% of the nodes need be altruistic.

The following examples, quantify the improvements. For simplicity, in most discussions we drop the O-notation, since the constant factors should be the same for our architecture and for DHT-style architectures.

Routing Performance at Larger Scales: Example. Consider a $(N =)$ one million node network. Then, routing in a traditional DHT overlay requires $(logN =)$ 20 hops, in the steady-state. In the highly-dynamic case, DHT routing requires $O(N)$ hops – a gloomy prospect!

For altruism-based routing we assume that 5% (50,000) of peers are altruistic. Having one altruistic node per cluster, each cluster will have about $logN \approx 20$ peer nodes and the routing within each cluster will require $log(logN) \approx 4$ hops and 6 in total, after adding the two hops needed to get to the source and destination clusters' altruistic nodes, in the steady-state case. Therefore, in similarly-sized networks, routing hop-count efficiency is improved by a factor of better than $3\times$.

In the highly-dynamic case, when large numbers of peers join and leave the network concurrently and frequently and the special neighbors structure of the DHT cluster breaks, altruism-based routing requires $O(S) = O(logN) \approx 20$ DHT hops, plus 2 for reaching the target cluster. This yields an impressive improvement of several orders of magnitude!

Routing Performance at Smaller Scales: Example. For smaller size networks, with one thousand peer nodes, traditional solutions yield a routing hop count about $(logN =)$

10 and 1000 in the steady-state and highly-dynamic cases, respectively. With altruism-based routing, the steady-state routing hop count is about 3 (i.e. $log(log1000)$) and the highly-dynamic case is about $S = log1000 = 10$, yielding improvement factors of about $2\times$ (after accounting for altruistic network hops) and about two orders of magnitude, respectively.

2.4   PLANES Architecture Extensions

In dynamic systems, the main concern is the overhead for maintaining freshness of routing state about altruists, which may become expensive or even impossible to maintain, breaking the complete-connectivity of the altruistic network. We first work in two dimensions: (i) reduce the required number of altruists and (ii) reduce their routing state. Then, we discuss an architecture without complete connectivity for the altruists network.

PLANES with Fewer Altruists: Riding the $Log()$ Factor... We present an extended architecture, showing how to offer small sacrifices in routing speedups, to secure dramatic reductions in the overhead for maintaining altruist network routing state.

We architect the network to consist of $C = \frac{N}{z \times logN}$ clusters, yielding a cluster size of $S = z \times logN$ for an appropriately-valued integer z. The key is to note that: (i) the required number of altruists (which is equal to C) decreases by a factor equal to z; and (ii) the routing hop count within each DHT cluster increases by $logz$, since $logS = log(z \times logN) = logz + log(logN)$.

Example: with one million nodes and $z = 6$, $C \approx 8335$ clusters, cutting the state and freshness overhead requirements by a factor of $6\times$ (going from a 50,000 altruistic-nodes network down to 8335 nodes). In return, instead of routing in <5 hops within the DHT cluster, we now require about <7 hops ($log120 \approx 7$). Taking this point further, using $z = 50$, results in 1000 clusters, each with 1000 nodes in it. Routing within each cluster now needs 10 hops; and the required number of altruists are now reduced by a factor of $50\times$.

Thus, we can still ensure significant speedups in routing (by a factor of about $2\times$ for the steady-state case and by orders of magnitude in the highly-dynamic case). At the same time, the overhead for maintaining high connectivity within the altruistic network, is dramatically reduced, since the number of altruists has been drastically reduced. Finally, we stress that requiring such a small percentage (0.1%) of altruistic nodes is not unrealistic [11, 12, 13].

PLANES with Less Altruism, and/or Less Power: Keep on Clustering... Alternatively (or complementarily) to the previous architecture, one can adopt the same layering principle recursively with respect now to the altruistic network. The motivation for this is twofold: (i) reduce further the overhead for maintaining complete/high connectivity between altruists, and (ii) exploit possible heterogeneities among altruists.

Fig. 3 outlines our approach for a three-layer P2P network. This network now includes a clustered altruistic P2P network with $A = 50,000$ altruistic nodes, partitioned in $C = 390$ clusters (AltNets), each of $S = 128$ altruistic nodes. This configuration is obtained by employing the $C = \frac{A}{z \times logA}$ configuration presented earlier and applied now for the altruistic network of A nodes, with $z = 8$.

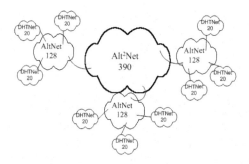

Fig. 3. A Multilevel Altruism-based P2P Network

Altruists belong in AltNet, or in Alt2Net. In the network in Figure 3 the network has $N = 1,000,000$ nodes, with 5% (50,000) altruistic nodes being organized into two levels (of 390 altruistic clusters - AltNets - with 128 altruists each and an Alt2Net network of 390 altruists, one for each AltNet cluster). Each DHT cluster (DHTNet) consists of 20 nodes. Each DHTNet is served by an AltNet, with each AltNet serving 128 DHTNets. All AltNets and the Alt2Net are as before (almost) completely connected. The requirements in order to maintain this high connectivity are further drastically reduced: altruists within an AltNet (Alt2Net) need have 128 (390) neighbors. This represents a reduction by a factor of about 400 to 128, respectively.

At the same time, the significant routing speedups are maintained. For the example one-million-node network, instead of requiring two hops to reach the target DHT cluster, now two or four hops are required for this purpose (depending on whether the source and destination nodes are served by the same AltNet overlay, or not, respectively). So a total of about 6-8 hops are required: 2-4 to reach the target DHT cluster and about 4 to reach the target node within it. This gives a speedup of about 2.5 to $3\times$, compared to the 20 hops required in the steady-state case for the plain DHT architecture. Again, in the highly-dynamic case, the speedup is several orders of magnitude.

Note that, the more layers we deploy, the less the routing state powerful peers have to maintain. The latter, however, comes at the expense of routing hops. Whether more layers are suitable or not is highly dependent on the characteristics of the network and the actual application.

PLANES Without Altruistic Network Complete Connectivity. Altruistic networks can also be structured using a DHT, doing away with the completely-connected network. The layered routing algorithm presented earlier, needs to be updated to combine steps 3 and 4 and call on the DHT's routing operation to send the request to the target cluster.

Routing without Complete Connectivity: The altruists form a Chord unit ring onto which altruistic node ids are placed. In addition, cluster ids are mapped to the same ring (like document ids are mapped to Chord rings). Thus, altruists are responsible for clusters, as nodes are responsible for documents in Chord networks. Routing then at the top layer (i.e., from a source-cluster altruist to the destination cluster altruist) is done by routing through the altruists' Chord ring for the destination cluster id. The other steps remain the same.

Consider a network with $N = 1,000,000$, nodes with $S = C = \sqrt{N} = 1,000$. Employing a DHT for the $C = 1,000$ altruists does not improve hop counts in the steady-state case: about $logC$ (=10) hops would be required to route through the altruists' DHT and $logS$ (=10) hops to route within the target cluster's DHT.

However, this still leverages the characteristics of altruists to yield high routing performance in the highly-dynamic case. Since we assume that the altruist routing state about their neighbors can be maintained even in the highly- dynamic case, routing within it requires $O(logC) = O(log\sqrt{N})$. But even in the unlikely case where this cannot be achieved, routing within the altruists' DHT will require $O(C) = O(\sqrt{N})$. Routing within the cluster DHTs requires in the highly-dynamic case $O(S) = O(\sqrt{N})$. Thus, overall, $O(\sqrt{N})$ hops are required, a drastic improvement compared to DHTs, making this architecture highly desirable.

Finally, in the architecture of sec. 2.4, altruist DHTs can be used at one level only. This still enjoys smaller hop counts in the steady-state and highly-dynamic cases, and requires a percentage of completely-connected nodes.

3 AltSeAl: Altruism Sealed

SeAl[23] is a software layer we have developed for identifying selfish peers and giving them incentives to behave fairly so to improve load balancing and overall data-access performance. SeAl can be transparently incorporated in structured and unstructured networks. Here we outline AltSeAl, a modified version of SeAl, addresssing the needs of AESOP.

3.1 The Monitoring/Accounting Layer

The basic idea is that all transactions between peers result in the creation of tokens (called "Transaction Receipts" or TRs) that can be used much like "favors" in real life; the peers rendering favors (i.e. sharing resources) gain the right to ask peers receiving favors to somehow pay them back in the future or get "punished" otherwise.

All of these operations are performed transparently to the user. Nodes keep track of the favors they render or receive (i.e. store the corresponding TRs) in two "favor lists": the "Favors-Done" (F_d) and "Favors-Owed" (F_o) lists. Moreover, nodes in AltSeAl are characterized by their "altruism score" (denoted by $n_i.\mathcal{A}$). This is simply a function of $|F_d|$ and $|F_o|$, where $|X|$ denotes the size of the set X. For example, we can consider $|F_d| - |F_o|$ or $\frac{|F_d|}{|F_o|}$ as possible altruism score functions.

If node n_1 shares a resource r_1 and node n_2 accesses it, the favor-lists mechanism enables n_1 to selectively redirect a subsequent incoming request for r_1 to n_2. AltSeAl nodes autonomously and independently set an upper ($n_i.\mathcal{A}_{max}$) and a lower ($n_i.\mathcal{A}_{min}$) threshold value for their score. When they rate higher than $n_i.\mathcal{A}_{max}$ they always redirect incoming requests (if possible), while never redirecting when rating lower than $n_i.\mathcal{A}_{min}$. In all other cases, nodes with a tunable probability decide whether to serve or redirect.

3.2   Favors and Complaints

In the previous scenario, if n_2 serves the redirected request, then the corresponding favor is marked as paid-back. Otherwise, n_1 may choose to use the corresponding TR – i.e. $TR_{n_1}^{n_2}(r_1)$ – as a means of accusing n_2 of acting selfishly. This is accomplished in the following manner. AltSeAl uses a DHT overlay of its own to store "complaints". n_1 sends $TR_{n_1}^{n_2}(r_1)$ to the appropriate node – say n_3 – on this DHT (found by hashing the TR itself). n_3 then acts as an arbitrator between n_1 and n_2; it can ask (both) nodes to verify $TR_{n_1}^{n_2}(r_1)$ and have n_2 pay back the corresponding favor. If the verification succeeds but n_2 still refuses to play fair, n_3 stores $TR_{n_1}^{n_2}(r_1)$ for other nodes to know. If the verification fails, n_3 may choose to similarly "complain" about the perjurer peer.

What's more interesting is that, if n_2 chooses to go altruist at some time, it can go out on the DHT, collect all filed complaints, and selectively pay them back, thus improving its status with respect to the community. Note that, while complaints are sent out to the DHT, TRs concerning favors done or paid-back are kept locally at the altruistic peer. Moreover, to keep storage requirements constant as the system evolves, we use an aging scheme for stored TRs.

TRs are constructed using strong (e.g. public-key) cryptographic primitives, while nodes in AltSeAl are equipped with a public/private key-pair and identified using a digest of their public key, also used to verify TRs. Thus, nodes can't fake TRs or refuse the validity of a TR, unless they change their ID (key-pair). Furthermore, AltSeAl deploys a feedback mechanism rather than a penalizing one – requests are queued and served in a prioritized manner, while the actual resources allocated for serving these requests (e.g. bandwidth, storage, etc.) vary, based on the overall "score" of the served peers. Moreover, peers commence their lifecycle in the system with the worst possible score, thus having no incentive to change their ID or mount a Sybil [24]-class attack.

3.3   SeAled PLANES: AltSeAl and AltNets

AESOP requires the capability to find the IDs of a number of altruistic peers, asynchronously with respect to when they assumed such a status. In the context of AltSeAl, altruism can be expressed using the "altruism score". For example, only peers with $\frac{|F_d|}{|F_o|} \geq 2$ may be deemed altruists. Proofs of altruism are also needed. In AltSeAl, TRs of favors rendered or paid-back can serve for this purpose[5]. Using these TRs, further auditing is possible, validating a peer's claims for altruism.

Finally, AESOP needs a structure to manage altruists. We use a second DHT-based (e.g. Chord[2]) overlay for the altruists – the *AltDHT*. As soon as a node n is proved to be an altruist, the *AddToAltDHT(n)* routine is called. This routine:

1. Is directed to the node n', responsible for maintaining the "complaints" for n.
2. n' audits n, retrieving its white records and checking the locally-stored black records for it.
3. If the audit is successful (i.e. n's altruism score is higher than the system's altruism threshold), n' computes an altruist ID (e.g. by hashing the concatenation of the string

---

[5] We'll call such "positive" TRs the *white records*, as opposed to "negative" TRs called the *black records*.

"Altruist" and n's ID) and, using the DHT node addition protocol, it adds n to the AltDHT. If the audit fails, n' returns an error to n.

4. Whenever a node is promoted to the AltDHT it assumes special responsibilities (e.g. routing).
5. When a peer loses its altruist status (e.g. its altruism score drops below the corresponding threshold), it is removed from the AltDHT using the DHT's node deletion protocol.

Note that peers have a natural incentive not to cheat staying in AltDHT when they wish not to be altruists, since they receive extra load. In addition, peers in AltDHT can perform random audits: periodically, they choose a random ID n'' from those in AltDHT and calculate its altruism score. Peers that are discovered to cheat can be ejected! A more elaborate (but also more resource-hungry) approach to verifiable monitoring and auditing is described in [23].

With this infrastructure in place, discovering altruists is straightforward. To discover k altruists we can, for example, compute a random ID, use AltDHT to locate the node responsible for it and then follow k successor pointers (if AltDHT is implemented using Chord).

4   The Performance of AltSeAl

We have simulated AltSeAl. Our performance results show that AltSeAl performs very well in terms of network/storage overhead and the number of transactions required to audit all nodes.

4.1   Experimental Setup

Our experimental setup assumes that AltSeAl operates in a music-file sharing context, with file sizes (in Mbytes) uniformly distributed in the range 3-10 (for an average size of 6.5 Mbytes). The simulated network consists of 2,500 nodes, sharing 50,000 distinct documents, replicated across peers following a Zipf access distribution, with $\alpha = 0.7$ and 1.2 [25] (for a total of approximately 50.200 and 51,350 documents respectively). We have also tested our system with larger node populations (with similar results), but with not as many queries, due to CPU and memory constraints, and thus report only on the 2500-node case here. The simulation runs for 200,000 requests. Requests arrive at the system following a Poisson distribution, such that every peer will make approximately 5 requests per day of simulated time. The documents requested follow a Zipf distribution too, with similar results for both α values (0.7 and 1.2). Due to space considerations, we report only on the $\alpha = 1.2$ cases.

The peer population consists of 90% (70%) free-riders and 10% (30%) altruists, with network connections ranging (uniformly) from 33.6kbps (modem) to 256kbps (cable) lines for selfish peers, and from 256kbps to 2Mbps (T1) lines for altruists. Furthermore, all peers may fail or deny service with a probability of 0.2, and delete/unshare files with a probability of 0.1.

Finding a peer sharing a file and downloading the file are both 1-hop operations. All AltSeAl operations are run on top of a DHT, thus every AltSeAl transfer is assumed

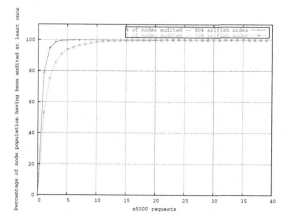

Fig. 4. Performance of the Auditing Mechanism

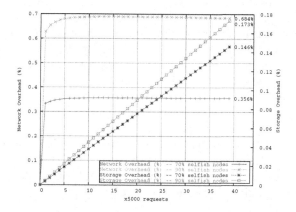

Fig. 5. Network & Storage Overhead of AltSeAl

to take $O(log(N)) = 11$ hops on average (for the 2500-node network). As we'll show shortly, in spite of this handicap, AltSeAl incurs negligible network overhead. Moreover, should AltSeAl be operating on top of store-and-forward networks, such as FreeNet or AChord, the observed network and storage overhead would be orders of magnitudes smaller.

Peers compute their scores using $|F_d| - |F_o|$. Altruistic (selfish) peers redirect incoming requests with probabilities 0, 1, and 0.5, when their score is below their lower threshold, above their upper threshold, or within these values respectively.

The simulation results are depicted in fig. 4 and 5. In the simulation the TR aging mechanism was off, hence the linear growth of the storage overhead (fig. 5). Even with this handicap, AltSeAl inflicts on average a mere 0.16% storage overhead. Moreover, the network overhead stabilizes to at most approximately 0.7%, while more than 90% of the total node population has been audited, after the first 5k requests (fig. 4).

5   Conclusions

The coexistence of altruistic and selfish peers in P2P networks has been well documented. With this paper we PLANES; an architectural paradigm harnessing these characteristics, weaving them into the structured network architecture. We argued for the need and have shown how to achieve significantly greater routing efficiency in such networks for both the steady-state and highly-dynamic cases, without transferring routing overheads to other system functionalities, and while introducing significant efficiency gains in terms of hop counts, routing state size and maintenance requirements, and robustness.

We presented several architectures and algorithms offering trade-offs between routing speedups vs the required number of altruists and their routing state and between routing path lengths in the steady-state case vs altruist-network connectivity requirements. The end result is that extremely small percentages of altruistic nodes are required, being burdened with small overheads, and introducing steady-state routing speedups by factors of up to 2-4×, and by several orders of magnitude in the highly-dynamic case. At the same time, total routing state size is reduced by a factor of about 2×, which leads to improved robustness.

Furthermore, routing robustness is improved due to the smaller total routing state and the isolation of the ill-effects of selfish behavior within small clusters of peers. Because of the above and its simplicity, we believe the proposed paradigm is viable and realizable and we offer it as the way to structure the P2P networks of the future.

Finally, we presented a number of open problems whose solution can ensure significant further performance gains. In a related thread we are developing a software monitoring/auditing layer that can seamlessly and efficiently discover altruistic nodes within the network [23]. In addition, we are developing a protocol suite integrating this layer with the PLANES architecture. The two components lead to a self-organizing, altruist-inspired, dynamic P2P network architecture, maintaining the highly desirable performance characteristics of PLANES, as presented here.

References

1. Druschel, P., Rowstron, A.: Pastry: Scalable, distributed object location and routing for large-scale peer-to-peer systems. (In: Proc. Middleware '01)
2. Stoica, I., et al.: Chord: A scalable Peer-To-Peer lookup service for internet applications. (In: Proc. ACM SIGCOMM '01)
3. Ratnasamy, S., et al.: A scalable content-addressable network. (In: Proc. ACM SIGCOMM '01)
4. Zhao, B., Kubiatowicz, J., Joseph, A.: Tapestry: An infrastructure for fault-tolerant wide-area location and routing. (Technical Report UCB/CSD-01-1141)
5. Gnutella: (http://rfc-gnutella.sourceforge.net/)
6. Clarke, I., Sandberg, O., Wiley, B., Hong, T.: Freenet: A distributed anonymous information storage and retrieval system. (In: Proc. ICSI Workshop on Design Issues in Anonymity and Unobservability '00)
7. LimeWire: (http://www.limewire.org/)
8. Mnet: (http://mnetproject.org/)
9. Mojonation: (http://www.mojonation.com/)

10. Castro, M., Costa, M., Rowstron, A.: Should we build gnutella on a structured overlay? (In: Proc. HotNets II '03)
11. Adar, E., Huberman, B.: Free riding on Gnutella. Technical report, Xerox PARC (2000)
12. Saroiu, S., Gummadi, K., Gribble, S.: A measurement study of peer-to-peer file sharing systems. (In: Proc. MMCN '02)
13. Wilcox-O'Hearn, B.: Experiences deploying a large-scale emergent network. (In: Proc. IPTPS '02)
14. Liben-Nowell, D., Balakrsihnan, H., Karger, D.: Observations on the dynamic evolution of peer-to-peer networks. (In: Proc. IPTPS '02)
15. Ratnasamy, S., Shenker, S., Stoica, I.: Routing algorithms for DHTs: Some open questions. (In: Proc. IPTPS '02)
16. Lv, Q., Ratnasamy, S., Shenker, S.: Can heterogeneity make Gnutella scalable? (In: Proc. IPTPS '02)
17. Chawathe, Y., et al.: Making Gnutella-like P2P systems scalable. (In: Proc. SIGCOMM '03)
18. Rhea, S., Geels, D.: Handling churn in a DHT. (In: Proc. USENIX Technical Conference '04)
19. Gummadi, K., et al.: The impact of DHT routing geometry on routing resilience and proximity. (In: Proc. SIGCOMM '03)
20. Malkhi, D., Naor, M., Ratajczak, D.: Viceroy: A scalable and dynamic emulation of the butterfly. (In: Proc. ACM PODC '02)
21. Aberer, K., Hauswirth, M., Punceva, M., Schmidt, R.: Improving data access in P2P systems. IEEE Internet Computing **6** (2002)
22. Karger, D., et al.: Consistent hashing and random trees: Distributed caching protocols for relieving hot spots on the world wide web. (In: Proc. ACM STOC '97)
23. Ntarmos, N., Triantafillou, P.: SeAl: Managing accesses and data in peer-to-peer sharing networks. (In: Proc. IEEE P2P '04)
24. Douceur, J.: The Sybil attack. (In: Proc. IPTPS '02)
25. Sripanidkulchai, K.: (The popularity of gnutella queries and its implications on scalability) White paper, Feb. 2001.

Search Tree Patterns for Mobile and Distributed XML Processing

Adelhard Türling and Stefan Böttcher

University of Paderborn,
Faculty of Electrical Engineering, Computer Science and Mathematics,
Fürstenallee 11, D-33102 Paderborn, Germany
{Adelhard.Tuerling, stb}@uni-paderborn.de

Abstract. As in a centralized environment, XML data processing in a peer-to-peer environment relies on basic relations between two XML fragments such as containment, subset, difference and intersection. Fast calculation of such relations based only on logical expressions like XPath is known to be a major challenge. Recently XML patterns have been introduced to model and to identify handy subclasses of XPath. We introduce a model for XML data based on their DTDs, tailored to the needs of distributed data processing. In order to meet the required granularity for data processing, our model combines concepts of tree patterns and search trees to represent XML fragments. Besides the given overview and properties of our *search tree pattern* model, we give an introductive example of the usage of such patterns in a peer-to-peer XML caching environment. It enables a peer's cache manager to partially contribute to other peer's requests. Identifying suitable and flexible classes of our newly introduced search tree patterns, we show that our model supports fast and resource preserving logical XML data processing, and we show how such classes can be tailored to a specific application domain and how access focus changes to XML data can be adapted.

Keywords: mobile databases, XML, query patterns, XPath, caching, peer-to-peer.

1 Introduction

Whenever XML data is exchanged, processed and cached on computers within a network, data management meets new challenges. For example, in networks of resource-limited mobile devices, efficient usage of data storage and data transportation over a wireless network is a key requirement [17,6,5]. In such a network, a common situation is that a client queries for data of a dedicated source. Within such a network, it may be of considerable advantage to share and exchange cached XML data among several neighboring clients, compared to a solution where data is only transferred between each requesting client and a dedicated server. One of the main new challenges in such a data sharing scenario is the organization of the data space which is shared among the clients.

This includes specifying how the data space can be divided into handy fragments, how to profit from the distribution of data according to these fragments, and how cooperative usage in a network can enhance data processing.

W.S. Ng et al. (Eds.): DBISP2P 2004, LNCS 3367, pp. 166–184, 2005.
© Springer-Verlag Berlin Heidelberg 2005

A basic challenge is to identify handy classes of logical representations for XML fragments to build a cooperative framework for data sharing and data exchange. Data processing components in such a framework must decide on the fly, i.e. without losing time for extensive intersection tests and difference fragment computations on XML data, whether or not an XML fragment can be used in order to fulfill an operation.

To enable collaborative use of partial XML information, we identify two requirements. Firstly, for any such fragments used in the framework, it shall be easy to decide whether or not they intersect, which parts intersect and which parts differ and to easily (re-)join them *(with minimal operating costs)*. Secondly, most XPath query results can be represented by such fragments or joins of such segments with little or no dispensable offset *(fitting granularity)*. Obviously, there is a conflict between the requirement of a fitting granularity and the need for an overall fast processable set of fragments accepted by all collaborative clients. We address this conflict and present a suitable subset of fragments, that can be adjusted based on access frequency analysis.

The remainder of our paper is organized as follows. In Section 2, we shortly introduce ST-patterns and give an introductory example for their usage in a peer-to-peer environment. In order to express the required granularity of XML fragments, we introduce our formal framework in Section 3. We present the properties of ST-patterns in Section 4 and present ST-pattern processing in Section 5. We show how to use ST-patterns for the distributed caching example in Section 6. In Section 7, we discuss related work and summarize and conclude our contribution in Section 8.

2   Motivation

In the field of mobile data processing where mobile clients might use their resources in cooperation, data management optimization concepts are limited by processing power, available memory and the amount of available energy. Thus, a collaborative use of data fragments will only be accepted if it is easy to manage.

This chapter gives an introductory example of how a fragmentation of an XML data source can be used to decrease response time and save communication resources using a collaborative caching mechanism.

2.1   Brief Introduction into the Concept and Terminology

Within Section 3, we introduce so called *ST-patterns*, which can be regarded as a subclass of XPath expressions used to select specific XML fragments of a global master XML document. We use particular ST-patterns belonging to a predefined subclass of ST-patterns, called ST_{SET}, in order to logically describe the partitioning of the XML document's schema space. In the framework, ST-patterns describe so called *pattern fragments* containing partial application data that are stored, exchanged and processed as handy data units in a data processing network.

2.2 Overview and Scenario

Within our system, each participating node that provides XML data is called a *dedicated server* for that data. The dedicated server, as with other participants, organizes its data space and its data according to a class of ST-patterns called ST_{SET}. The union of all these ST-patterns forms an ST-pattern ST_U that describes the logically available data in the cache. Besides the dedicated server, other participants, called *caching servers*, might offer a caching service.

Whenever a client wants to request data using an XPath query, it looks up its cache for any partial fragments of the answer and sends the request for the missing fragments as an ST-pattern ST_{REQ} to a caching server.

If the caching server cannot completely answer the request, it can forward a reduced version of the incoming request and at the same time send the pattern fragments of the request it has cached as a partial response. The originator of the request collects and (re-)joins the pattern fragments as they arrive, and might store the result in its own cache.

2.3 Segmentation Caching in Peer-to-Peer Environments

In a peer-to-peer environment, each client could act as an intermediate caching server. As routing delivers the request to a master server, each client on the route can contribute locally available pattern fragments, send them immediately to the originator of the query, and in parallel rewrite the original query and thus reduce the amount of requested data.

This is possible and attractive for two major reasons. First, the costs for another client to contribute are minimized by using the concept of ST-patterns. We expect that the savings of time and transport costs by data sharing will clearly come out as an average advantage for each participating client. Second, costs for contributing are dominated by transmitting the locally available pattern fragments. In networks where a (potentially contributing) client is a routing node between server and originator of the request, it would have communication costs in any case. Since it would receive and send the data as a router anyway, as an intermediate caching server, some data has to be looked up and sent in the case of contributing partial results.

2.4 Expected Behavior in Peer-to-Peer Environments

For applications with hot spots and frequent similar requests, we expect enormous savings, if the choice of the ST-pattern class guarantees that frequent requests can be represented by pattern fragments with minimal or no dispensable offset. Each cached pattern fragment found in the local cache or an intermediate cache server guarantees a saving of time and transmission resources. For infrequent requests, it is acceptable to have some overhead.

Especially in networks with limited bandwidth such as Bluetooth or clients with other wireless access, we expect enormous savings. For example, self organizing ad-hoc networks of mobile clients organize their routing dynamically. In such a scenario, the discussed peer-to-peer approach, where each client on the requested route can contribute pattern fragments, seems very promising. We can formulate the cost reduction as follows. Let C be a set of tuples (j, i) where each tuple represents the client c_i that contributes the pattern fragment p_j to the actual request. Furthermore, the costs for transporting a pattern fragment p_j from client c_i to c_{i-1} are expressed as costs (p_j, c_i) and can depend, for example, on distance, bandwidth, sending power and power supply. For a client c_0 that requests n frequent pattern fragments $\{p_1, ..., p_n\}$ from a master XML document of client c_m, routing its request through the path of nodes c_i with i ϵ $\{1, ..., m-1\}$, transport costs can be reduced to:

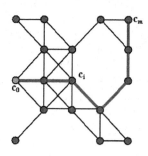

$$\underbrace{\sum_{j=1 \text{ to } n} \sum_{i=1 \text{ to } m} \text{costs} (p_j, c_i)}_{} - \underbrace{\sum_{\text{each } (j, i) \in C} \sum_{k=i \text{ to } m} \text{costs} (p_j, c_i).}_{}$$

Fig. 1. Example topology

Without caching: Each p_j has to be transported over a link m times.

Savings because of caching.

See Figure 1 for an example topology. Besides the reduction of transport costs, we also expect a time saving based on two observations. First, since all c_i know the request earlier than c_m, the response is already started as the request reaches the first c_i that can contribute a pattern fragment. Second, the time period between the start of the first response package in c_m and the arrival in c_0 (known as pipeline initiation time) is reduced, since data packages to be transferred are already spread along the route from c_m to c_0.

3   Framework for ST-Patterns

We use XML patterns as logical data descriptions for data processing. In this context we need logical descriptions that are easy to handle and that allow a good degree of granularity. By granularity, we mean that it must be possible to split any logical description into several parts. This technique can be used to archive handy sizes of the fragments represented by the description. For an example (compare the DTD of Figure 2), standard tree patterns allow us to describe a fragment that holds all the contact nodes and to split it into two patterns. One part holding all contact names and the other holding all the corresponding images. Assuming that the names are the most frequently needed information, the split separating two fragments by the condition of the sibling's labels 'name' and 'image' is a good partitioning. However, the latter pattern describes an XML fragment including all images of all offers and this fragment might still be too large for efficient processing. Because tree patterns like these can't be split any more, we expand the definition of XML patterns to so called ST-patterns which support a higher granularity.

To achieve this granularity, we introduce ST-patterns based on split nodes that partition a node's child set and introduce operations and properties on ST-patterns.

3.1 Formal Framework

```
<!ELEMENT car EMPTY>
<!ATTLIST car
    name CDATA #REQUIRED
    year CDATA #REQUIRED
    price CDATA #REQUIRED
    type (truck | convert | limo)
#REQUIRED
>
<!ELEMENT contact EMPTY>
<!ATTLIST contact
    name CDATA #REQUIRED
    image CDATA #REQUIRED
>
<!ELEMENT offer (seller, car+)>
<!ELEMENT offers (offer+)>
<!ELEMENT seller (contact+)>
<!ATTLIST seller
    town CDATA #REQUIRED
>
```

We next introduce models for basic objects of our framework. Starting with simple models for DTDs, XML documents and XML patterns, we develop a formal framework for so called *ST-patterns* and *ST-pattern fragments* used as basic components in our data processing. As a running example, we use a car-selling catalog based on the DTD given in Figure 2.

Similar to [20], in the following we use $N = \{n_1, n_2, n_3, ...\}$ as an infinite set of nodes, $\Sigma = \{e_1, e_2, e_3, ...\}$ as a finite set of element names and $Q = \{v_1, v_2, v_3, ...\}$ as a infinite, ordered set of data values.

Fig. 2. Example DTD

3.2 DTD Trees

DTDs describe the structure of valid XML documents. DTD trees are a simplified model for DTDs. Each element, text-node and attribute occurring in such a DTD is converted to a node in our DTD model, i.e. in the *DTD tree*. The parent-child relation (and the attribute-relation) between the elements and the attributes of a DTD are represented by directed edges within the DTD tree. For each element name, the model formally expresses these relations by using its *branching constraints*. A branching constraint describes the set of allowed children element names and for each allowed child it specifies the *multiplicity relation* as being one-to-many or one-to-one (short * or 1). For example in Figure 3, a DTD tree is shown that allows car nodes to occur in arbitrary quantity under an offer node, whereas attribute nodes are always restricted to a single occurrence per parent element.

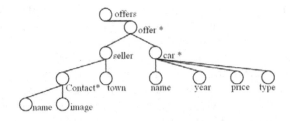

Fig. 3. Example DTD tree

Definition 3.2.1. A *DTD tree D* (over alphabet Σ) is a triple (Σ, r, b), where
(1) $r \in \Sigma$ is the root label
(2) $b: \Sigma \to \{(e_1, m_1), \ldots, (e_k, m_k) \mid e_i \in \Sigma, m_i \in \{1,*\}$ with $i \in \{1, \ldots, k\}$, $e_i = e_j \Leftrightarrow i = j$, $k <= |\Sigma| \}$ associates to each node name a branching constraint $\{(e_1, m_1), \ldots, (e_k, m_k)\}$.

A graphical representation for a DTD tree can be seen in Figure 3. Usually the '*' multiplicity relation is denoted to the edges whereas the '1' is omitted. The DTD tree can be easily constructed from a DTD, extracting the branching constraints as parent-child relations and converting multiplicity relations as follows: $1, ? \to 1$ and $+, * \to *$. Recall that a DTD is in general stricter than the corresponding DTD tree, since the DTD tree is a simplified model.

3.3 XML Data Model

XML data models can be distinguished by whether or not they support sibling order. Whereas, for content centric documents sibling order is considered to be important, we stick to unordered siblings as commonly expected in the context of data centric documents. XML data trees are simplified models for these data centric XML documents. They simplify the richness of XML syntax to labeled trees containing data. There are two commonly known data tree models for XML data. In contrast to a single node type model [20], we use a *leaf data tree model* that distinguishes between *data* and *navigation nodes*. Attributes and all elements being leaf nodes are represented as data nodes, whereas internal elements are represented as navigation nodes. Non-empty element nodes are split into a pair of nodes containing a navigation node and a data node.

The *leaf data tree* model represents an XML document as a set of tree-connected *element names* with attached *data values* in its leaf nodes. We next define the containment property, the three operations union, intersection and difference for leaf data trees and give a classification for such trees based on DTD trees.

Definition 3.3.1. An *XML leaf data tree (short LDT)* T (over alphabet Σ) is a triple (t, λ, υ), where:

(1) t is a finite rooted tree with navigation nodes $N_n(t) \in N$ and data nodes $N_d(t) \in N$,
(2) $\lambda: N_n(t) \cup N_d(t) \to \Sigma$ is the node labeling function and
(3) $\upsilon: N_d(t) \to Q$ is the value mapping, mapping a value to each node $\in N_d(t)$

Definition 3.3.2. An LDT T_1 $(t_1, \lambda_1, \upsilon_1)$ is *contained* in an LDT T (t, λ, υ) if

(1) t_1 is a subtree of t containing the root and
(2) $\lambda_1, \upsilon 1$ are the restrictions of λ, υ to the nodes of t_1.

The following two definitions are required for the formal definition of the difference operation in 3.3.5.

Definition 3.3.3. Whenever t is a finite rooted tree and $n \in t$ is a node in t, we use dln(n, t) as a shortcut for the *set of descendent leaf nodes* of n in t.

Definition 3.3.4. For two LDTs T' (t', λ', υ'), T'' (t'', λ'', υ'') where T' and T'' are both contained in a master LTD M (t_m, λ_m, υ_m), let N_{disp} (t_m, t', t'') be the *dispensable set of navigation nodes for a difference operation* of T' and T''. N_{disp} is defined as:

$$N_{disp}(t_m, t', t'') = \{n \in t_m \mid n \in N(t'), n \in N(t'') \text{ and } (dln(n, t') \subseteq dln(n, t''))\}.$$

Definition 3.3.5. The (a) *union (b) intersection (c) difference of two LDTs* T' (t', λ', υ'), T'' (t'', λ'', υ'') where T' and T'' are both contained in a master LTD M (t_m, λ_m, υ_m) is an LDT T (t, λ, υ), where:

(1) t is a subtree of t_m reduced to $N_n(t) \cup N_d(t)$ with

    (a) $N_n(t) = N_n(t') \cup N_n(t'')$ and $N_d(t) = N_d(t') \cup N_d(t'')$

    (b) $N_n(t) = N_n(t') \cap N_n(t'')$ and $N_d(t) = N_d(t') \cap N_d(t'')$

    (c) $N_n(t) = N_n(t') \setminus N_{disp}(t, t', t'')$ and $N_d(t) = N_d(t') \setminus N_d(t'')$

(2) λ is the restrictions of $\lambda' \cup \lambda''$ to the nodes of t.

(3) υ is the restrictions of $\upsilon' \cup \upsilon''$ to the nodes of t.

Notice that λ', λ'' and υ', υ'' map to identical values for nodes in $N_n(t') \cap N_n(t'')$ and $N_d(t') \cap N_d(t'')$ because T', T'' are both contained in M. Thus there is no conflict and the restriction is well defined.

Definition 3.3.6. An LTD T=(t, λ, υ) is *valid* according to a DTD tree D=(Σ, r, b), if the root of t is labeled r and if for each node $n \in t$ its branching constraint $b(\lambda(n)) = \{(e_1, m_1), \dots, (e_q, m_q)\}$ *holds*. The branching constraint for a node $n \in t$ holds, if n has only children with label e_i, $i \in \{1, .., q\}$ in t and for each $(e_i\ m_i)$ in $b(\lambda(n))$ with $m_i=1$, n has only one or zero child nodes c in t with label $\lambda(c) = e_i$.

Definition 3.3.7. The set of all LDTs, that are valid according to a given DTD tree D, is denoted by *valid(D)*.

3.4 ST-Patterns

Tree patterns are used in the context of XML as expressions that describe XML fragments (LTDs) of a master XML document. These patterns can be regarded as tree models for XML queries. Nodes of a pattern can be labeled with any tag name in Σ. To keep our model simple, we here withhold common abbreviations such as the wildcard '*' or the relative paths '//', used to express 'any label' and 'a node sequence of zero or more interconnected nodes'. The directed edges in XML patterns represent parent-child relations defined in the DTD.

In contrast to basic XML patterns [9], we are only interested in rooted patterns because they describe XML fragments that correspond to absolute XPath expressions.

Furthermore, we use the same terminology for patterns as used for XML documents. For example, we call all nodes that can be reached from a current node by outgoing edges, the node's *children*. The incoming edge of a current node starts from the node's *parent*, all children of a node are in *sibling relation*, and the transitive closure of all nodes reached by outgoing (incoming) edges is called the set of *descendent (ancestor)* nodes. We say that a pattern is formed of *pattern nodes* N_p, and we formally define:

Definition 3.4.1. A *simple root pattern* SRP = (t, λ, D) is a labeled tree under a DTD tree D=(Σ, r, b) where

(1) t is a rooted tree and N_p is the set of the nodes of t,
(2) λ associates with each $n_p \in N_p$ a node name in Σ
(3) sibling pattern nodes $n_p \in N_p$ in t must have distinct labels.

The nodes $n_p \in N_p$ are called *pattern nodes of SRP*.

ST-patterns are an extension of simple root pattern by additional nodes called *split nodes*. They form a simple intuitive query language for XML data that is sufficient for a wide range of applications. We don't want to present another query language for XML here, since XPath and XQuery are widely accepted standards. We formally introduce ST-patterns to provide a simple and flexible data representation model for fast intermediate XML data processing. See Figure 4 to 6 for example ST-patterns.

ST-patterns are associated to the DTD tree D=(Σ, r, b) of the master document they query. We again represent ST-patterns as trees, composed of *pattern nodes* and *split nodes*. As in simple root patterns, starting at the root, pattern nodes select nodes of an LDT by specifying node names for child nodes. We call a pattern node for which an equally labeled leaf node in D exists a *data node representative* and a pattern node for which an equally labeled inner node in D exists a *navigation node representative*.

Additionally, an ST-pattern can restrict the former selection by conditions on data values. Such conditions are expressed as membership of the data value in a certain interval I over Q and are represented as *split nodes*. We treat the equality relation as a special case where left- and right boundary of the interval have equal values. A special condition is the *remaining set,* meaning: 'any value in Q that is not specified by a given sibling split node's condition'. Combinations of disjunctions and conjunctions of split nodes are organized as *(sub-)decision trees*. Split nodes in a parent-child relation form conjunctions, whereas split nodes not being in a parent-child relation form disjunctions.

Split nodes are related to two nodes in the corresponding DTD tree which might have equally named corresponding nodes in the ST-pattern. See figure 5 for an example. The two related nodes are called *split parent* and *reference node* (short ref. node). The split parent always has a corresponding, equally labeled pattern node in the ST-pattern. It is the first pattern node on the split node's ancestor-axis. The corresponding node in the DTD tree is equally labeled and has a one-to-many multiplicity relation. This relation indicates that the sub-fragment rooted at the split parent is constrained by the split node. The ref. node points out the node values that are tested by the split node's interval condition. It must be a descendent leaf node of the split parent in the DTD tree. A pattern node corresponding to the ref. node might also be found in the ST-pattern, representing the selection of the constrained node. The path from split parent to ref. node in the DTD tree is stored together with the interval constraint in the split node of the ST-pattern. Formally we define an ST pattern as an extended root pattern.

Definition 3.4.2. Given a DTD tree D and an order O for D's leaf nodes, an *ST-pattern STP*=(t, λ, I, p, D, O) is a labeled tree where

(1) t is a rooted tree and $N = N_p \cup N_s$ is the set of nodes of t, $n_p \in N_p$ are called *pattern nodes*, $n_s \in N_s$ are called *split nodes*.
(2) λ associates with each node a node name in Σ.
- Sibling pattern nodes $n_p \in N_p$ in t must have distinct labels.
- Sibling split nodes $n_s \in N_s$ in t must have the same label.
(3) I associates to each split node an interval condition $[i_{left}, i_{right}]$ or the special condition *remaining set*.
- At most one node in each set of sibling split nodes can have the condition *remaining set*.
- Sibling split nodes n_s must not have overlapping intervals.
(4) p specifies a relative path identifying a dedicated ref. node for each split node.
Moreover, t is constrained by the following:
- the root must be a pattern node;
- Each split node n_s is either a child of another split node according to a predefined *ref. node order O*, or n_s is a child of a pattern node n_p, for which the following holds. Let n_{pp} be the first node on the ancestor axis of n_p in the pattern that is a pattern node. The node labeled $\lambda(n_{pp})$ in the corresponding DTD tree D has a branching constraint that contains a one-to-many multiplicity relation for $\lambda(n_s)$, i.e. $(\lambda(n_s),*)$.

3.5 Pattern Fragments: Answers to ST-Pattern

When we use the ST-pattern as a query on a master LDT M, the answer itself forms an LDT T' called *pattern fragment*. Before we formally define a pattern fragment, we introduce *mixed edges, split node sequences* and the *fulfillment* of a split node's condition.

Definition 3.5.1. A *mixed edge* in an ST-pattern P=(t, λ, I, p, D, O) is an edge {n_s, n_p} from a split node to a pattern node in t. We call all ancestor nodes, starting at n_p up to the first split parent, a *split node sequence*.

For example in Figure 5 the edge (year, year[2000,∞]) in the left pattern is a mixed edge indicating that all nodes with additional arrow reference form a the split node sequence of the split node labeled 'year[2000,∞]'.

Proposition 3.5.2. We observe that by definition a split node sequence is of the following form: n_{p1}, n_{s1} ... n_{sn}, n_{p2}, where the n_{si}, $i \in \{1,...,n\}$ are an arbitrary amount of split nodes, n_{p1} is a pattern node (the related split parent) and n_{p2} is the pattern node belonging to a mixed edge.

Like in database theory, we regard a given valid XML document X as an *interpretation* of the DTD tree D, that assigns the truth value `true` to every rooted path found in the XML document X and assigns the truth value false to every rooted path allowed by D but not found in X. Furthermore, the interpretation X maps a path from the document root to an attribute value v or to a text value v in X to the value v.

Definition 3.5.3. Let a given XML document X be an interpretation of a DTD tree D, let an ST-pattern P=(t, λ, I, p, D, O) describe an LTD T=(t', λ', υ') where t' is a subtree of X, let C be a condition of a split node n_s with a given split parent n_p in t. Let $p(n_p)$ be a path in t' that corresponds to the labels found on the path to n_p in t. Then we call C *fulfilled in t'*, if X maps the path $p(n_p)$ + '/' + λ (n_s) to a value v that is in the interval $i(n_s)$.

Definition 3.5.4. Given an ST-pattern P=(t, λ, I, p, D, O) for an LDT M=(t_m, $λ_m$, $υ_m$) corresponding to a DTD tree D. A *pattern fragment* (also called an answer to P) is an LTD T', created by the mapping from the nodes of t into the nodes of t_m such that:

(1) Each edge {n_1, n_2} between pattern nodes in t is mapped into an edge {m_1, m_2} of t_m, if λ(n_1)= $λ_m$ (m_1) and λ(n_2)= $λ_m$ (m_2) and n_1 has at least one descendent data node representative in P.
(2) Given a split node sequence n_{p1}, n_{s1} ... n_{sn}, n_{p2}, each mixed edge {n_s, n_{p2}} in t is mapped onto an edge {m_1, m_2} of t_m, if λ(n_{p1})= $λ_m$ (m_1) and λ(n_{p2})= $λ_m$ (m_2), if for each split node in the split node sequence the condition can be fulfilled in M.

Definition 3.5.5. Two pattern fragments that are contained in an LDT M *intersect*, if their ST-patterns map to some identical data nodes in T.

Corollary 3.5.6. *Properties of pattern fragments* T', T" contained in an LDT M
- T', T" have at least one overlapping navigation node in T (the root)
- T', T" might intersect.

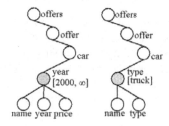

Fig. 4. Two ST-patterns: ST_1 and ST_2

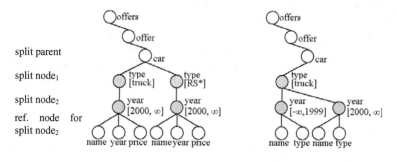

Fig. 5. The two ST-patterns of figure 4 expanded for the ref. nodes 'type' and 'year'

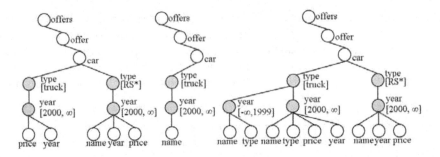

Fig. 6. The ST-patterns: difference(ST$_1$, ST$_2$), intersection(ST$_1$, ST$_2$), union(ST$_1$, ST$_2$)

4 Properties and Operations on ST-Patterns

In this paragraph, we introduce the three operations *union, intersection* and *difference,* mapping two given ST-patterns onto a resulting ST-pattern. Therefore, we firstly define *space equality* for ST-patterns and the two operations *compress* and *extend,* used to 'space equally' transform ST-patterns e.g. for normalization purposes.

Definition 4.0.1. Two ST-patterns are *space equal* for a given DTD tree D, if the pattern fragments T', T" they describe are identical for *any* T ε valid(D).

4.1 Expansion and Compression of ST-Patterns

Split nodes in an ST-pattern being siblings are called a *decision group*. For example, in Figure 5 the two split nodes being siblings with the intervals [-∞, 1999] and [2000, ∞] form a decision group. For simplicity, let's assume that the set Q of data values is the rational numbers. If the union of all intervals found in a decision group forms Q, as in the above example, the decision group is called *complete*. Thus, a decision group containing a split node with the special constraint *remaining set* is always complete.

Expansion adds additional split nodes underneath a split parent to the pattern, expanding the sub-decision trees for a specific ref. node. See Figure 5 for the expanded patterns of Figure 4.

Algorithm 4.1.1. (Expansion of an ST-Pattern)
Given (1) an ST-pattern P=(t, λ, i, p, D, O), (2) a split parent n_p ε t, (3) a ref. node n_r that is not used as a ref. node in t and that has a corresponding node in D that is both, labeled $\lambda(n_r)$ and descendent to the node labeled $\lambda(n_p)$ and (4) a decomposition of Q as a set of non-overlapping intervals I = {i_1, … , i_n} where the union of all elements of I forms Q, the *expansion* of an ST-pattern P' = (t, λ, i, p, D, O) can be constructed as follows:

```
01    for each edge (n₁, n₂) in t with p(n₁) < p(n_r) < p(n₂) according to the pre-defined
      ref. node order O, do the following in t {
02        t.edges.removeEdge(n₁, n₂) ;
03        for each interval i in I {
04            n_si = new splitNode (n_si.λ= λ(n_r), n_si.p= path(n_r), n_si.i = i_i) ;
```

```
05          t.nodes.addNode(n_si) ;
06          t.edges.addEdge(n_1, n_si) ;
07          n_si.append(descendentTree(n_2)) ;
08   }}
```

The algorithm of 4.1.1 can be extended for split parents n_p that are not in $N_p \cup N_s$ but in D and to ref. nodes n_r that are already used as ref. nodes in P. The reverse operation of an expansion is called a *compression* (both, the extended expansion and the compression is not shown in this paper). The following corollary holds for these extended conditions too.

Corollary 4.1.2. An expansion P' of an ST-pattern P for a given DTD tree is space equal to its origin P for any split parent in D, any allowed ref. node in D and any decomposition of Q.

We are now ready to define the three operations union, intersection and difference for ST-patterns.

Definition 4.1.3. The *(a) union (b) intersection (c) difference* of two ST-patterns P', P" for a given DTD tree D and DTD tree leaf order O, is an ST-pattern P, where the answer to P for *any* LTD M ∈ valid(D) is identical to the (a) union (b) intersection (c) difference of the answers of P' and P" for M.

Within the next Section we show how to compute the union, intersection and difference of two ST-patterns. We close this Section by defining the property of intersection for ST-patterns by their data node representatives.

Definition 4.1.4. Based on the intersection operation, we define two ST-patterns to *intersect*, if their intersection contains data node representatives. - If two ST-patterns do not intersect, we call them disjointed.

5   Evaluating ST-Patterns

After completely presenting our formal framework for ST-patterns, in section 3 and 4, we show in the following, how the operations for ST-patterns can be computed and present fast processable ST-pattern subclasses.

5.1   Node Matching for ST-Patterns

A classification for ST-patterns can be given by their ref. node sets and the ref. nodes predefined order.

Definition 5.1.1. The *ref. node set* of an ST-pattern P (t, λ, I, p, D, O) $RN_{SET}(P)$, is the set containing all node names of nodes in t referred to as ref. nodes.

Definition 5.1.2. Two ST-patterns P' = (t', λ', I', p', D', O'), P" = (t", λ", I", p", D", O") corresponding to the same DTD tree D' = D", are said to be *built on the same ref. node base* ($RN_{SET}(P')$, O'), if $RN_{SET}(P')=RN_{SET}(P")$ and the orders O' and O" order all pairs of elements of $RN_{SET}(P")$ in the same way.

Definition 5.1.3. The set of all ST-patterns built on the same ref. node base ($\{r_1, ...,$ $r_n\}$, O) for a given DTD D and is called *subclass($\{r_1, ..., r_n\}$, D, O)*.

Corollary 5.1.4. The set of ST-patterns under D and O, as well as subclass($\{r_1, ...,$ $r_n\}$, D, O) is closed under union, intersection, and difference.

In Section 6 we will discuss the runtime of ST-pattern processing. Therefore, we here shortly define the level distance as a further classification.

Definition 5.1.5. The *level distance* of a set of ST-patterns $ST_{SET} = \{P_1, ... , P_i\}$ corresponding to a DTD tree D is
$| \bigcup RN_{SET}(P_i)$ where $P_i \in ST_{SET} | - min (\{ (| RN_{SET}(P_i) |) | P_i \in ST_{SET}\})$

Corollary 5.1.6. Each set of ST-patterns ST_{SET} for a given DTD can be transformed by space equal expansions of ST_{SET} members, into a set ST'_{SET} that is in subclass($\{r_1,$ $..., r_n\}$, D, O) for $\{r_1, ..., r_n\} = \bigcup RN_{SET}(P_i)$ where $P_i \in ST_{SET}$.

5.2 Node Matching as Basic ST-Patterns Algorithm

Next, we shortly introduce node matching as a basic algorithm for ST-pattern operations. After showing how to process ST-patterns, we address the needed adjustments for the intersection operation in 5.3.

Definition 5.2.1. A *root path* rpath(n) of a node n, in an (ST-)pattern is the path containing all pattern nodes on the ancestor axis of n.

Definition 5.2.2. Given two ST-patterns $P' = (t', \lambda', I', p', D, O)$, $P'' = (t'', \lambda'', I'', p'', D,$ O) in subclass($\{r_1, ..., r_n\}$, D, O) for any $\{r_1, ..., r_n\}$, two nodes $n_1 \in t'$ and $n_2 \in t''$ are a *match*, if

1. their root paths are equal: $rpath(n_1) = rpath(n_2)$
2. their node names are equal: $\lambda(n_1) = \lambda(n_2)$
3. if n_1, n_2 are spit nodes:
    *   they refer to the same ref. node: $p(n_1) = p(n_2)$
    *   their interval conditions intersect: $I(n_1) \cap I(n_2) \neq \emptyset$

The node matching algorithm maps two given ST-patterns $P' (t', \lambda', I', p', D, O)$, $P'' (t'',$ $\lambda'', I'', p'', D, O)$ onto a resulting ST-pattern P. It starts at the root of both patterns and compares and tries to match equivalent nodes in each pattern by traversing both patterns in parallel. The algorithm is initiated with $n_1= root(t')$ and $n_2= root(t'')$.

Whenever a match is found, the pair's child nodes can be processed by an operation-dependent function calling e.g. Algorithm 5.3.1 or Algorithm 5.3.2.

Algorithm 5.2.3. Function Node Matching

```
01    ST-pattern nodeMatching (Operation oper, Node n₁, Node n₂) {
02        ST-pattern P = new ST-pattern(D, O) ; n = new Node() ;
03        case oper of
              intersect:     n = intersection(n₁, n₂) ;
```

```
            union:        n = union(n₁, n₂) ;
            difference:   n = difference(n₁, n₂) ;
         end case;
04       for each n₁.child() c₁ᵢ {
05          if (c₁ᵢ.isInMatch = (c₁ᵢ, c₂ᵢ)) then n.append( nodeMatching(oper, c₁ᵢ, c₂ᵢ));}
06       P.append (n) ;
07    return P ; }
```

To apply the node matching algorithm to any two ST-patterns corresponding to a given DTD tree, we need to adjust them to the same ref. node base. For example, if in ST_1 a split node referring to 'year' is found and no such node exists in ST_2, we expand ST_2 for the ref. node 'year'. As input for the expansion, we use the conditions found in ST_1 and add the *remaining set* condition to complete the decision group, if needed.

The needed adjustment can be seen as a preprocessing step. To keep the processing fast, this adjustment can be done on the fly in the matching process using no additional parsing runs. A drawback of expansion is in the possible exponential growth of the ST-pattern, because each expansion adds a level to the ST-pattern. Therefore, we will restrict ST-patterns in the following section, to keep the level distance minimal.

5.3 Processing of ST-Patterns

The processing of any two nodes compared in the matching algorithm depends on whether or not they are a match, and it follows operation-dependent tasks. We describe how to handle some operations next. For example, for the operator-patterns ST_1 and ST_2 of Figure 4, the expanded ST-patterns can be seen in Figure 5. Here, we identify the needed expansions for each ST-pattern, one for the ref. node 'type', the other for the ref. node 'year' and thus expand both initial patterns. The calculated result for the three discussed operations for ST-patterns is shown in Figure 6.

Given two ST-patterns P', P'' $\in$ subclass($\{r_1, ..., r_n\}$, D, O) for some r_i, D, O, the intersection operation on P', P'' defined in 4.1.3 can be computed using the node matching algorithm of 5.2.3 with the following function intersection.

Algorithm 5.3.1. Function **intersection**

```
01   Node intersection(Node n₁, Node n₂) {
02      Node n = new SplitNode( ) ; n.λ= λ(n₁) ; n.p= p(n₁) ; n.I = I(n₁) ∩ I(n₂) ;
03   return n ; }
```

Given two ST-patterns P', P'' $\in$ subclass($\{r_1, ..., r_n\}$, D, O) for some r_i, D, O, the union operation on P', P'' defined in 4.1.3 can be computed using the node matching algorithm of 5.2.3 with the following function union.

Algorithm 5.3.2. Function **union**

```
01   Node union(Node n₁, Node n₂) {
02      Node n = new Node ( ) ;
03      if (n₁ ,n₂) is a match of split nodes with Intervals I(n₁), I(n₂){
04         create the intervals I₁ = I(n₁) \ I(n₂), I₂ = I(n₂) \ I(n₁), I₃ = I₄ = I(n₁) ∩ I(n₂) ;
```

```
05      for each such not empty interval I_{i=1 to 4} do {
06          s_i = new SplitNode( ) ; s_i.λ= λ(n_1) ; s_i.p= p(n_1) ; s_i.I = I_i ; }
07      s_1.append(descendentTree(n_1)) ;  s_3.append(descendentTree(n_1)) ;
08      s_2.append(descendentTree(n_2)) ;  s_4.append(descendentTree(n_2)) ;
09      n.append(s_1) ;   n.append(s_2) ;
10      n.append (nodeMatching(union,s_3, s_4)) ; }
11  else{  //(n_1 ,n_2) is a match of pattern nodes
12      n = n_1;
13      for each child node c_i of n_1 in P' or n_2 in P" with c_i.isInMatch does not exist{
14              n.appendTree(c_i) ; }
15      for each child node c_i of n_1 in P' or n_2 in P" with c_i.isInMatch = (n'_{1i}, n'_{2i}) {
16              n.appendTree( nodeMatching(union,n'_{1i}, n'_{2i}) ) ; }}
17  return (n) ; }
```

Given two ST-patterns P', P" $\in$ subclass($\{r_1, ..., r_n\}$, D, O) for some r_i, D, O, the difference operation on P', P" defined in 4.1.3 can be computed similar to 5.3.2.

As the algorithms show, we mainly need one node matching run to calculate any of the three operations, visiting each node of P' and P" at maximum once. For the union and difference operations, recursive calls organize the correct splitting of matching split nodes with intersecting intervals into three nonintersecting intervals. This process can expand a sub-decision tree by the factor 3. Thus, an upper bound for the size of a union ST-pattern for two ST-patterns P', P" on the same expansion level as operands is $3*(max(|P'|, |P"|))$. An upper bound for the size of a difference ST-pattern is $3*|P'|$, for an intersection ST-pattern it is $min(|P'|, |P"|)$.

5.3.3. Proposition
Intersection, union and difference operations for ST-patterns P', P" on the same expansion level can be done in p-time and p-space.

6 Data Processing Based on ST-Patterns

As motivated in Section 2, we use ST-patterns to describe XML data fragments (pattern fragments) during data processing in our distributed system.

6.1 Choice of the ST-Pattern Set

We restrict participating clients to the use of a certain subset ST_{SET} of ST-patterns. This set must be chosen with care, taking into account the addressable granularity and the complexity of processing. In Definition 5.1.3 we introduce the class subclass($\{r_1, ..., r_n\}$, D, O) that is closed under union, intersection and difference. Any two ST-patterns in such a subclass have a level distance of 0, which guarantees fast processing in time and space. Such a subclass might be a good choice for ST_{SET}. As long as the level distance is kept small, any other choice will do, if the granularity is set up according to the application domain's need. The granularity of a subclass($\{r_1, ..., r_n\}$, D, O) can be adjusted by the right choice of the set of ref. nodes $\{r_1, ..., r_n\}$. Whereas the amount of ref. nodes is a degree for the granularity, the ref. nodes themselves specify the attribute values in the master document that are selection criteria. The order O is a weighting on these nodes. An access frequency analysis for queries can be used to identify the n most frequently constrained data node names in queries to set up a well adjusted ref. node set and order. The decomposition of Q for each node in the ref. node set is not discussed in this paper and left open as an individual degree.

This setup of ST_{SET} is even flexible in the context of focus changes. Recurrent access frequency analysis can update the set of ref. nodes by adding and deleting nodes or by changes in the node order O. Such updates can be easily applied to ST-patterns by expansion, compression or rearrangements in the ST-patterns' sub-decision trees. Alternatively, an expanded interim set ST_{SET}, including the old and new ST-pattern class can be used, accepting a temporary higher level distance. This will lead to a higher robustness, as the processing of requests which conform to both the old and new setup is still possible.

As a client wants to query XML data e.g. by an XPath query, this XPath query first has to be mapped on an ST-pattern in ST_{SET}. As the granularity of ST_{SET} is still restricted, this mapping will map the XPath query to an ST-pattern that might address a pattern fragment that is a superset of the fragment addressed by the XPath query. We call the difference between these two fragments the *mapping offset*. If ST_{SET} is set up with care, this mapping offset should be small or none for frequent queries and acceptable for infrequent queries.

6.2 Use of ST-Patterns in the Caching Scenario

In the distributed caching example, each participating client holds an ST-pattern expression ST_U, describing all available XML data in its cache. As a client wants to request data by an XPath expression, it first maps the XPath expression to an ST-pattern ST_{REQ} in ST_{SET} with minimal mapping offset. This can be done by querying a so called schema tree, that is extended for the given ST-pattern subclass with the XPath expression [1]. The client then calculates, whether its local cache contains any needed data by computing $ST_{LOCAL} = \text{intersect}(ST_{SET}, ST_U)$. If $ST_{LOCAL} \neq \emptyset$ it can send a reduced request $ST'_{REQ} = \text{difference}(ST_{REQ}, ST_{LOCAL})$ to a neighbour client. These steps can be accomplished by any participating client using a minimum of resources, because of two reasons. First, only small logical representatives for XML fragments are processed, and no 'physical data' is involved so far. Second, the involved operations generate only a small workload. As a participating client finds out that it can contribute to a request, it has to extract the partial result from its cache. This again can be done very fast, if the ST_U is used as an index tree for the cached data, especially for the intervals of sibling split nodes.

As partial fragments reach the requesting client, they have to be joined for further processing. Therefore, the XML data must support IDs for each node with a multiplicity constraint 'one-to-many'. Prepared like this, any two pattern fragments that are answers to ST-patterns can be joined on the deepest node with a multiplicity constraint 'one-to-many' in the intersection ST-pattern of the two patterns. Depending on the caching strategy, the client also might update its cache with the newly obtained data and update ST_U by $ST_U = \text{union}(ST_U, ST_{REQ})$.

6.3 Properties of Pattern Operations

ST-patterns are a light-weight solution for XML data processing, not only restricted to cache management. To summarize, evaluating operations on ST-patterns can be done by adapting basic XML match algorithms using a single parsing run. For the difference operation and the union operation, the generation of series of descendent split nodes can cause exponential expansion of sub-decision trees. This expansion can be prevented by keeping the level distance of the class of ST-patterns that is used minimal, for example by restricting the used ST-patterns to a specific ref. node set subclass of D and O.

Similar to the more complex XPath expressions, ST-patterns are used to select fragments of an underlying XML document and thereby address the document with a fine granularity, allowing conjunctions and disjunctions. For example, any ST-pattern can be split into two patterns, where each of the resulting patterns addresses a fragment with about half the size of the fragment the original patterns addressed. Thus, any fragmentation granularity can be achieved.

Patterns can be represented as short strings, e.g. in so called *numbering scheme representation form*. For example, the pattern ST_1 shown in Figure 4 can be encoded as the string 1,2,8,[2000,∞]10,9,10,11. Numbers in the string correspond to the document order position of a node in the DTD tree and act as the node's ID. Special notation must only be introduced for our extensions. The entry [2000, ∞]10 represents the interval of a split node that is related to the ref. node 10.

Moreover, ST-patterns enable us to virtually process any XML data for a given DTD by the operations union, intersection and difference, as long as we work on XML fragments (LTD trees) that can be expressed as ST-patterns.

7 Related Work

Tree patterns are well known in the context of XML data processing and are especially used to improve query response times. To search frequent XML tree patterns in XML documents [11] is a widely adapted technique and is used for various applications, ranging from indexing optimal access paths [3, 20, 14] to the formulation of various classes of XML queries [16, 13]. We follow these approaches, as we use frequent access tree patterns to achieve optimization goals. With the latter two approaches, we have in common to use tree patterns to specify subclasses of queries. Tree patterns represent the tree-structure of XML query languages like XPath [9] or XQuery [4]. In the context of querying and maintaining XML data, Abiteboul [15] shows a solution for representing and querying incomplete XML data. The presented incomplete data trees have similarities to our ST_U representations in each client, in that they use conditions on the elements' data values and that they are based on DTDs. Different to our approach, their incomplete tree focuses on missing data, whereas our approach argues on partially available data.

In comparison to all these approaches, we use tree patterns to identify sets of pattern fragments and include not only DTD restrictions but also constraints on selected data values. A caching strategy based on frequently accessed tree patterns is introduced in Yang [12]. We extend the approach of classical patterns presented in Yang [12] to ST-patterns including predicate filters, which enable us to express finer XML granularity. Our approach also differs in that we support cooperative caching by restricting the allowed ST-patterns to an easy to handle and resource preserving subclass ST_{SET}.

A different approach for XML caching is to check whether cached data can contribute to a new request by testing the intersection of cache entries and an XPath query [18] and thereafter compute difference fragments as partial results [19]. Such tests are known to be NP-hard for XPath expressions [10, 8] and difference computations are known to be resource consuming. In comparison, our approach focuses on efficient computation and thereby requires only minimal resource consumption.

8 Summary and Conclusions

We expect ST-pattern fragmentation to be a solution for splitting a huge XML document into handy atomic units to support fast data processing based on simple and fast intersection and containment decisions, e.g. in the area of caching, replication or query processing.

The drawback of using normalized data units is a clipping offset caused by answering a request by a slightly bigger superset. This is acceptable, since frequent requests can be answered with minimal or no clipping offset based on a well adjusted restriction to a subclass of ST-patterns.

Especially in the area of mobile data processing, it is important to minimize communication costs and to preserve the mobile client's resources. Besides communication resources, we keep shared CPU resources to a minimum because costly intersection or containment tests are reduced to fast operations on simple logical expressions. In the context of collaborative data processing, it is important that participating clients interact and interchange data based on a set of predefined data units. Otherwise, advantages of collaboration will be consumed by adjusting and comparing (slightly) different data objects.

[1] describes a continuative approach using an ST-pattern's partitioning, that is restricted to a set of not intersecting ST-patterns. Currently, we implement a mobile peer-to-peer approach which will use ST-pattern caching for any data exchange. In our further research, we address the challenge of segmentation adaptation and update propagation for the overall system. Adapting ST-patterns towards dependent patterns, not containing the decision criteria, and distributed query processing [21, 2] based on ST-patterns, seem to be further promising steps.

As far as we know, we are the first to expand tree patterns for XML using additional selection criteria at the node level containing conjunctions and disjunctions to support fine granularity.

We use these ST-patterns to model virtual schema expansion. Our solution is especially tailored to adapt to continuous context switches in query behavior, supporting e.g. a fine granularity in hot spot areas.

References

1. Adelhard Türling, Stefan Böttcher: Finite segmentation for XML caching, IFIP TC8 Working Conference on Mobile Information Systems (MOBIS), Oslo, Norway, 2004.
2. Alan Halverson, Josef Burger, Leonidas Galanis, Ameet Kini, Rajasekar Krishnamurthy, Ajith Nagaraja Rao, Feng Tian, Stratis Viglas, Yuan Wang, Jeffrey F. Naughton, David J. DeWitt: Mixed Mode XML Query Processing. VLDB, Berlin, Germany, 2003, pages 225-236.
3. Chin-Wan Chung, Jun-Ki Min, Kyuseok Shim: APEX: an adaptive path index for XML data. SIGMOD 2002, pages 121-132.
4. D. Chamberlin, D. Florescu, J. Robie, J. Simon, and M. Stefanescu. XQuery: A Query Language for XML W3C working draft, 2001.
5. Douglas B. Terry, Venugopalan Ramasubramanian: Caching XML Web Services for Mobility. Journal ACM Queue 1, 3/2003.
6. Franky Lam, Nicole Lam, Raymond K. Wong: Efficient synchronization for mobile XML data. CIKM 2002: 153-160.
7. Georg Gottlob, Christoph Koch, Reinhard Pichler: XPath Query Evaluation: Improving Time and Space Efficiency. ICDE, Bangalore, India, 2003, pages 379-390.
8. Georg Gottlob, Christoph Koch, Reinhard Pichler: The complexity of XPath query evaluation. PODS, San Diego, California, 2003, pages 179-190.
9. J. Clark and S. DeRose. XML Path Language (XPath) version 1.0 W3C recommendation, 1999.
10. Jan Hidders: Satisfiability of XPath Expressions. DBPL, Potsdam, Germany, 2003, pages 21-36.
11. L. H. Yang, M. L. Lee, W. Hsu. Mining Frequent Query Patterns in XML. 8th Int. Conference on Database Systems for Advanced Applications (DASFAA), 2003.
12. Liang Huai Yang, Mong-Li Lee, Wynne Hsu: Efficient Mining of XML Query Patterns for Caching. VLDB, Berlin, Germany, 2003, pages 69-80.
13. Nicolas Bruno, Nick Koudas, Divesh Srivastava: Holistic twig joins: optimal XML pattern matching. SIGMOD 2002, pages 310-321.
14. Raghav Kaushik, Philip Bohannon, Jeffrey F. Naughton, Henry F. Korth: Covering indexes for branching path queries. SIGMOD 2002, pages 133-144.
15. Serge Abiteboul, Luc Segoufin, Victor Vianu: Representing and Querying XML with Incomplete Information. PODS, Santa Barbara, California, 2001.
16. Shurug Al-Khalifa, H. V. Jagadish, Jignesh M. Patel, Yuqing Wu, Nick Koudas, Divesh Srivastava: Structural Joins: A Primitive for Efficient XML Query Pattern Matching. ICDE, San Jose, 2002.
17. Stefan Böttcher, Adelhard Türling: XML Fragment Caching for Small Mobile Internet Devices. Web, Web-Services, and Database Systems, NODe 2002 Web and Database-Related, booktitle: Web, Web-Services, and Database Systems, Erfurt, Germany, pages 268-279.
18. S. Böttcher: Testing Intersection of XPath Expressions under DTDs. International Database Engineering & Applications Symposium. Coimbra, Portugal, July 2004.
19. S. Böttcher, Adelhard Türling: Caching XML Data for Mobile Web Clients. International Conference on Internet Computing, IC'04, Las Vegas, USA, 2004.
20. Torsten Grust: Accelerating XPath location steps. SIGMOD 2002, pages 109-120.
21. Yanlei Diao, Michael J. Franklin: Query Processing for High-Volume XML Message Brokering. VLDB, Berlin, Germany, 2003, pages 261-272.

Dissemination of Spatial-Temporal Information in Mobile Networks with Hotspots[1]

Ouri Wolfson, Bo Xu, and Huabei Yin

Department of Computer Science, University of Illinois at Chicago
{wolfson, boxu, hyin}@cs.uic.edu

Abstract. In this paper we examine the dissemination of reports about resources in mobile networks with hotspots, where hotspots, vehicles and sensors communicate with each other via short-range wireless transmission. Each disseminated report represents information about a spatial-temporal event, such as the availability of a parking slot at a particular time or the detection of an injured in an earthquake damaged building. We propose an opportunistic dissemination paradigm, in which a moving object transmits the reports it carries to encountered peers and obtains new reports in exchange. We address two issues in such an environment. First, we develop an architecture that allows a moving object to receive resource reports opportunistically. Second, we study how the received reports are used by a consumer to reduce resource discovery time. The proposed system has the potential to create a completely new information marketplace.

1 Introduction

Consider an urban area with hundreds of thousands of vehicles. Drivers and passengers in these vehicles are interested in information relevant to their trip. For example, a driver would like his/her vehicle to continuously display on a map, at any time, the available parking spaces around the current location of the vehicle. Or, the driver may be interested in the traffic conditions (e.g. average speed) one mile ahead. Such information is important for drivers to optimize their travel, to alleviate traffic congestion, or to avoid wasteful driving. The challenge is processing queries in this highly mobile environment, with an acceptable delay, overhead and accuracy. One approach to solving this problem is maintaining a distributed database stored at fixed sites that is updated and queried by the moving vehicles via the infrastructure wireless networks. Potential drawbacks of this approach are (i) the responses to queries may be outdated, (ii) the response time may not meet the real-time requirements, and (iii) access to infrastructure communication service is costly, (iv) currently there is no business model to provide a return-on-investment for setting up and operating the fixed sites, and (v) the solution is not robust; particularly, it is vulnerable to failures of the fixed servers. In this paper we explore a new paradigm that is based on peer-to-peer communications.

---

[1] Research supported by NSF Grants 0326284, 0330342, ITR-0086144, and 0209190.

W.S. Ng et al. (Eds.): DBISP2P 2004, LNCS 3367, pp. 185–199, 2005.

We assume that each moving object (e.g. vehicle) has processing power (see [14]), and the capability of communicating with its neighbors. This communication can be enabled by a local area wireless protocol such as IEEE 802.11 [8], Ultra Wide Band (UWB) [22], or CALM [6]. These protocols provide broadband (typically tens of Mbps) but short-range (typically 50-100 meters) peer-to-peer communication. These communication capabilities exist already in experimental projects [23, 2] and are being planned for deployment on a large scale environment [9]. Similar communication capabilities are being planned between sensors in the infrastructure and moving vehicles [9]. With such communication mechanisms, a moving object receives the desired information from its neighbors, or from remote objects by multi-hop transmission relayed by intermediate moving objects. Thus, resource dissemination is performed in a *mobile peer-to-peer network.*

Compared to the traditional fixed-site based information query, this paradigm ("of the vehicles, by the vehicles, for the vehicles") has the following advantages. First, it provides better information authenticity, accuracy, and reliability, especially for real-time information. Consider for example parking space availability. Information collected from a vehicle that is leaving a parking slot tends to be more reliable than that from the fixed site. Second, it is free of charge, assuming that vehicles are willing to relay messages for free (in exchange for their messages being relayed). A back of the envelope calculation reveals that the cost (in terms of fuel) of communicating with encountered vehicles is less than a cent per day, even if the communication is continuous throughout the day.

The mobile peer-to-peer approach can also be used in matching resource producers and consumers among pedestrians. For example, an individual wishing to sell a pair of tickets for an event (e.g. ball game, concert), may use this approach right before the event, at the event site, to propagate the resource information. For another example, the approach can be used in singles matchmaking; when two singles whose profiles match are in close geographic proximity, then one can call the other's cell phone and suggest a short face-to-face meeting.

The approach can also be used for emergency response and disaster recovery, in order to match specific needs with expertise (e.g. burn victim and dermatologist) or to locate injured. For example, scientists are developing cockroach-sized robots that are able to search victims in exploded or earthquake-damaged buildings [18]. These robots are equipped with radio transmitters. When a robot discovers a victim, it can use the mobile peer-to-peer approach to disseminate the discovery, and home in on the target far more quickly than searchers using more conventional means. Thus we use the term moving objects to refer to all, vehicles, pedestrians, and robots.

We would like to comment at this moment that in our model a peer does not have to be a moving object. In many cases there are both moving peers and fixed peers, and they collaborate in data dissemination. For example, a sensor in the parking slot (or the meter for the slot) monitors the slot, and, while unoccupied, transmits the availability information to vehicles nearby. Or all the slots in a parking lot may transmit the information to a fixed 802.11 hotspot via a wired network, and the hotspot announces the information. In either case, the vehicles that receive the information may propagate it to a wider area via the mobile peer-to-peer approach. In such an environment the mobile peer-to-peer network serves as a supplement/extension to the fixed-site based solution.

In this paper we propose to examine an *opportunistic* approach to dissemination of reports regarding availability of resources (parking slot, taxi-cab customer, dermatologist, etc.). In this approach, an object propagates the reports it carries to encountered objects, and obtains new reports in exchange. For example, an object finds out about available parking spaces from other objects. These spaces may either have been vacated by these encountered objects or these objects have obtained this information from other previously encountered ones. Thus the parking space information transitively spreads out across objects. Similarly, information about an accident or a taxi cab customer is propagated transitively. In this paper we explore this information propagation paradigm, which we call *opportunistic peer-to-peer* (or OP2P).

In this paper, we will study how a resource consumer should use the received reports to discover a resource type. This is important when the resource can only be exclusively used by one object at one time. Consider for example a driver who is looking for a parking slot. The driver may receive reports of multiple parking slots, and these parking slots may be in different orientation with regard to the driver's current location. Then the question is which parking slot the driver should go to (namely, pursue). In this paper we propose an information usage strategy called *Information Guided Searching* (or IGS), that takes both the distance and the age of the resource report into considerations. With IGS, a consumer chooses resource-reports based on a spatial-temporal relevance function that represents the likelihood that the resource is available when the consumer reaches it. The consumer always pursues the resource whose relevance is the highest and is above a certain threshold. We experimentally compare IGS with the naive strategy where the information is not used, in terms of resource discovery time, namely the length of the period of time starting when the consumer starts to look for a resource type until the consumer captures a resource. The experiments show that IGS always results in reduced discovery time compared to blind search (i.e. the information is not used). In some cases IGS cuts discovery time by more than 75%.

In summary, this paper makes the following contributions. First, we introduce a data model for spatio-temporal resources in applications related to transportation, disaster recovery, and mobile electronic commerce, and we develop an architecture for opportunistic dissemination of information about these resources. Second, we propose an information usage strategy and compare it with the naive strategy for resource discovery. We show that the information usage strategy is consistently better than the naive strategy and may cut discovery time by more than 75%.

Let us emphasize that although the experiments conducted in this paper use the peer-to-peer model, the developed resource data model and the information usage strategy hold in a cellular wireless communication environment as well. These approaches are applicable to applications that need match making based on attributes, regardless whether the resource information is received from a peer or from a server through the cellular infrastructure.

The rest of the paper is organized as follows. Section 2 develops the architecture. Section 3 discusses the information usage strategy and evaluates the benefit of resource information. Section 4 discusses relevant work. Section 5 concludes the paper and discusses future work.

2 System Architecture

2.1 Resource Model

In our system, resources may be spatial, temporal, or spatio-temporal. Information about the location of a gas station is a spatial resource. Information about the price of a stock on 11/12/03 at 2pm is temporal. There are various types of spatio-temporal resources, including parking slots, car accidents (reports about such resources provide traffic-jam information), taxi-cab requests, ride-sharing invitations, demands of expertise in disaster situations, and so on. Formally in our model there are N *resource types* $T_1, T_2, ..., T_N$. At any point in time there are M *resources* $R_1, R_2, ..., R_M$, where each resource belongs to a resource type. Each resource pertains to a particular point location and a particular time point, e.g. a parking slot that is available at a certain time, a cab request at a street intersection, invitation of cab-sharing from airport to downtown from a passenger wishing to split the cost of the cab, or the demand of certain expertise at a certain location at a certain time. We assume that resources are located at points in two-dimensional geospace. The location of the resource is referred to as the *home* of the resource. For example, the home of an available parking space is the location of the space, and the home of a cab request or a cab-sharing invitation is the location of the customer. For each resource there is a *valid duration*. For example, the valid duration of the cab request resource is the time period since the request is issued, until the request is satisfied or canceled. The valid duration of the cab-sharing invitation starts when the invitation is announced and ends when an agreement is reached between the invitation initiator and another passenger. The valid duration of an accident starts when it occurs, and lasts until it is cleaned up. The valid duration of a victim-assistance-request starts when the person is injured, and lasts until a rescuer reaches him/her. We say that a resource is *valid* during its valid duration.

Let us comment further about spatial resources, such as gas stations, ATM machines, etc. In these cases the valid duration is infinite. Opportunistic dissemination of reports about such resources is an alternative paradigm to geographic web searching (see e.g. [13]). Geographic web searching has generated a lot of interest since many search-engine queries pertain to a geographic area, e.g. find the Italian restaurants in the town of Highland Park. Thus instead of putting up a web site to be searched geographically, an Italian restaurant may decide to put a short-range transmitter and advertise via opportunistic dissemination. In mobile systems, this also solves some privacy concerns that arise when a user asks for the closest restaurant or gas station. Traditionally, the user would have had to provide her location to the cellular provider; but she does not need to do so in our scheme. In our scheme, the transmission between two vehicles can be totally anonymous.

2.2 Peers and Validity Reports

The system consists of two types of peers, namely fixed hotspots and moving objects. Each peer o (either hotspot or moving object) that senses the validity of resources produces *validity reports*. Denote by $a(R)$ a report for a resource R. For each resource R there is a single peer o that produces validity reports, called the *report producer* for R. o is referred to as the *producer* of each report it produces. A peer may be the report producer for multiple resources. Report $a(R)$ contains the home of R and a *timestamp*.

The timestamp is the time at which the report is transmitted to a peer by its producer. Report $a(R)$ is *valid* as long as R is valid. For each resource type T, a peer o has a *validity reports database*, or *reports database*.

In the parking slots example, a sensor in the parking slot (or the meter for the slot) monitors the slot, and, when the slot becomes free, it produces a validity report. When the parking slot is occupied, the report is removed from the reports database. In the cab request example, the customer who needs a cab may click an application icon on her PDA, or press a button in a station at the closest intersection (similar to road-crossing buttons in the USA). The PDA or the station produces a report that indicates the location of the customer. The report is removed from the reports database once the customer takes a cab (this can be sensed, for example, by the cab sending a notification to the station). In the car accident example, the report is produced by the sensor that deploys the air-bag.

At any point in time, the reports database for a resource type in a peer o stores two categories of validity reports. The first category are the reports produced by o for resources that are currently valid. These are referred to as the *native reports* of o. The second group are the reports received by o from other peers (when and how the reports are received is discussed in 2.3). These are referred to as the *foreign reports* of o. A native report $a(R)$ is inserted into the reports database once it is produced, and it is deleted from the reports database when R becomes invalid. For example, if the meter for a parking slot is also a hotspot (i.e. a peer), then its reports about the monitored parking slot are native, and other reports are foreign. If a hotspot monitors all the parking slots in a lot, then all the reports about these slots are native.

2.3 Relevance Model

With OP2P, a peer constantly receives validity reports from the peers it encounters. If not controlled, the number of reports saved and communicated by a peer may continuously increase. In order to limit the data exchange volume, we employ a relevance function that prioritizes the availability reports. The relevance of a report a(R) to a peer o, the *consumer*, is determined by a spatio-temporal function, which decreases as the distance of the reported resource from o and the time elapsed from report-generation increase. In this paper we use the following relevance function:

$$\text{Rel}(a(R)) = e^{-\alpha \cdot t - \beta \cdot d} \quad (\alpha, \beta \geq 0) \tag{1}$$

where t is the number of time units since $a(R)$ is transmitted by its producer, and d is the travel distance from the home-location of R to the consumer. α and β are non-negative constants that represent the decay factors of time and distance respectively. α and β may vary per resource type and per each individual peer. Observe that this function is always positive, indicating that each report always has some relevance, and it decreases as t and d increase.

Let us consider *competitive* resources, i.e. resources that require a consumer to physically reach them ahead of other consumers in order to occupy or possess them (e.g. parking slots, cab requests, or highway assistance requests). Accident reports may inform many consumers of the accident, thus they are not competitive. We now show that for a competitive resource R, under some conditions the relevance of a report $a(R)$ equals to the probability that R is valid when the consumer reaches it.

Theorem: Assume that the length of the valid duration (see subsection 2.1) of R is a random variable with an exponential distribution having mean u. Assume further that the speed of the consumer is v. If $\alpha = 1/u$ and $\beta = 1/(u \cdot v)$, then the relevance of a report $a(R)$ is the probability (at report acquisition time) that the resource R is valid when the consumer reaches R. $\square$

Proof idea: Consider a consumer that receives a(R) t time units after the report has been transmitted by the producer of a(R), and at that time the consumer is at distance d from R. If $\alpha = 1/u$ and $\beta = 1/(u \cdot v)$, then the relevance of the report is:

$$\text{Rel}(R) = e^{-\frac{1}{u} \cdot (t + \frac{d}{v})} \qquad (2)$$

For an exponential distribution, the probability that R is still valid b time units after a validity report is transmitted is $e^{-b/u}$. Observe that the consumer will reach the resource t+d/v time units after the validity report has been transmitted, thus the theorem follows. $\square$

The theorem motivates our definition of the relevance function (at least for resources with exponentially distributed valid-duration).

Observe that we implicitly made two assumptions in order to determine d and t. The first assumption is that each consumer knows its location when receiving $a(R)$, so d can be computed. The second assumption is that the clock between the report producer and the consumer is synchronized, so t can be accurately computed. Both assumptions can be satisfied if each peer is equipped with a GPS that reports both location and time.

The relevance function we use in this paper is one example in which the relevance decays exponentially per time and distance. But there are other possible types of relevance functions in which other behaviors may be exhibited. Furthermore, other factors such as the travel direction with respect to the home of a resource may be considered in the relevance function. However, in this paper we confine ourselves to time and distance alone.

2.4 Peer-to-Peer Report Exchange

Each peer is capable of communicating with the neighboring peers within a maximum of a few hundred meters. One example is an 802.11 hotspot or a PDA with Bluetooth support. The underlying communication module provides a mechanism to resolve interference and conflicts. Each peer is also capable of discovering peers that enter into or leave out of its transmission range. For example, in 802.11 a node detects appearance and leaving of neighboring nodes via periodical beacon messages [8].

The user of a peer specifies to the communication module what types of validity reports she is interested in exchanging. And for each such type, the user further specifies the maximum number of reports she wishes to receive during an exchange. This number is referred to as the *interest threshold* and is denoted by M. When two peers A and B encounter each other, if both A and B have their communication module open, then A and B start a session to exchange validity reports. During each encounter, for each resource type T that B is interested in, A computes the relevance of each report a(R) in its reports database. If a(R) is a native report, then A updates the timestamp of a(R) to be the current time before computing the relevance of a(R). Finally, A chooses the top M relevant reports and transmits them to B. Upon receiving each report a(R), B checks whether there is a report a(R)' in its reports database that reports R. If not, B saves a(R). Otherwise, B saves a(R) if the timestamp of a(R) is greater than that of a(R)', and discards a(R) otherwise.

We would like to emphasize that in our model, the interactions among peers are completely self-organized. The association between a pair of peers is established when they encounter each other and is ended when they finish the trading or when they are out of the transmission range of each other. Other than this there is no other procedure for a peer to join or leave the network.

3 Benefit of Report Dissemination

In this section we evaluate how much a consumer gains when searching for a resource using the validity reports it receives, compared to not using the resource information. Specifically, we evaluate how much time is saved when a consumer uses validity reports to capture a resource. First we describe two strategies for a consumer to discover resources, one using validity reports and the other which does not do so. Then we compare these two strategies.

3.1 Resource Discovery Strategies

The first resource discovery strategy is a naive one, called *blind search*, or BS. With this strategy, a consumer moves around the area where a resource of interest could possibly be located, and it takes possession of the first resource that is valid at the time when the consumer reaches it. For example, a driver who is looking for a parking slot simply drives around all the streets that are within walking distance from the place to visit and parks at the first parking slot that is seen available. The area within which the consumer looks for a resource is referred to as the *search space*.

The second strategy is *information guided search*, or IGS. With this strategy, a consumer starts with a blind search, and a relevance threshold H_0. The search continues until either a resource is valid at the time the consumer reaches it, or some validity report $a(R)$ is received. In the latter case, the consumer evaluates the relevance of $a(R)$ and goes to R (i.e. attempts to capture R) if the relevance of $a(R)$ (i.e. Rel($a(R)$)) is higher than the predefined threshold H_0. If R is invalid when the consumer reaches it, then the consumer discards $a(R)$, returns to the closest point in the search space, and continues the blind search. Clearly, if a valid resource is passed by on the way to R, then the consumer captures it and the search ends. If another report $a(R')$ is received during the trip to R, and the relevance of $a(R')$ (i.e. Rel($a(R')$)) is higher than Rel($a(R)$), then the consumer goes to R' and sets the relevance threshold to Rel($a(R')$). Thus the relevance threshold keeps increasing while the consumer receives more relevant reports.

Our concept of the relevance threshold is used to alleviate the phenomenon of herding, which occurs when the consumers that hear about the same resource all head to that resource, leading to high contention. The relevance threshold prevents all, but the most likely to capture it, from pursuing the resource. In subsection 3.2 we will provide an approach to determining the threshold H_0.

3.2 Comparison of Resource Discovery Strategies

In this subsection we compare IGS and BS in terms of how long it takes a consumer to discover a resource, with each one of them. First we define the performance measure, and then we describe the simulation method. Finally we present the simulation results.

3.2.1 Definition of Discovery Time

For a competitive resource, discovery means that the moving object captures the resource, i.e. it arrives to the resource while the resource is still valid. For example, discovering a parking slot means that the driver reaches the parking slot before it is occupied; discovering a cab customer resource means that the cab driver reaches the customer before the customer hires another cab; The *discovery time* is the length of the time period starting when the user starts to search the resource type, and ending when a resource of that type is captured.

3.2.2 Simulation Method

We synthetically generated and moved objects within a 1mile×1mile grid network. The distance between two neighboring grid points is 0.1 mile (approximately the length of one street block). Hotspots are placed on intersections (see Fig. 1). There is only one consumer in the system. The search space of the consumer is a square centered at the center of the grid network and with side length 0.6 mile. This square is referred to as the *search square*. All the other moving objects participate in opportunistic data dissemination but are not interested in capturing any resource. These objects are referred to as *brokers*.

For each broker i, we randomly chose two points on the grid network, and assigned them as the start point and the first stop of i respectively. The path of i is the shortest path between the start point and the first stop. i moves along its path from the start point to the first stop at a constant speed. When the first stop is reached, another random point is chosen as the second stop of i, and i moves from the first stop to the

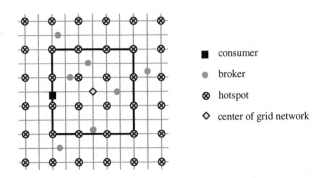

Fig. 1. The grid network, hotspots, search square, brokers and the consumer

second stop at the same constant speed. And so on. The motion speed of a broker is randomly chosen from the interval $[v-5, v+5]$ where v is a parameter.

Resources are generated only at hotspots. At each hotspot, the length of the valid duration of a resource follows an exponential distribution with mean 30 seconds, and the time length of the invalid duration follows an exponential distribution with mean $30 \times k$ seconds. k is a parameter. It represents the ratio between the length of time a resource is invalid, and the length of time it is valid. We use this ratio to model the competition for the resource generated by other consumers, and refer to this ratio as the *invalidity-to-validity ratio*. In other words, instead of simulating multiple consumers competing for resources, we simulate a single consumer; but each resource is valid for only 30 seconds approximately, and $30 \times k$ seconds it is unavailable.

Each hotspot announces exactly one resource, and the home of that resource is the location of the hotspot. The transmission range is the same for all the hotspots and all the moving objects. We use Equation (2) defined in section 2.3 as the relevance function and use the *route-distance* as the distance metric. The *route-distance* between two locations on the grid network is the length in miles of the shortest path between them on the grid network.

In each exchange a peer acquires the single most relevant report.

There are six parameters for each simulation run (see Table 1). Among these parameters, the transmission range r, the motion speed v, the broker density g, the hotspot density s, and the invalidity-to-validity ratio k are referred to as *environmental parameters* since they define the environment with respect to communication, traffic and resource generation. The relevance threshold is not an environmental parameter.

Table 1. Parameters and their values

Parameter	Symbol	Unit	Value
Transmission range	r	meter	50, 100, 150, 200
Motion speed	v	miles/hour	10, 20, 30, 40, 50, 60
Broker density	g	brokers/mile^2	0, 50, 100, 150, 200
Invalidity-to-validity ratio	k		10, 20, 30, 40, 50
Relevance threshold	H_0		0, 0.1, 0.2, 0.3, 0.4, 0.5, 0.6, 0.7, 0.8, 0.9
Hotspot density	s	hotspots/mile^2	17, 36, 100

If the hotspot density is 100, then there is a hotspot at each intersection. If the hotspot density is 36, then there is a hotspot for every two intersections, i.e. the distance between any two neighboring hotspots is 0.2 miles. If the hotspot density is 17, then there is a hotspot for every three intersections, i.e. the distance between any two neighboring hotspots is 0.3 miles.

Each simulation run is executed as follows. At the beginning of the simulation run, g brokers are generated and they start to move at the same time (time 0). Resources are generated and the initial state of each resource is either valid or invalid with the probability of being valid $1/(k+1)$. When two peers are with the transmission range, they exchange reports. Each exchange completes instantaneously, i.e. it takes time 0. At the 500-th simulated second, the consumer is introduced at a random point along the search square and its initial moving direction is either clockwise or counter-clockwise with equal probability. The consumer moves at the constant speed v. The consumer looks for resources using the search square as the search space. The simulation run terminates when the consumer successfully captures a resource. The length of the time period since the consumer is introduced up to the end of the simulation run is the discovery time of that run.

For each set of parameters, we ran 1000 simulation runs and averaged the discovery times of each simulation run. The average discovery time is the discovery time for that set of parameters.

3.2.3 Simulation Results

The results show that IGS consistently outperforms BS. In some cases the discovery time of IGS is less than one-fourth that of BS. This indicates that the validity reports help shortening the discovery time dramatically.

Relevance threshold. Fig. 2 shows how the discovery time of IGS changes per the relevance threshold H_0. From the figure it can be seen that IGS has the best performance (i.e. the minimum discovery time) when $H_0=0.1$. Above 0.1, the discovery time of IGS increases as H_0 increases. This is because as the relevance threshold increases, the consumer uses fewer reports. This means that even reports with a low relevance are better than no reports at all. IGS is equivalent to BS when $H_0=1.0$, because in this case IGS degenerates to BS (both strategies capture the resource only when the consumer is at the resource). Let us point out that the optimal relevance threshold varies depending on the environmental parameters. However, our simulations provide an approach to determining the optimal H_0 given the environmental parameters.

We identified the optimal H_0 for each set of environmental parameters. We found that in all the cases the optimal H_0 varies within a small range from 0.0 to 0.2. In many cases the optimal H_0 is 0.0. Even when the optimal H_0 is not 0.0, the discovery time obtained with the optimal H_0 is very close to that obtained with $H_0=0.0$. This is because, during the consumer's trip to the reported resource, it has the same chance of capturing a valid resource as if it uses the BS strategy. Thus going to a reported resource can only decrease but not increase the discovery time, regardless of the report relevance. Note that H_0 is the threshold for the first candidate resource that the consumer attempts to capture. However, it does not necessarily indicate the relevance (of the report) of the resource that is eventually captured.

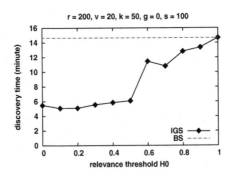

Fig. 2. Discovery time versus initial relevance threshold H_0

From now on throughout the rest of this section, when we present the performance of IGS, we use the discovery time that is obtained with the optimal H_0.

Impact of broker density and transmission range. The discovery time of IGS decreases as the transmission range increases, and as the broker density increases (Fig. 3 and Fig. 4). Intuitively, as the values of these two parameters increase, the interactions among peers become more frequent, and thus the newly generated reports get propagated more quickly and reach the consumer sooner. These reports have higher relevance and therefore give the consumer a higher probability of capturing a resource. The fact that the discovery time decreases as the broker density increases indicates the effect of peer-to-peer interactions on speeding up information propagation. Note that the discovery time of BS is not affected by the transmission range and the broker density.

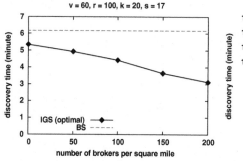
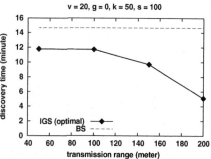

Fig. 3. Discovery time versus broker density

Fig. 4. Discovery time versus transmission range

Impact of invalidity-to-validity ratio. Fig. 5 shows the discovery time of IGS and that of BS as functions of the invalidity-to-validity ratio. It can be seen that the discovery time of IGS and that of BS both increase as the invalidity-to-validity ratio increases, which is natural. However, the discovery time of IGS increases with a lower rate than that of BS. This suggests that IGS is particularly useful in an environment where the competition for the resources is high.

Hotspots density. Fig. 6 shows the discovery time of IGS and that of BS as functions of the hotspot density. It can be seen that the discovery time of IGS and that of BS both decrease as the hotspot density increases. This is because in our simulation resources are generated only at hotspots. So with a lower hotspot density, fewer valid resources exist in the system at a time. Further observe that the difference between IGS and BS does not change per hotspot density. This suggests that the hotspot density has little impact on the advantage of IGS over BS.

Motion speed. Fig. 7 shows the discovery time of IGS and that of BS as functions of the motion speed of the consumer. The discovery time of IGS and that of BS both decrease as the motion speed increases. This is clearly due to the fact that a higher motion speed gives the consumer a better chance to reach a valid resource before the resource is re-captured. Further observe that the ratio between the discovery time of

IGS and that of BS decreases as the motion speed increases. This suggests that IGS is particularly suitable for a higher speed environment.

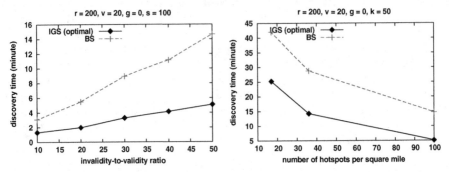

Fig. 5. Discovery time versus invalidity-to-validity ratio

Fig. 6. Discovery time versus hotspot density

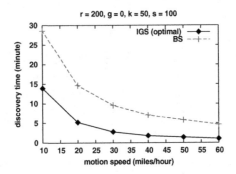

Fig. 7. Discovery time versus motion speed

4 Relevant Work

Different resource discovery architectures (SLP [4], Jini [12], Salutation [7], and UpnP [21]) have been developed for ubiquitous computing environments over the last few years. Typically these architectures consist of a dedicated directory agent that stores information about different services or data, a set of protocols that allow resource providers to find a directory agent and to register with it, and a naming convention for resources. In highly mobile environments, due to high variability of the network topology we cannot rely on any one component being always available. Therefore, it is important to develop methods that use opportunistic exchanges rather than a dedicated directory.

Peer-to-peer networks [10, 15] and architectures [16] have all been studied in previous works. There are two major differences between our model and traditional peer-to-peer approach. First, in our environment the participating parties are physically mobile, and sometimes can be highly mobile (consider vehicles that move in opposite directions at 120 miles/hour relative speed). The object density can vary in a big range from rush hours to midnight. The underlying communication network is thus subject to topology changes and disconnections. In such an environment a moving object does not necessarily always have neighboring objects to communicate with, and even if it does, the set of the neighbors is not fixed. Furthermore, there does not always exist a communication path between a pair of peers. These characteristics defeat the applicability of typical peer-to-peer frameworks that rely on peers to forward queries (e.g. Gnutella [3], DHTs like [20]). Second, in our environment information sharing is opportunistic. Pre-defined data access structures such as search routing tables used in Gridella [1] are impractical in mobile ad hoc networks. They are replaced by opportunistic peer-to-peer interactions.

A lot of work has been done on data dissemination in mobile environments (e.g. [17, 19, 11, 5]). However, all this work considers regular data items but not spatial-temporal ones. So the benefit of data dissemination is measured differently than here. In the existing work, the benefit of data dissemination is usually measured by the level of the consistency between the disseminated copies and the master copy. It does not consider how the data is used. In our work we use the spatio-temporal relevance function to express the utility of data (loosely speaking, to measure the consistency), and we analyze how the information is used, and what benefit in terms of time-saving it provides.

Goel et al [27] study the dissemination of traffic-speed information in both peer-to-peer and infrastructure environments, and evaluates the benefit of traffic-speed information in terms of travel time reduced compared to if information is not used. However, the approach considers only non-competitive resources (traffic-speeds) whereas we consider both non-competitive resources and competitive resources in our model, and we evaluate the benefit of competitive resources. Moreover, they do not discuss information prioritization of reports in terms of their relevance.

Finally, this paper differs from our prior work [24, 25, 26] in multiple aspects. The model is more general in the sense that it allows resources to be advertised by the stationary hotspots in addition to moving objects (in [24] resources are advertised by moving objects only). The hotspots not only announce reports but also exchange reports with moving objects. In other words, hotspots announce resources other than their own (in [25] hotspots only announce resources they produce). The information usage is new, and the evaluation of the benefit of information is also new ([25] also evaluates benefit but using a much simpler simulation model and it does not discusses information usage).

5   Conclusion

In this paper we devised an architecture and a data model for dissemination of spatial and temporal resource-information in a mobile peer-to-peer communication environment, in which the database is distributed among the hotspots and moving objects. We analyzed IGS, the information guided resource discovery strategy, and determined that IGS reduces search time compared to blind search, and by how much. We also determined how the time savings varies as a function of the environmental parameters, such as the number of brokers, the competition for resources reflected in the valid/invalid time ratio, the speed of the moving objects, the number of hotspots producing resources, and the transmission range.

In general, we feel that the P2P paradigm is a tidal wave that has tremendous potential, as Napster and Gnutella have already demonstrated for entertainment resources. Mobile P2P is the next step, and it will revolutionize dissemination of spatial and temporal resources. For example, location based services have been considered a hot topic for quite some time, and it has been assumed that they have to be provided by a separate commercial entity such as the cellular service providers. The approach outlined in this paper can provide an alternative that bypasses the commercial entity. Although in this paper we used traffic examples, as mentioned in the introduction, the applications range from social networks to disaster recovery to mobile electronic commerce.

In terms of future work, much remains to be done. For example, incentive mechanisms need to be developed to stimulate peers to participate as suppliers of resource information and/or intermediaries for information propagation. Strategies that best utilize the received information need to be investigated in a realistic traffic and resource operation environment. Other forms of interactions, e.g. peer-to-peer broadcast rather than pair-wise exchange, are also worth studying. In this paper, we assumed a memory-less probabilistic distribution for the valid-time of a resource. We will examine with other distributions such as a normal distribution.

Acknowledgements: We thank Aris Ouksel for helpful discussions.

References

1. Karl Aberer, Manfred Hauswirth, Magdalena Punceva, Roman Schmidt. Improving Data Access in P2P Systems, *IEEE Internet Computing*, 6(1), January/February 2002.
2. CarTalk. http://www.cartalk2000.net/
3. Gnutella website. http://gnutella.wego.com
4. E. Guttman, C. Perkins, J. Veizades, M. Day, Service Location Protocol, Version 2. *RFC2608*, June 1999. http://www.ietf.org/rfc/rfc2608.txt
5. H. Hayashi, T. Hara, and S. Nishio. *Cache Invalidation for Updated Data in Ad Hoc Networks*. Proc. Int'l Conf. on Cooperative Information Systems (CoopIS'03), 2003.
6. http://www.etsi.org/etsi_radar/cooking/rub11/transport_a.htm
7. http://www.salutation.org/
8. IEEE Computer Society. *Wireless LAN Medium Access Control (MAC) and Physical Layer (PHY) Specifications*. 1997.
9. Intelligent Safety Efforts in America. http://www.its.dot.gov/speeches/madridvii2003.ppt
10. V. Kalogeraki, A. Delis, D. Gunopulos: Peer-to-Peer Architectures for Scalable, Efficient and Reliable Media Services. IPDPS 2003.
11. G. Karumanchi, S. Muralidharan, and R. Prakash. Information Dissemination in Partitionable Mobile Ad Hoc Networks. *Proc. Symposium on Reliable Distributed Systems* (SRDS'99), pp.4-13, 1999.
12. W. Keith Edwards, *Core JINI*, Prentice Hall, 1999.
13. A. Markowetz, et al. Exploiting the Internet As a Geospatial Database, *International Workshop on Next Generation Geospatial Information*, 2003.
14. New Microsoft Goal: A computer in every car. http://www.usatoday.com/tech/news/2003-12-01-ms-cars_x.htm

15. W.S. Ng, B. C. Ooi, K.L. Tan, A. Zhou. PeerDB: A P2P-based System for Distributed Data Sharing. International Conference on Data Engineering (ICDE'2003), Bangalore, 2003.

16. M. Papazoglou, B. Krämer, J. Yang. Leveraging Web-Services and Peer-to-Peer Networks. In *Proceedings of* CAiSE 2003, June, 2003.

17. M. Papadopouli and H. Schulzrinne. Effects of Power Conservation, Wireless Coverage and Cooperation on Data Dissemination Among Mobile Devices. *MobiHoc 2001*, October 4-5, 2001, Long Beach, California.

18. Robo-rescuers increase disaster victims' chances.
http://firechief.com/ar/firefighting_roborescuers_increase_disaster/

19. K. Rothermel, C. Becker, and J. Hahner. Consistent Update Diffusion in Mobile Ad Hoc Networks. *Technical Report 2002/04*, Computer Science Department, University of Stuttgart, 2002.

20. Stoica, R. Morris, D. Karger, M. Kaashoek, and H. Balakrishnan. Chord: A Scalable Peer-to-Peer Lookup Service for Internet Applications. In *Procs. ACM SIGCOMM*, 2001.

21. Universal Plug-and-Play (UPnP) Forum, *Microsoft Corporation*.http://www.upnp.org.

22. Ultra-wideband (UWB). http://www.ubisense.net/technology/uwb.html

23. E. Welsh, P. Murphy, P. Frantz. A Mobile Testbed for GPS-Based ITS/IVC and Ad Hoc Routing Experimentation. *International Symposium on Wireless Personal Multimedia Communications* (WPMC), Honolulu, HI, Oct. 2002.

24. B. Xu, A. Ouksel, O. Wolfson, Opportunistic Resource Exchange in Inter-vehicle Ad Hoc Networks, *Proc. of 2004 IEEE International Conference on Mobile Data Management*, Berkeley, California, Jan. 2004.

25. O. Wolfson, B. Xu, P. Sistla. An Economic Model for Resource Exchange in Mobile Peer-to-Peer Networks. *Proceedings of the 16th International Conference on Scientific and Statistical Database Management* (SSDBM'04), Santorini Island, Greece, June 2004.

26. O. Wolfson, B. Xu. Opportunistic Dissemination of Spatio-Temporal Resource Information in Mobile Peer-to-Peer Networks. Accepted, to appear in *1st International Workshop on P2P Data Management, Security and Trust (PDMST'04)*, Zaragoza, Spain, Sept. 2004.

27. S. Goel, T. Imielinski, K. Ozbay, and B. Nath, Grassroots: A Scalable and Robust Information Architecture. *Technical Report DCS-TR-523*, Department of Computer Science, Rutgers University, June 2003. http://paul.rutgers.edu/~gsamir

Wayfinder: Navigating and Sharing Information in a Decentralized World

Christopher Peery, Francisco Matias Cuenca-Acuna,
Richard P. Martin, and Thu D. Nguyen

Department of Computer Science, Rutgers University, Piscataway, NJ 08854
{peery, mcuenca, rmartin, tdnguyen}@cs.rutgers.edu

Abstract. Social networks offering unprecedented content sharing are rapidly developing over the Internet. Unfortunately, it is often difficult to both locate and manage content in these networks, particularly when they are implemented on current peer-to-peer technologies. In this paper, we describe Wayfinder, a peer-to-peer file system that targets the needs of medium-sized content sharing communities. Wayfinder seeks to advance the state-of-the-art by providing three synergistic abstractions: a global namespace that is uniformly accessible across connected and disconnected operation, content-based queries that can be persistently embedded into the global namespace, and automatic availability management. Interestingly, Wayfinder achieves much of its functionality through the use of a peer-to-peer indexed data storage system called PlanetP: essentially, Wayfinder constructs the global namespace, locates specific files, and performs content searches by posing appropriate queries to PlanetP. We describe this query-based design and present preliminary performance measurements of a prototype implementation.

1 Introduction

Social networks offering unprecedented content sharing such as Gnutella, KaZaA, and DMOZ are rapidly developing over the Internet. Unfortunately, locating specific information in these networks can often be frustrating, particularly when they are implemented using current peer-to-peer (P2P) technologies. For example, the Direct Connect system (http://www.neo-modus.com) used by a local file sharing community allows the browsing of each individual node's shared content but does not support a global browsable namespace. Consequently, over 25TB of data is completely fragmented across more than 8000 individual listings without any way for the users to collaboratively organized this shared information. To exacerbate the problem, content search is quite primitive, content ranking is not supported, and it is impossible to reason about data availability because of extensive disconnected operation[1]. This state-of-the-art is common to other P2P systems such as KaZaA (http://www.kazaa.com) and eMule (http://www.emule-project.net).

Managing shared content is also difficult, particularly when users participate in multiple networks, as users must manually track content replicas across multiple publishing infrastructures and their local writable storage systems. This problem is further exacerbated as users increasingly depend on multiple devices such as PCs, laptops, and PDAs,

---

[1] Consistent with [2, 24], traces show that most users connect for less than a few hours a day.

W.S. Ng et al. (Eds.): DBISP2P 2004, LNCS 3367, pp. 200–214, 2005.

some of which may frequently change their connectivity and bandwidth status, requiring explicit reasoning about the impact of disconnected operation.

In this paper, we present Wayfinder, a novel P2P file system that seeks to address the above limitations by presenting three synergistic abstractions: a global namespace that is uniformly accessible across connected and disconnected operation, content-based queries that can be persistently embedded into the global namespace, and automatic availability management. We choose to build around a file system paradigm for wide accessibility: data stored in files are easily accessible through a wide range of applications, including simple utilities such as `cat`, `grep`, and `awk`. Given this central paradigm, the three abstractions then serve to unify the fragmented views of data spread across multiple users and their devices, providing device-independent name *and* content addressing that naturally encompasses disconnected operation. Underneath the global data view, Wayfinder automatically manages the replication and placement of data to achieve specified availability targets.

In the remainder of this section, we describe the three abstractions mentioned above in more details. In the body of the paper, we describe Wayfinder's design and a prototype implementation; in particular, a key aspect of Wayfinder's design is that its abstractions are all implemented as queries against meta-data stored in an underlying P2P indexed storage layer called PlanetP [7]. Thus, we briefly describe PlanetP, how Wayfinder leverages PlanetP's indexing capabilities and query language to implement its exported abstractions, and how Wayfinder uses a light-weight distributed hash table (DHT) as a caching infrastructure to make its query-based design efficient. Finally, we close with some thoughts on the benefits that can be derived from enhancing PlanetP's query language, particularly as shared content are increasingly structured via XML.

Global Namespace. Wayfinder constructs its global namespace by overlaying the local namespaces of individual nodes within a sharing community as shown in Figure 1. Each node's local namespace is called its *hoard* and consists of a directory structure and files stored in a local persistent storage system. The community may, at any point, split into multiple connected subsets, each with its own shared namespace, and later rejoin to recreate the entire global namespace. In essence, Wayfinder presents a shared view of all data stored across any set of connected nodes that expands and contracts smoothly on node arrival and departure.

Wayfinder adopts the above merging approach as opposed to today's mounting approach because it provides three important advantages. First, it provides users with a consistent browsing experience similar to the web but avoids the binding of names to specific devices. In particular, it allows any user to contribute content to any portion of the namespace by binding files to appropriate names within the local namespace of any of his devices; indeed, a user can modify any portion of the namespace by modifying, adding, and deleting files and directories provided that they have the necessary rights to do so[2]. This makes it possible for any Wayfinder community to collaboratively organize shared information in a manner similar to the web-based DMOZ project (http://dmoz.org).

---

[2] Wayfinder implements a security model that allows a community to control write access to files and directories. A discussion of this model is beyond the scope of this paper, however. We refer the interested reader to [19].

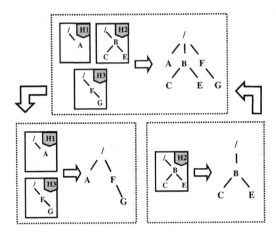

Fig. 1. Wayfinder dynamically constructs a shared namespace across any set of connected devices by merging their local hoards. This figure shows 3 nodes originally being connected so that the shared namespace is the merged view of hoards H1 through H3. When the community is partitioned into 2 connected subsets, Wayfinder maintains a merged view for each subset. When the subsets reconnect, Wayfinder dynamically re-merges the shared namespace

Second, it reduces the data management overheads by removing the need for users to explicitly reason about what replica resides on which device. As shall be seen, when a user accesses a file, Wayfinder will locate the latest version of that file within the connected community. Wayfinder also detects and automatically resolves conflicts that arise because of changes made during disconnected or partitioned operation. Wayfinder maintains sufficient information for users to manually resolve these conflicts if the automatic resolution is semantically incorrect.

Finally, a merging approach naturally encompasses partitioned and disconnected operation as shown in Figure 1. At the extreme, disconnected operation simply means that the namespace will include only the local hoard; thus, while the amount of accessible content may change, the manner in which users browse the namespace and access files does not.

Semantic Directories. A key lesson from the web is that successful management and sharing of large volumes of data require both *browsing*, i.e., name addressing, and *content search*, i.e., content addressing. To date, however, browsing and content search have typically been viewed as two separate approaches for locating and organizing information. Wayfinder seeks to integrate these two approaches through the implementation of semantic directories [11, 12], which are search queries that are embedded into the persistent file system namespace.

Semantic directories provide a powerful organizational paradigm because they allow users to create a persistent namespace that automatically binds content to multiple browsing paths. For example, a file discussing content search in P2P file systems might be found through two completely different pathnames, with one leading to a query for "content search" and the other to a query for "P2P file systems," *without requiring users to explicitly create these name bindings.* While individual users can of course pose either of these queries independent of the namespace, devising "good" queries is often a difficult art. In our lab, we often share good web queries with each other; e.g., "look this up using the following query." Embedding queries into the namespace will allow users to easily preserve and share good queries. Users will also benefit from each other' fine-tuning of search results; for example, each addition of a file that is relevant to but does not match a query benefits the next user that browses the semantic directory looking for relevant information.

As shall be seen, semantic directories are periodically reevaluated to reflect changes in the shared data collection, thus turning the file system namespace into an *active* organizational tool. Further, similar to the HAC file system [12], Wayfinder allows users to explicitly fine-tune the content of a semantic directory rather than having to manipulate the query until it returns the exact set of desired files. Finally, Wayfinder implements an approximation of the TFxIDF vector space ranking algorithm so that files inside a semantic directory can be ordered based on their relevance to the directory's query.

Automatic Availability Management. Providing high data availability is a fundamental aspect of a file system. Achieving high availability in P2P systems, however, can be quite difficult because of the extensive disconnection already mentioned. Wayfinder addresses this problem by automatically replicating data to achieve explicitly specified availability targets. Wayfinder continuously monitors and predicts the availability of nodes in a sharing community in order to make replication and placement decisions. In addition, we are exploring a novel user-centric availability model that addresses the combined problem of hoarding, that is, ensuring the presence of data on a specific device for disconnected operation, and availability, which is typically defined as the probability of successful access when connected to a server. Our ultimate goal is to support a unified metric where a file is available if it can be accessed, regardless of the accessing device's connectivity state. Wayfinder seeks to provide high user-centric availability, which works together with the dynamic global namespace to remove the need for users to explicitly reason about what replica resides on which device across connected and disconnected operations. This aspect of Wayfinder is still at the exploratory stage, however, and so will not be described further in this paper.

Design and Implementation Status. Wayfinder stores each node's hoard in the node's local file system and stores its meta-data in PlanetP, which is a P2P indexed data storage layer that supports a simple boolean query language for data retrieval. Wayfinder then uniformly constructs its file system namespace, locates specific files, and performs content searches by posing appropriate queries to PlanetP.

We have implemented a Wayfinder prototype that is sufficiently complete to support the transparent execution of common applications such as cvs, emacs, latex, gv, etc. on Linux. Currently, Wayfinder targets medium size communities of hundreds to several thousands of users as the common unit of social interaction. A good example of such a social group is the local P2P network already mentioned above that is comprised of several thousand students sharing approximately 25TB of data. Sharing within our laboratory (and department) is another example environment where we are deploying and using Wayfinder.

Our Contributions Include:

- The design and preliminary evaluation of a P2P file system that unifies name and content addressing in the context of a global browsable and writable namespace. Critically, our system supports content addressing and ranking without requiring any centralized indexing.
- The unification of two recent paradigms for building robust decentralized systems, distributed hash tables (DHT) [26] and replication using gossiping, to build a robust and efficient P2P file system.

2   Background: PlanetP

We begin by briefly describing PlanetP since Wayfinder uses it as a distributed data store for its meta-data. PlanetP is a toolkit that provides three building blocks for the construction of robust, medium-scale P2P applications: a gossiping module [7,9], an indexed storage system and distributed query processing engine, and a lightweight active DHT. PlanetP's indexed storage system stores information as bindings of the form $\{k_1, k_2, ..., k_n\} \rightarrow o$, where k_i is a text key, o is an arbitrary object, and we say that $keys(o) = \{k_1, k_2, ..., k_n\}$. Stored objects are retrieved by specifying queries comprised of text keys combined using three operators, *and* ($\wedge$), *or* ($\vee$), and *without* ($-$). For example, a query ("cat" $\wedge$ "dog" $-$ "bird") would retrieve the set $\{o \mid (\{cat, dog\} \subseteq keys(o)) \wedge (\{bird\} \nsubseteq keys(o))\}$.

When a binding $\{k_1, k_2, ..., k_n\} \rightarrow o$ is inserted into PlanetP[3] at a particular node, PlanetP stores o in a persistent store local to that node, e.g., a BerkeleyDB database [25], and $k_1, k_2, ..., k_n$ in a two-level index. The top level of this two-level structure is a globally replicated key-to-node index, where a mapping $k \rightarrow n$ is in the index if and only if at least one binding $\{..., k, ...\} \rightarrow o$ has been inserted at node n. The second level is comprised of a set of *local* indexes, one per node, which maintains the key-to-object mappings for all bindings inserted at each node. The global index is currently implemented as a set of Bloom filters [4], one per participating node, and is loosely synchronized over time using the gossiping module [7].

To evaluate a query posed at some node n, PlanetP uses n's replica of the global index to identify target nodes that may contain relevant bindings. Then, PlanetP can either forward the query to all targets for exhaustive retrieval or to only a subset of targets that are likely to contain the most relevant objects. Contacted target nodes evaluate the query against their local indexes and return URLs and relevance rankings for matching objects to n. PlanetP's relevance ranking is computed using an approximation of the text-based TFxIDF vector space ranking algorithm [6].

To complement the gossip-based persistent indexed store, PlanetP also implements an active unreliable DHT. This DHT is active in that stored objects can execute on the hosting nodes but unreliable in that it may loose objects arbitrarily because nodes may leave (fail) without redistributing their portions of the DHT. There are two main

---

[3] We often refer to the indexed data store as just PlanetP when the reference is clear within the surrounding context.

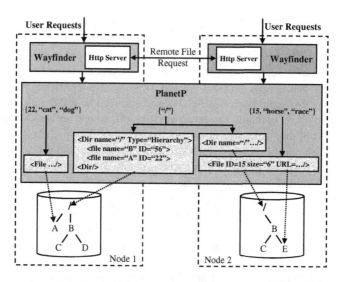

Fig. 2. An overview of Wayfinder's architecture. Solid arrows inside PlanetP indicate bindings of keys to waynodes while dashed lines indicate implicit bindings of waynodes to file/directory replicas. Note that only a few waynodes are shown for clarity

expected use of this DHT: weak serialization of potentially conflicting operations and caching of *soft* state such as those reconstructible from data in the indexed store to enhance performance.

We have shown that PlanetP's content ranking algorithm can achieve similar accuracy to a centralized implementation of TFxIDF [6]. In addition, PlanetP is extremely robust, even for highly volatile communities, and currently scales well to thousands of nodes [7] (hence the "medium-scale" label).

3   Files and Directories

We now describe how Wayfinder implements files and directories. As already mentioned, Wayfinder stores each node's hoard in the node's local file system and stores its meta-data in PlanetP (Figure 2). More specifically, each hoard is a sub-directory comprised of a portion of the files in the global namespace and the corresponding directory structure. Each file and directory can have many replicas across the community, with each replica described by a small data structure called a *waynode*. The set of all waynodes comprises Wayfinder's meta-data and is stored in PlanetP, where each waynode is bound to a set of content keys and a unique file or directory ID key. Wayfinder then constructs the global namespace, locates individual files, and performs content searches by posing appropriate queries to PlanetP. To make this query-based design efficient, Wayfinder caches query results in PlanetP's DHT. As shall be seen, Wayfinder only caches *soft state*, which can be arbitrarily lost at any point in time without affecting its correctness.

Files. Each Wayfinder file is identified by a unique identifier while each replica is described by a waynode. Each waynode contains a file ID, a version, a content hash, and a URL indicating where the replica can be retrieved. Each waynode is stored in Plan-etP, bounded to the replica's file ID and keys extracted from the replica's content. Each replica of a file */path/name* is stored at *path/name* in some hoard.

More specifically, suppose that the hoard of a node n is stored at */WFRoot* in n's local file system. When a file */path/f* is opened, Wayfinder first retrieves f's ID from the meta-data associated with */path* (see below) and queries PlanetP for all the waynodes of all replicas of f to compute the latest version and where replicas or diffs can be retrieved. To avoid this expensive operation in the future, Wayfinder caches the result in the DHT. Cache entries are active objects that can receive and process information about updates and so can persist in the cache indefinitely; in our current implementa-tion, they are discarded after not having been accessed within some threshold period of time.

Then, if n does not have a local replica of f, Wayfinder retrieves a copy, stores it at */WFRoot/path/f*, and creates a new waynode for this replica and inserts it into PlanetP. The new waynode contains the same file ID and version number but has a new URL pointing to n's hoard. On the other hand, if n has an old version, Wayfinder updates the local copy to the latest version and updates the waynode to the new version number. Finally, Wayfinder completes the open on the local replica. Creation works similar to open except that Wayfinder generates a new file ID for the newly created file.

If f was opened for write, on closing, Wayfinder increments the replica's version number (in the waynode) and updates the meta-data object cached in the DHT for f if one exists. Wayfinder also computes a diff that contains all changes since the open and stores it in */WFRoot/path* together with f. (Of course, diffs are hidden from the user's view of the directory in the global namespace.) Diffs allow nodes to update replicas of large files without downloading the entire file. Diffs also allow Wayfinder to unroll changes as necessary to resolve write conflicts (see Section 4). Finally, Wayfinder schedules the file to be indexed in the background; if the file has already been indexed in the past, then Wayfinder can do an incremental index using just the diff. Once the index is completed, Wayfinder rebinds the waynode to the extracted content keys.

Directories. When a user opens or creates a file */path/f* at a node n, Wayfinder creates the directory *path* in n's hoard if it does not already exist. Thus, directories are replicated across nodes' hoards as well, although as shall be seen, they are only partially replicated. Directories are uniquely identified by their pathnames since directories with the same name are merged in the global view.

Each directory replica is represented by a waynode that stores all the name-to-replica bindings in the *local* hoard. That is, if a directory *path* in n's hoard contains two files, f_1 and f_2, then the waynode for */path* would contain two bindings, one binding the name f_1 to f_1's ID and one binding f_2 to f_2's ID. Each directory waynode w is inserted into PlanetP as a binding $\{"/path"\} \rightarrow w$. Then, to construct a global view of a directory */path* (for example, when the user does an *ls*), Wayfinder retrieves all waynodes bound to the key "/path" and merges their content.

We also cache directory views for efficiency. Similar to our caching of file meta-data, we choose to continuously update cached directory views; thus, whenever a node adds or deletes a file, if a view of the file's parent directory exists in the cache, then it updates the cache view to reflect the operation.

Semantic Directories. A semantic directory is one whose name maps to a content query [11]. In Wayfinder, mkdir creates a semantic directory if the first character of the name is a "$". Currently, a semantic directory's name just consists of a sequence of space-separated terms that are combined using the "and" operator to form the query. Each semantic directory has a set of attributes that can optionally be set to direct the ranking and display of matching files.

On creation, a semantic directory is populated with files within its scope that matches the directory's query. A file is defined to match a query if the keys that its waynodes, i.e., the waynodes of the replicas with the latest version, are bound to satisfy the query. Depending on its attributes, a semantic directory can be populated with all matching files or only a subset of highly ranked files. Wayfinder periodically reevaluates each semantic directory's query to refresh its content; the reevaluation period is a user-specifiable attribute of the directory.

When a user creates a semantic directory $/a/b$, if a is a regular directory, then the user has a choice of populating b with matching files from the entire file system (global scope) or only files contained in a (parent scope). If a is a semantic directory, however, then only parent scoping is allowed. Thus, a chain of three semantic directories $b/c/d$ would give three sets of files equivalent to the queries b, $b \wedge c$, and $b \wedge c \wedge d$.

Similar to [12], Wayfinder's semantic directories can be directly manipulated by users. That is, users can add files to or remove files from a semantic directory just like a normal directory. Files explicitly removed by a user are never brought back by a reevaluation although they can be added back explicitly. Likewise explicitly added files are never removed by reevaluation, even if their content do not match the directory's query.

Semantic directories are implemented as follows. When a node accesses a semantic directory, a replica is created in its hoard along with a waynode. The waynode is used to record explicit user manipulations of the semantic directory at that node, i.e., additions and deletions. On (re)evaluation, Wayfinder poses the directory's query to PlanetP and retrieves all waynodes that matches the query. Wayfinder also gathers all waynodes describing replicas of the directory. It then modifies the set of matching file by the union of the actions contains in the directory waynodes. Actions are ordered using logical timestamps; conflicting operations are resolved conservatively, favoring addition over deletion.

The result of the above evaluation is cached in memory until the next evaluation. When a file inside a semantic directory is accessed, a copy of it is downloaded to the hoard just as for a normal directory. If that file is later accessed through another pathname, or if a local replica already exists, Wayfinder only keeps one copy in the hoard and uses hard links to support accesses through the different pathnames.

4   Consistency

Wayfinder exports a weak consistency model similar to that of Bayou [20] for both directories and files to support partitioned operation—recall that Wayfinder continues to operate even when the sharing community is splintered into several disconnected parts. In this section, we describe this consistency model and its implications for users.

Files. Recall that when a user attempts to access a file f at some node n, n simply opens the latest version of f that it can find. This essentially implements a "single copy, any version availability" model [13]. Under partitioned operation, this model can lead to users seeing stale data and conflicting non-concurrent writes because of incomplete hoarding within n's partition or recent writes outside of n's partition. (Note that these problems can arise even when the entire community is connected: when cached entries in the DHT are lost, gossiping delays may give rise to inconsistent views of the global index, which in turn may lead to inconsistent actions. These inconsistencies are subsumed by those arising from partitioned operation, however, and so are dealt with similarly.)

The above inconsistencies are *inherent* to any system that supports partitioned operation. Wayfinder's replication approach (not described here) reduces the probability of accessing stale data. To address write conflicts, Wayfinder maintains a version vector in each waynode, where a new version extends the vector with a monotonically increasing number and the ID (a hash of a public key) of the writer. Then, when Wayfinder detects write conflicts, it imposes an arbitrary but deterministic and globally consistent ordering on the changes. This allows nodes to resolve conflicts without the need to reach a communal consensus.

For example, suppose Wayfinder detects two waynodes for the same file with conflicting versions $[(x,1)(y,2)]$ and $[(x,1)(z,2)]$. Further suppose that $y < z$ according to their integer values. Wayfinder would then apply the diff between $[(x,1)]$ and $[(x,1)(z,2)]$ to $[(x,1)(y,2)]$ to get the version $[(x,1)(y,2)(z,2)]$. To address the cases when this resolution is semantically incorrect—although often, similar to CVS conflict resolution, this automatic resolution may be correct—Wayfinder allows users to manually merge diffs to create a new, semantically correct version. Continuing the example, Wayfinder allows a user to create a new version $[(x,1)(y,2)(z,2)(u,3)]$ by providing the $[(x,1)]$ version using diff rollback and the two conflicting diffs.

Directories. Wayfinder also supports a "single copy availability" model for directory accesses. Suppose a user at some node n attempts to access a directory */path/dir*. This access will succeed if any node in n's partition has a replica of */path/dir*. For similar reasons as above, this model can cause users to not see bindings that actually exist, see bindings that have been deleted, and create conflicting bindings. Since replicating files involve replicating their ancestor directories, our replication approach also reduces the probability of incomplete views. To resolve conflicting bindings when creating a directory view, Wayfinder renames the bindings in the DHT cache entry and notes this rebinding. When a user attempts to access a file through the renamed binding, Wayfinder notifies the user of the conflict so that a permanent rebinding can be affected.

To delete a binding */path/f*, Wayfinder unlinks *path/f* in the local hoard, removes f from the cached entry of */path* in the DHT, and publishes a delete notification to PlanetP. Whenever a node accesses */path*, it will see the delete and remove its own local replica if it has one. Each node also periodically looks for delete notices and removes any corresponding local replicas. Delete notifications are discarded after an expiration period currently set to four weeks. Thus, it is possible for a node that was offline for longer than this period to bring back a copy of a deleted file when it comes back on-line.

Table 1. Results of the Modified Andrew Benchmark using the Linux NFS, original JNFSD and the JNFSD linked with Wayfinder running in isolation and connected to a large community of nodes

Modified Andrew Benchmark				
Phase	Linux NFS	JNFSD	Wayfinder: 1 Node	Wayfinder: Worst Case
1	0.02 s	0.04 s	0.04 s	0.10 s
2	0.18 s	0.37 s	0.82 s	1.51 s
3	1.03 s	0.82 s	0.85 s	1.08 s
4	0.84 s	1.58 s	1.64 s	1.82 s
5	2.09 s	3.13 s	3.30 s	3.49 s
Total	4.16 s	5.94 s	6.65 s	8.01 s

To delete a directory, Wayfinder deletes all files within the directory as described above and deletes the directory itself from the hoard. When processing delete notifications, a node also recursively delete ancestor directories if the deleted binding was the last in that directory. This implementation has two implications. First, since deleted files can reappear, so can deleted directories. Second, deleting the last binding in a directory effectively deletes that directory as well.

Finally, since we depend on nodes to update cached directory entries in the DHT to reflect changes, these entries may become stale when a node goes offline, modifies its local hoard, then returns. To address this problem, cached entries are automatically discarded after an expiration period. Also, when a node rejoins an online community, it lazily walks through its hoard and updates any stale cached entries. When two connected subsets join, cached entries for the same directory are merged.

5   Performance

We now consider the performance and robustness of a prototype implementation. Results presented here are preliminary since we are just starting to use Wayfinder on a daily basis.

Our prototype is written in Java and uses a modified JNFSD server [16] to export its services as a locally mounted user-level NFS system. All experiments are performed on a cluster of PCs, each equipped with an 800MHz PIII processor, 512MB of memory, and a 9GB SCSI disk. Nodes run Linux 2.2.14 and Sun's Java 1.4.1_2 SDK. The cluster is interconnected by a 100Mb/s Ethernet switch.

Each Wayfinder node caches meta-data retrieved from the DHT in local memory for 10 seconds. In our current setup, this reduces the impact of accessing the DHT through Java RMI, which requires on order of 2.5ms for a single RPC. When Wayfinder is used by communities connected over the Internet, this caching reduces the impact of communication over the WAN. Note that this caching is similar to caching done by the Linux NFS client (3–30 seconds), although Linux has a more sophisticated policy of when to disregard the cache.

Andrew Benchmark. Table 1 shows the running time for the Modified Andrew Benchmark [15] for Linux NFS, the unmodified JNFSD, and Wayfinder. The benchmark consists of five phases executed by a single client: (1) create a directory structure, (2) copy a set of files into the directory structure, (3) stat each file, (4) grep through the files, and (5) compile the files. In all cases, the NFS server and client ran on the same machine for comparison against when Wayfinder is running on a single node. For Wayfinder, "Worst Case" reflects performance for the hypothetical scenario where the community is very large so that each access to the DHT requires a message exchange. Since all operations are performed on a single client, these remote DHT accesses are the most significant source of overhead for this benchmark.

Observe that Wayfinder imposes little overhead when the workload is not entirely comprised of file system operations. In particular, Wayfinder imposes insignificant overheads for phases 4 and 5, when the client is grepping and compiling, respectively. Phase 1 and 2 impose higher performance penalty, particular phase 2 where each copy requires Wayfinder to compute a diff and to synchronously flush the corresponding waynode from the local cache, forcing a remote DHT update. Currently, the computation of a diff involves copying the entire file at an open which we plan to optimize in the future by implementing copy-on-write. Phase 3 benefits from the cache footprint resulting from phase 2 and so imposes only a modest amount of overhead.

We thus conclude that while Wayfinder does impose visible overheads on basic file system operations. These overheads are quite acceptable given that the prototype is a largely un-tuned Java program. We also observe that the Andrew Benchmark gives the worst case scenario for Wayfinder: all operations are performed at a single client and so gives no measure of Wayfinder's effectiveness for collaborative workloads.

Scalability and Robustness. We now show the advantage of Wayfinder's dual nature, using gossiping for robustness to failures and caching in the DHT for scalable performance. In this experiment, we turn off the caching at the local node to force accesses to use either the DHT or PlanetP's retrieval.

Figure 3(a) plots the time required for a single node to perform a complete traversal of a namespace, e.g., doing an "ls -R" vs. community size with, and without, the use of caching in the DHT. The namespace is a complete trinary directory tree of depth 3, giving a total of 41 directories with each directory containing 1 file. Each node hoards the entire namespace.

As expected, the scan time without caching in the DHT grows linearly with community size since computing each directory view requires contacting all nodes. With caching, however, the scan time rises only slightly with community size as more and more cached entries are stored at remote nodes; this curve has an asymptote, however, corresponding to the cost of a network access per directory access.

On the other hand, Figure 3(b) shows Wayfinder's robustness to loss of DHT data. In this experiment, we run a sequence of scans and, in two instances, we simulate node crashes by causing 2 and 4 nodes, respectively, to drop all of their DHT entries and leave the community. The scan is performed over a similar (albeit slightly smaller) directory structure as before but where each file is replicated only twice so that each crash leaves some files with only one replica. Observe the rise in scan time right after the simulated failures because some directory views had to be reconstructed. These scans correctly recreated all views, however, and re-cached them.

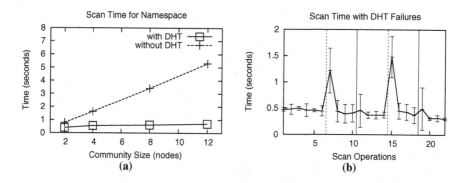

Fig. 3. (a) Time required to scan a namespace plotted against community size. (b) Scan time in the presence of node failures; x-axis is a sequence of scans, dotted vertical lines indicate node failures, and solid vertical lines indicate the return of failed nodes. 2 nodes failed after scan 6 while 4 nodes failed after scan 14. The vertical bar gives the standard deviation for scan time across 10 samples

6   Related Work

Several previous efforts have investigated the provision of a global namespace spanning multiple file and publishing systems [18, 21]. However, these efforts were more focused on providing individual users with logical namespaces that span multiple file systems rather than a communal namespace that can be collaboratively organized. The Federated File System (FFS) [27] is probably closest to our work with respect to namespace construction but FFS is targeted specifically for a cluster rather than a P2P community.

The Semantic File System [11] introduced the concept of semantic directories, which was further developed in the HAC File System [12]. Wayfinder implements this abstraction in the context of P2P systems. Wayfinder also introduces content ranking within semantic directories.

Many projects have recently explored P2P file systems. However, to our knowledge, none of these systems have considered content search and ranking. Further differences are as follows. The Secure Read-Only File System [10] and the Cooperative File System [8] are read-only publishing file systems. Farsite [1], a general read/write server-less file system, shares many common goals with our work. However, Farsite targets a corporate environment with significantly different characteristics than our target environments and so its design and implementation is significantly different from Wayfinder. Oceanstore [22] and Pangaea [23] are more concerned with extreme scaling than Wayfinder and so their designs and implementations are also significantly different than Wayfinder. Ivy [17] is a P2P file system that stores its data blocks in a DHT. This approach is fundamentally different than ours and may lead to unacceptably high data movement for highly dynamic communities [5, 3]. Finally, Bhagwan et al. have considered automatic availability management in the context of a storage system built around a DHT [3]. This system's replication approach is similar to that of Wayfinder (although this aspect of our work is not described here) but it does not target disconnected operation nor content search and ranking.

Several projects have addressed the enhancement of data management capabilities in P2P networks. For example, Harren et al. are exploring the introduction of complex query languages to P2P systems, particular in the context of systems built on DHTs [14]. The Piazza project is seeking to support the sharing of heterogeneous, semantically rich data in P2P systems [29]. These efforts are complementary to ours in that more powerful querying languages and engines on top of semantically rich data will likely increase Wayfinder's capability for providing a convenient yet powerful collaborative information sharing environment.

Tang and Dwarkadas recently investigated content search and ranking for DHT-based P2P systems [28]. This work is similar to PlanetP's content search and ranking albeit it targets a different underlying building block for P2P systems.

7   Conclusions and Future Work

We have presented Wayfinder, a novel P2P file system that seeks to unify publishing, searching, and collaborative organization within the context of a file system to better support the needs of medium-sized content sharing networks. Specifically, we have described two of the three critical abstractions exported by Wayfinder: a global namespace that merges devices' local namespaces into a unified view and semantic directories that allow the namespace to actively organize the shared information. We have shown how Wayfinder implements these abstractions on top of a P2P indexed data store; specifically, Wayfinder stores all of its meta-data in this data store. Wayfinder then constructs the global namespace, locates specific files, and performs content searches by posing appropriate queries to the underlying storage system. We have also described how to make this query-based design efficient by caching the query results in an unreliable DHT. Finally, we have given preliminary performance measurements collected from a prototype to show that we can achieve reasonable performance.

We are currently in the process of deploying Wayfinder inside our lab (and hopefully within our department) for actual use to evaluate Wayfinder's impact on everyday data management tasks. We are also pursuing two directions of future work. First, we are exploring the usefulness of Wayfinder's semantic directories as well as the opportunity to improve its content ranking capabilities by observing users' access patterns and explicit manipulations of semantic directories. For example, if a user explicitly adds a file to a semantic directory or accesses a lowly ranked file frequently, we might be able to use the content of these files to "improve" the query through keyword expansion.

Second, we are exploring how PlanetP can support a more complex query language. Harren et al. [14] have pointed out that such an effort can be rewarding as it can significantly enrich ways in which applications like Wayfinder can help users locate and manage shared content more effectively[4]. Concurrently, we will also explore the storage of Wayfinder's files as well as its meta-data in PlanetP. In essence, we seek to explore a

---

[4] Interestingly, PlanetP already supports part of the API identified by Harren et al. as being useful for implementing complex query languages in P2P systems.

content management and sharing system where coherent views, e.g., files and directories, are just results of appropriate queries posed on an underlying "sea of data." Such a hybrid system is powerful in that it supports a simple file system API yet also provides the benefits of a powerful underlying data management system. For example, in our current system, a semantic directory can be thought of as a dynamic "attraction" point, where new content entering the system related to a set of keywords will automatically be listed. Yet, applications accessing such a directory simply opens, reads, and writes the directory without having to know anything about the underlying data management capabilities. One can imagine equivalent *semantic* files that can serve to attract snippets of information; current PDA address books and calendars are examples of how such semantic files might be useful.

Acknowledgements. We thank Kien Le for developing Wayfinder's content indexer. We thank the reviewers for their thoughtful comments.

References

1. A. Adya, W. J. Bolosky, M. Castro, G. Cermak, R. Chaiken, J. R. Douceur, J. Howell, J. R. Lorch, M. Theimer, and R. P. Wattenhofer. FARSITE: Federated, Available, and Reliable Storage for an Incompletely Trusted Environment. In *Proceedings of the Symposium on Operating Systems Design and Implementation (OSDI)*, Dec. 2002.
2. R. Bhagwan, S. Savage, and G. Voelker. Understanding Availability. In *Proceedings of the International Workshop on Peer-to-Peer Systems (IPTPS)*, Feb. 2003.
3. R. Bhagwan, K. Tati, Y. Cheng, S. Savage, and G. M. Voelker. Total Recall: System Support for Automated Availability Management. In *Proceedings of the Symposium on Networked Systems Design and Implementation (NSDI)*, June 2004.
4. B. H. Bloom. Space/Time Trade-offs in Hash Coding with Allowable Errors. *Communications of the ACM*, July 1970.
5. F. M. Cuenca-Acuna, R. P. Martin, and T. D. Nguyen. Autonomous Replication for High Availability in Unstructured P2P Systems. In *Proceedings of the Symposium on Reliable Distributed Systems (SRDS)*, Oct. 2003.
6. F. M. Cuenca-Acuna and T. D. Nguyen. Text-Based Content Search and Retrieval in ad hoc P2P Communities. In *Proceedings of the International Workshop on Peer-to-Peer Computing*, May 2002.
7. F. M. Cuenca-Acuna, C. Peery, R. P. Martin, and T. D. Nguyen. PlanetP: Using Gossiping to Build Content Addressable Peer-to-Peer Information Sharing Communities. In *Proceedings of the International Symposium on High Performance Distributed Computing (HPDC)*, June 2003.
8. F. Dabek, M. F. Kaashoek, D. Karger, R. Morris, and I. Stoica. Wide-area cooperative storage with CFS. In *Proceedings of the Symposium on Operating Systems Principles (SOSP)*, Oct. 2001.
9. A. Demers, D. Greene, C. Hauser, W. Irish, J. Larson, S. Shenker, H. Sturgis, D. Swinehart, and D. Terry. Epidemic Algorithms for Replicated Database Maintenance. In *Proceedings of the Sixth Annual ACM Symposium on Principles of Distributed Computing*, 1987.
10. K. Fu, M. F. Kaashoek, and D. MaziÃ¨res. Fast and secure distributed read-only file system. In *Proceedings of the Symposium on Operating Systems Design and Implementation (OSDI)*, Oct. 2000.
11. D. K. Gifford, P. Jouvelot, M. A. Sheldon, and J. W. O. Jr. Semantic File Systems. In *Proceedings of the Symposium on Operating Systems Principles (SOSP)*, Oct. 1991.

12. B. Gopal and U. Manber. Integrating Content-Based Access Mechanisms with Hierarchical File System. In *Proceedings of the Symposium on Operating Systems Design and Implementation (OSDI)*, Feb. 1999.

13. R. G. Guy, J. S. Heidemann, W. Mak, T. W. Page, Jr., G. J. Popek, and D. Rothmeir. Implementation of the Ficus Replicated File System. In *Proceedings of the Summer USENIX Conference*, June 1990.

14. M. Harren, J. M. Hellerstein, R. Huebsch, B. T. Loo, S. Shenker, , and I. Stoica. Complex Queries in DHT-based Peer-to-Peer Networks. In *Proceedings of the International Workshop on Peer-to-Peer Systems (IPTPS)*, Apr. 2002.

15. J. H. Howard, M. L. Kazar, S. G. Menees, D. A. Nichols, M. Satyanarayanan, R. N. Sidebotham, and M. J. West. Scale and Performance in a Distributed File System. *ACM Transactions on Computer Systems (TOC)*, 6(1), Feb. 1988.

16. Java nfs server. http://members.aol.com/_ht_a/ markmitche11/jnfsd.htm, Oct. 2002.

17. A. Muthitacharoen, R. Morris, T. Gil, and I. B. Chen. Ivy: A Read/Write Peer-to-Peer File System. In *Proceedings of the Symposium on Operating Systems Design and Implementation (OSDI)*, Dec. 2002.

18. B. C. Neuman. The Prospero File System: A Global File System Based on the Virtual System Model. In *Proceedings of the Workshop on File Systems*, May 1992.

19. C. Peery, F. M. Cuenca-Acuna, R. P. Martin, and T. D. Nguyen. Wayfinder: Navigating and sharing information in a decentralized world. Technical Report DCS-TR-534, Department of Computer Science, Rutgers University, Oct. 2003.

20. K. Petersen, M. Spreitzer, D. Terry, and M. Theimer. Bayou: Replicated Database Services for World-Wide Applications. In *Proceedings of the Conference on Operating Systems (SIGOPS)*, Sept. 1996.

21. H. C. Rao and L. L. Peterson. Accessing Files in an Internet: The Jade File System. *Software Engineering*, 19(6), June 1993.

22. S. Rhea, P. Eaton, D. Geels, H. Weatherspoon, B. Zhao, and J. Kubiatowicz. Pond: The oceanstore prototype. In *Proceedings of the Conference on File and Storage Technologies (FAST)*, 2003.

23. Y. Saito and C. Karamanolis. Pangaea: a symbiotic wide-area file system. In *Proceedings of the Conference on Operating Systems (SIGOPS)*, Sept. 2002.

24. S. Saroiu, P. K. Gummadi, and S. D. Gribble. A Measurement Study of Peer-to-Peer File Sharing Systems. In *Proceedings of Multimedia Computing and Networking (MMCN)*, Jan. 2002.

25. S. Software. Berkeley DB. http://www.sleepycat.com/.

26. I. Stoica, R. Morris, D. Karger, M. F. Kaashoek, and H. Balakrishnan. Chord: A Scalable Peer-to-peer Lookup Service for Internet Applications. In *Proceedings of the Conference on Data Communications (SIGCOMM)*, Aug. 2001.

27. L. I. Suresh Gopalakrishnan, Ashok Arumugam. Federated File Systems for Clusters with Remote Memory Communication . Technical Report DCS-TR-472, Department of Computer Science, Rutgers University, Dec. 2001.

28. C. Tang and S. Dwarkadas. Hybrid Global-Local Indexing for Efficient Peer-to-Peer Information Retrieval. In *Proceedings of the Symposium on Networked Systems Design and Implementation (NSDI)*, June 2004.

29. I. Tatarinov, Z. Ives, J. Madhavan, A. Halevy, D. Suciu, N. Dalvi, X. Dong, Y. Kadiyska, G. Miklau, and P. Mork. The Piazza Peer Data Management Project. In *Proceedings of the Conference on Management of Data (SIGMOD)*, June 2003.

CISS: An Efficient Object Clustering Framework for DHT-Based Peer-to-Peer Applications

Jinwon Lee, Hyonik Lee, Seungwoo Kang, Sungwon Choe, and Junehwa Song

Division of Computer Science,
Department of Electrical Engineering & Computer Science,
Korea Advanced Institute of Science and Technology (KAIST), Daejeon, Korea
{jcircle, hyonigi, swkang, sungwon, junesong}@nclab.kaist.ac.kr

Abstract. Distributed Hash Tables (DHTs) have been widely adopted in many Internet-scale P2P systems. Emerging P2P applications such as massively multi player online games (MMOGs) and P2P catalog systems frequently update data or issue multi-dimensional range queries, but existing DHT-based P2P systems can not support these applications efficiently due to object declustering. Object declustering can result in significant inefficiencies in data update and multi-dimensional range query routing. In this paper, we propose CISS, a framework that supports efficient object clustering for DHT-based P2P applications. While utilizing DHT as a basic lookup layer, CISS uses a Locality Preserving Function (LPF) instead of a hash function. Thus, CISS achieves a high level of clustering without requiring any changes to existing DHT implementations. Technically, we study LPF encoding function, efficient routing protocols for data updates and multi-dimensional range queries, and cluster-preserving load balancing. We demonstrate the performance benefits of CISS through simulation.

1 Introduction

Distributed Hash Table (DHT)-based overlay networks [15][17][20][21] have recently emerged as a scalable and efficient infrastructure for wide-area data management. DHT is already adopted in many P2P systems including a wide-area file system [5] and an Internet-scale query processor [9]. These P2P systems mainly focus on an environment in which data updates are rare and exact match queries are the norm. However, emerging P2P applications frequently update data or issue range queries. For example, MMOGs intensively generate streams of updates such as players' locations and status [3][10]; P2P catalog systems intensively issue multi-dimensional range queries such as interest area queries [13].

Existing DHT-based P2P systems [5][9] can not support such applications efficiently due to object declustering. These P2P systems use a hash function to distribute objects randomly across different peer nodes. Thus, while they are effective in achieving a high level of load balancing, objects are totally declustered; even highly correlated objects are spread over different peer nodes. Such object declustering can result in significant inefficiencies in both data update and multi-dimensional range

W.S. Ng et al. (Eds.): DBISP2P 2004, LNCS 3367, pp. 215–229, 2005.

query routing. In data-intensive P2P applications such as MMOGs, DHT lookups have to be performed at every data update even though consecutive data updates are semantically close. Thus, it increases not only the communication overhead of the DHT layer, but also the latency of update routing. However, when objects are clustered, semantically close updates can be routed to the same peer node without having to perform additional lookups. In multi-dimensional range query-intensive P2P application such as P2P catalog systems, queries search for semantically related objects. Thus, when totally declustered, each key value in a query range should be enumerated and individually searched for via a separate DHT lookup. However, when objects are clustered, multiple key values can be searched for via a single lookup. Thus, the number of DHT lookups needed for query processing can be greatly reduced.

In this paper, we propose CISS (Cooperative Information Sharing System), a framework that supports efficient object clustering for DHT-based P2P applications. While utilizing DHT as a basic lookup layer, CISS uses a Locality Preserving Function (LPF) instead of a hash function. Thus, CISS achieves a high level of object clustering without requiring any changes to existing DHT implementations. Consequently, CISS significantly reduces the number of DHT lookups needed for data updates and multi-dimensional range queries.

In realizing CISS, there are three technical issues that must be taken into consideration. *First, CISS has to construct an N-bit key from multiple attributes for each object while preserving locality.* In order to preserve locality, the keys of two objects should be similar if attribute values of those objects are semantically related. The LPF is responsible for this key encoding. The LPF first encodes each attribute value to a shorter-length bit key. It then maps multiple such shorter-length bit keys to a one-dimensional N-bit key using the Hilbert SFC. Since the data types of each attribute can be diverse in practice, the LPF needs to be able to encode the attributes of various data types. We describe this encoding scheme in Section 4.1 with practical examples.

Second, CISS must support efficient routing protocols for data updates and multi-dimensional range queries in order to maximize the benefits of object clustering. To route data updates efficiently, we propose a caching-based update routing protocol. This routing protocol does not perform additional lookups if streams of updates belong to the key range of the most-recently-searched peer node. Each peer node manages semantically related objects and data updates are also usually semantically close. Thus, streams of updates belong to the same node with high probability. To route multi-dimensional range queries efficiently, we propose a forwarding-based query routing protocol that performs a minimal number of costly DHT lookups. In addition, our query routing protocol prevents query congestion.

Third, CISS must perform load balancing while preserving object clustering. Since each peer node in CISS manages semantically related objects, a skewed distribution of objects and queries results in significant load imbalance. To prevent hotspots, load balancing must be performed. However, load balancing mechanisms in existing DHT-based systems such as virtual servers [4][5][14][20] destroy the object clustering property. When using virtual servers, physical peer nodes can manage noncontiguous key ranges, *i.e.* multiple virtual servers. In order to preserve object clustering, physical peer nodes must manage contiguous key ranges. We propose two novel load balancing schemes, local-handover and global-handover, which preserve object clustering even after load balancing is achieved.

The rest of the paper is organized as follows. Section 2 reviews related work in the area of object clustering in P2P overlay networks. In Section 3, we describe the architecture of CISS. In Section 4, we explain technical issues faced in realizing CISS, including LPF, data and query routing protocols and cluster-preserving load balancing. Section 5 presents results from simulation studies of CISS. Finally, Section 6 concludes with a discussion of our plans for future work.

2 Related Work

In existing DHT-based P2P systems [5][9], exact matching queries are efficiently processed in $O(\log S)$ time, where S is the number of nodes in the P2P overlay network. However, streams of data updates and multi-dimensional range queries are not supported well due to object declustering in such systems. Recent research has focused on alleviating these shortcomings.

Much of this research [1][7][11][18] attempts to provide simple one-dimensional range queries over P2P overlay networks. In [1][18], the authors extend CAN [15] for range queries by utilizing query flooding techniques. In [7][11], they propose newly designed range addressable P2P frameworks which are not compatible with existing DHT implementations.

CLASH [12] and PHT [16] apply an extensible hashing technique to DHTs. They efficiently achieve an adaptive object clustering as well as support range queries. Due to the need for depth searching, an exact match lookup takes $O(\log(D)\cdot\log(S))$ time, where D is the maximum depth of the key and S is the number of nodes. However, multi-dimensional range queries have not been considered yet in these research projects.

Squid [19] supports multi-dimensional range queries over DHTs by using the Hilbert Space Filling Curve (SFC). Recursive refinement of queries in Squid significantly improves the performance of query routing, but it can incur query congestion. Thus, the overall scalability of a DHT-based P2P system is limited.

From the standpoint of real systems, much of this previous research did not consider several critical technical issues. First, it is not clear how to encode real attribute values to N-bit routing keys. In this paper, we clearly describe such an encoding scheme with practical examples. Second, even though many previous works focused on query routing, in fact it is data updates that are the major performance bottleneck of data-intensive P2P applications. We propose an efficient update routing protocol to address this. Finally, cluster-preserving load balancing has not been considered yet in those previous works. Load balancing is essential for such P2P systems to be able to work under real environments. However, the benefits of object clustering can be destroyed if we directly apply previous load balancing schemes [4][5][14][20]. Our cluster-preserving load balancing schemes are novel in that sense.

3 System Architecture

CISS is designed for a three-tier P2P system as shown in Figure 1. Such three-tier architecture is similar to existing DHT-based P2P systems [5][9]. While CISS uses DHT as a basic lookup layer by using DHT interfaces, P2P applications utilize CISS as an Internet-scale data management system. For data updates and queries, an interface using a simple conjunctive normal form language is provided to applications (see Table 1). CISS, like common P2P systems, consists of client and server modules. The client module of CISS receives data updates or queries from P2P applications. It then routes them to rendezvous peer nodes for processing. Before routing them, the client module leverages an LPF to encode multiple attributes of an object to an N-bit routing key. This key is used to perform a DHT lookup to search for rendezvous peer nodes in the P2P overlay network. The server module of CISS stores data to its repository and processes queries. It then returns matched results to requesting peer nodes. The load balancer in the server module is responsible for cluster-preserving load balancing.

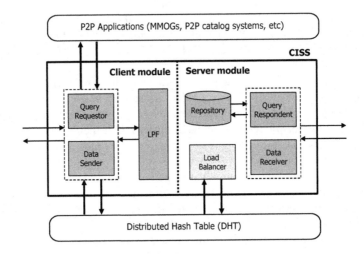

Fig. 1. CISS Architecture

Table 1. Interfaces for DHT and CISS

DHT	CISS
Lookup(key) → IP address	Update: (A1= value) $\wedge$ (A2=value) $\wedge$ ....
Join ()	Query: Predicate$_{A1}$ $\wedge$ Predicate$_{A2}$ $\wedge$ ....
Leave()	Predicate = Attribute **Operator** Value Operators = $\{>, <, \geq, \leq, =\}$

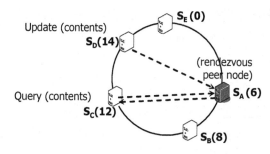

Fig. 2. Chord DHT

The scalable and robust nature of CISS stems primarily from utilizing DHT. We explain CISS using Chord [20] as an example DHT environment though any DHT implementation could be used. DHT [15][17][20][21] organizes highly distributed and loosely coupled peer nodes into an overlay network for storing and querying a massive number of objects. In a DHT environment, not only the placement of data objects on nodes, but also the join and leave of nodes in the overlay network can be done efficiently without any global knowledge. As shown in Figure 2, five peer nodes cooperatively manage an N-bit key space, where N is 4. Each node has a unique node identifier and is responsible for the key range between itself and its predecessor node.

From a database point of view, there are two attractive characteristics for using a DHT-based overlay network.

First, content-based searching in peer to peer networks – DHT makes it possible to implement content-based search networks. Multiple attributes of an object are encoded to form an N-bit key which is used to update and locate that object. Data updates and exact match queries which are encoded to the same N-bit key are routed to the same rendezvous peer node. After query processing, the matching results are returned to the querying nodes. This rendezvous point approach achieves content-based searching effectively by avoiding query flooding.

Second, efficient wide-area data indexing – It is critical that searches for the rendezvous peer node responsible for a given N-bit key should be done efficiently. DHT theoretically ensures that any peer node can look up any object using that object's N-bit key in $O(\log S)$ time, where S is the number of peer nodes in the overlay network. Lookups proceed in a multi-hop fashion; each node maintains information (IP addresses) about a small number of other nodes (neighbors) and forwards the lookup message recursively to the neighbor that is nearest to the N-bit key of the object.

4 Technical Issues

In this section, we describe three technical issues and novel solution approaches in realizing CISS. Specifically, the LPF encoding function, efficient routing protocols for data updates and multi-dimensional range queries and cluster-preserving load balancing are examined.

4.1 Locality Preserving Function (LPF)

The LPF constructs N-bit keys of objects while preserving locality. As shown below, this encoding is done in two steps.

> **Step1:** $\{(A1 = value) \wedge (A2 = value) \wedge ....\} \rightarrow \{bits_{A1} \wedge bits_{A2} \wedge ....\}$
>
> **Step2:** $\{bits_{A1} \wedge bits_{A2} \wedge ....\} \rightarrow$ **N-bit key of object**

The LPF first encodes each attribute value to a smaller-sized bit key. It then maps multiple bit keys to a one-dimensional N-bit key by using the Hilbert SFC. Both steps preserve the locality of objects. Each attribute is encoded to $N / D (= M)$ bits if D attributes are used for key encoding. As a practical value, we can use $N = 160$ and $D = 2$. Thus, $M = 80$. We select $N = 160$ to be compatible with Chord [20] implementation which uses 160-bit key. Also, $D = 2$ because two-dimensional range queries are dominantly issued in both MMOGs and P2P catalog systems. If an attribute of an object is not encoded as part of an N-bit key, queries on this attribute must be routed to all nodes in the P2P overlay networks. Thus, all attributes referred to in dominantly issued queries must be encoded to bit keys in order to avoid query flooding. We describe the technical details of each step as follows.

Step1: Bit key encoding of each attribute while preserving locality – LPF classifies data types of attributes into `Numerical` and `String` types, and applies different encoding schemes accordingly. We explain each encoding scheme with practical examples. The encoding scheme for the `Numerical` type handles `int`, `long`, `float`, `double` and `DATE` data-types.

For instance, MMOG (see Figure 3) use `Numerical` attributes. Players are the objects, and their x and y coordinates are the object attributes. In order to preserve locality, each attribute value is simply rescaled by multiplying a coefficient, 2^M / *(Maximum of attribute value)*. For example, $\{x=60 \wedge y=70\}$ where the maximum of each attribute value is 100 is encoded to $\{x=1010 \wedge y=1011\}$ if M is four. In the same way, a two-dimensional range query in Figure 3 is also encoded to $\{(0101 < x < 1110) \wedge (0011 < y < 1110)\}$. Therefore, objects will be clustered well if the positions of the objects are similar.

For the `String` type, we propose a *hash-concatenation encoding scheme*. P2P catalog systems (see Figure 4) use `String` attributes. Catalogs are the objects and categorized by two attributes, location and product. Each attribute value is represented using a hierarchical naming structure. For example,

> **A1: location** = USA.New York.White Plains.79 North Broadway
>
> ("USA" is the value of the topmost level in the hierarchy, "New York" is the second highest and so on)
>
> **A2: product** = Electronics.Computer.HP.Inkjet Pinter
>
> ("Electronics" is the value of the topmost level in the hierarchy, "Computer" is the second highest and so on)

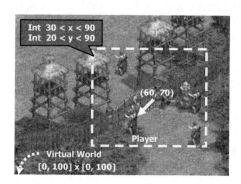

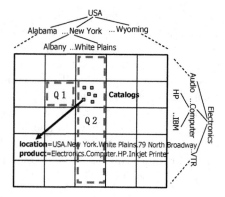

Fig. 3. MMOGs

Fig. 4. P2P catalog systems

Dominantly issued queries are two-dimensional range queries such as Q1 and Q2 in Figure 4[1]. Within each level in the hierarchy, partial string matching (*ex.* USA.N*.White Plains) is not usual. Thus, clustering according to the hierarchy is enough, while clustering between similar string values in same level is not necessary.

The hash-concatenation scheme hashes the value of each level in the hierarchy into M / d bits, where d is the hierarchy depth. It then concatenates the hashed values one after another. In practice, d is determined by an application. To hash a variable-length string value of each level to a fixed-length bit representation, a modified SHA-1[20] hash function is used[2]. Queries are also encoded in the same way. The tables below show encoding examples when M is 80 and the hierarchy depth d is 4. Thus, each string in the hierarchy is hashed to 20 bits.

A1: location = USA.New York.White Plains.79 North Broadway $\rightarrow$
h_{20}(USA)·h_{20}(New York)·h_{20}(White Plains)·h_{20}(79 North Broadway)

- -

A2: product = Electronics.Computer.HP.Inkjet Pinter $\rightarrow$
h_{20}(Electronics)·h_{20}(Computer)·h_{20}(HP)·h_{20}(Inkjet Printer)

•

Q1: location = h_{20}(USA)·h_{20}(New York)·h_{20}(Albany)* $\wedge$
product = h_{20}(Electronics)·h_{20}(Computer)·h_{20}(HP)*

- -

Q2: location = h_{20}(USA)·h_{20}(New York)·h_{20}(White Plains)* $\wedge$
product = * (* means a wild card)

---

[1] Although `String` type keyword queries such as "%keyword%" are popular in P2P file sharing, we do not tackle such queries because they do not benefit from object clustering.

[2] SHA-1[20] hashes a string to the randomized 160-bit. A string of each level has to be hashed to M / d bits which is less than 160. Thus, just M / d prefix bit of SHA-1 is used as a hashed value.

Our hash-concatenation scheme is useful in two aspects. First, due to hashing, a variable-length string is encoded to a fixed size bit length. Second, locality is preserved due to the concatenation scheme. Bit keys with similar hierarchical structures are closely clustered. In contrast, previous string-to-bit encoding schemes such as serial numbering and prefix encoding [3][19] are not feasible in P2P environments. The serial numbering scheme, which stores all mappings from strings to serial numbers, can not add new values easily. If new values in the hierarchy are added, all peer nodes have to update their mapping. Prefix encoding also can not categorize variable length strings well. Since this scheme encodes only the prefix characters of a string due to limited bit length, objects are not clustered well according to the hierarchy.

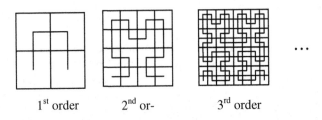

1st order   2nd or-   3rd order

Fig. 5. Hilbert SFC

Step2: Mapping multiple bit keys to a one-dimensional *N*-bit key while considering multi-dimension clustering – Many schemes have been studied to map multi-dimensional keys to a one-dimensional key [2]. Space Filling Curve (SFC) is a well-known scheme. It includes z-ordering, Gray code and the Hilbert SFC. We use the Hilbert SFC because it has better object clustering properties compared to other SFCs. It can be implemented with a simple state machine. As an example, the Hilbert SFC maps {x=1010 ∧ y=1011} to 10001011. The Hilbert SFC has two interesting properties: recursion and locality preservation. Figure 5 shows the recursion. The locality preserving property can be described as follows. Points which are close to each other along the space filling curve map to points which are close in the multi-dimensional space. We utilize this property for the multi-dimensional range query routing protocol.

4.2 Efficient Routing Protocols for Data Updates and Multi-dimensional Range Queries

CISS supports efficient routing protocols to maximize the benefit of object clustering: a *caching-based update routing protocol* for data updates and a *forwarding-based query routing protocol* for multi-dimensional range queries. Both of them significantly reduce the number of costly DHT lookups, and thus improve the efficiency of data-intensive and multi-dimensional range query-intensive P2P applications. We describe the technical details as follows.

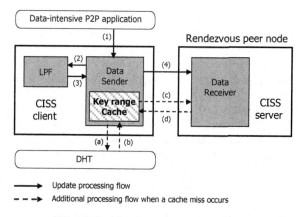

Fig. 6. Caching-based update routing protocol

Caching-based update routing protocol: As shown in Figure 6, the *CISS client* caches the key range of the most-recently-searched rendezvous node. Thus, the CISS client does not perform additional DHT lookups if streams of updates belong to the cached key range (cache hit). Streams of updates belong to the same node with high probability. It is because each peer node manages a semantically contiguous key range and data updates are usually semantically close. For example, in MMOGs, a subsection of the virtual world is managed by a peer node. Players will spend significant amounts of time in a given subsection and therefore their data will belong to the same node with high probability. To quantify the performance benefit of this update routing protocol, we measure the *hit ratio* of the key range cache. In our experiments, we also measure the hit ratio under various data mobility values because the hit ratio is directly affected by a data mobility value. The cached key range can be stale due to DHT topology changes (*e.g.* leave and join of nodes). Thus, a TTL (Time-To-Live) mechanism is utilized to maintain the consistency of the cached key range. After the TTL expires, the CISS client performs a DHT lookup to refresh the cached key range.

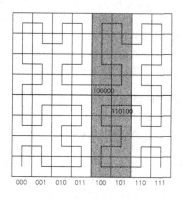

Fig. 7. Forwarding-based query routing protocol

Forwarding-based query routing protocol: For multi-dimensional range query routing, we propose a forwarding-based query routing protocol that reduces costly DHT lookups by forwarding a query to succeeding peer nodes. Multi-dimensional range queries involve multiple contiguous key ranges in CISS. To reduce the number of DHT lookups for those multiple key ranges, the forwarding-based query routing protocol utilizes the object clustering property of CISS. Assume that a user issues a multi-dimensional range query (10*, *) which is mapped to the two dotted curves in the gray area as shown in Figure 7. The Query Requester in CISS client module finds the first keys from the each contiguous curve using LPF, which are 100000 and 110100. The Query Requester then searches matching peer nodes via DHT lookups for the two keys. If matching peer nodes are found, the Query Requester sends the query (10*, *) to the Query Respondents in the CISS server modules of those peer nodes. The Query Respondent generates a result and sends it to the Query Requester. If the key range for the result is larger than the key range managed by the node, the Query Respondent forwards the query to the succeeding peer node without having to perform any more DHT lookups. Query forwarding is repeated until all relevant data are found for the result. In CISS, the number of DHT lookups is determined by the number of separate curves describing the query. In addition, the number of query forwarding messages depends on the size of the query range as well as the topology of a P2P overlay network. In experiments, we show that the forwarding-based routing protocol outperforms existing DHT-based query routing protocols in terms of the number of messages needed for query processing.

In Squid [19], authors suggested a mechanism to resolve a multi-dimensional keyword and range query by embedding a tree structure into the P2P overlay network topology. In this mechanism, all queries should be routed to the peer matching the cluster prefix 0 or 1 for query refinement. Thus, the peer can be the congestion point, which can result in one point of failure. However, our forwarding-based query routing protocol does not incur such a query congestion problem while supporting efficient query processing with few DHT lookups.

4.3 Cluster-Preserving Load Balancing

CISS supports two load balancing schemes: *local-handover* and *global-handover*. In order to achieve load balancing, both of them hand over the partial key range managed by an overloaded node to lightly loaded nodes. However, in contrast to the previous virtual server approach, our approach does not destroy the object clustering property. Thus, it still maintains the benefit of object clustering to process data update and multi-dimensional range queries.

In local-handover, the overloaded node hands over a part of its own key range to one of its neighbor nodes (predecessor or successor). This can be done easily by a leave followed by a join. Figure 8 shows a local-handover example. When node *B* gets overloaded, it hands over a part of its key range to its predecessor node *A* or successor node *C*. If *A* takes the load of *B*, *A* leaves the DHT-based overlay network and joins again closer to *B* so as to adopt the part of B's key range. This reduces the key range which *B* must manage, and the *B*'s key range is therefore decreased.

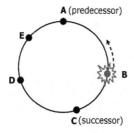

Fig. 8. Local-handover

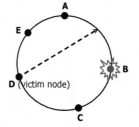

Fig. 9. Global-handover

Table 2. Load Balancing Cost

	Local-handover	Global-handover
DHT routing table updates	• $O(\log S)$ messages	• $O(\log S)$ messages
Object Transferring	• From the overloaded node to the neighbor node	• From the overloaded node to the victim node • From the victim node to the successor of victim node.
Victim Probing	• None	• n DHT lookups

Similarly, **C** can take **B**'s load if **B** leaves and joins again. Even after the local-handover is performed, each node still manages a contiguous key range. Thus, object clustering is preserved. However, cascading load propagation can occur in this scheme. If a neighbor node also gets overloaded due to the local-handover, it will also perform a local-handover to its neighbor node, and so on.

To alleviate this shortcoming, we propose global-handover. In this scheme, an overloaded node hands over a part of its key range to a victim node instead of a neighbor node. After probing randomly selected nodes in the DHT-based overlay network, the most lightly loaded node is determined as a victim node. Figure 9 shows a global-handover example. If node **D** is determined as a victim node, an overloaded node **B** makes **D** leave. Node **D** then joins as a predecessor of **B** and takes over a contiguous sub-range of **B**'s key range. Also, **D**'s successor node **E** manages contiguous key range. Thus, object clustering is still preserved.

Table 2 shows the load balancing cost of both schemes. First of all, the cost for updating the DHT routing table is the same since the node leave and the node join occurs only once in both schemes. The cost of the object transferring from the overloaded node to the lightly loaded node is also the same. However, global-handover requires additional object transferring cost as well as a victim-probing cost. The additional object transferring cost is required because the victim node should hand over all of its objects to its successor node before leaving the overlay network. For victim probing, it is necessary to collect load information from n randomly selected nodes. Thus, it requires **n** DHT lookups. To minimize the load balancing cost, CISS performs global-handover only when the cascading load propagation is expected if local-handover were to be used.

We are currently investigating some technical details for the proposed schemes including overload detection, load estimation and victim selection algorithms. For efficient load estimation, we are developing a histogram-based algorithm. To hand over the proper amount of load, all nodes have to know their own load information in detail. However, it is not practically possible to maintain load information for each key. Thus, each node divides its key range into several sub-ranges and then maintains a histogram for the number of requests in each sub-range.

5   Experiments

In this section, we demonstrate the performance benefit of CISS compared to existing DHT-based P2P systems which use a hash function. For our experiment, we have implemented a C++-based simulation engine which includes the Hilbert SFC-based LPF, the core functions of the CISS client and server module and a Chord-based DHT overlay network. The simulation has been performed for three overlay network topologies which consist of 1000, 10000 and 100000 peer nodes respectively. The identifier of each node is randomly generated. To exclude the effects of dynamic topology changes, we did not simulate node leaves or joins. We detail the performance of the proposed routing protocol in the simulation results below.

5.1   Data Update Performance

In each simulation, 1000, 10000 and 100000 mobile clients in a virtual world generate their position updates periodically for the workload of the simulator. Before updating its position, the mobile client checks whether its current position is in the cached key range. If a cache miss occurs, it looks up the node that is responsible for its current position. The mobile clients are designed to wander the $[0, 2^{12}] \times [0, 2^{12}]$ square virtual world based on the ns-2 *random waypoint mobility model* [6]. Each mobile client updates its position every 125 milliseconds (for comparison, the first-person shooter Quake II updates a player's position every 50ms); a position consists of two attributes: an x-coordinate and a y-coordinate. The simulation is run for 300 seconds.

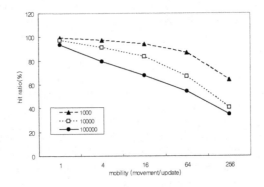

Fig. 10. Hit ratio of the key range cache

To measure the performance benefit of the caching-based update routing protocol, we use the hit ratio of the key range cache. Figure 10 depicts the average hit ratio of the key range cache over all the mobile clients having the same mobility value. A mobility value of 1 means that a mobile client can move maximum one pixel length in the $[0, 2^{12}] \times [0, 2^{12}]$ virtual world during one position update period. From the Figure 10, we see that this update routing protocol significantly reduces the number of look-ups for position updates (by up to 93% with 100000 nodes), whereas with hash function, the mobile client has to look up the node responsible for its current position at every position update. Because the range of mobile client movement is much smaller than the range managed by the responsible server, the hit ratio is high for low mobility values. The larger the mobility value, the lower the hit ratio. However, even with a high mobility value of 256, the update routing protocol achieves a 35% hit ratio with 100000 nodes. Figure 10 also shows the hit ratio variation according to the number of nodes. The range managed by each node increases as the number of peer nodes decreases. Thus, the hit ratio with a 1000 node topology, which has larger range size than the other ones, is the highest.

5.2 Multi-dimensional Range Query Performance

To implement multi-dimensional range queries, we used a P2P catalog system as an example application. The catalog is categorized by two attributes (**location** and **product**); each attribute consists of four levels. We have performed experiments for each of ten query types. For example,

- **Q(4,4):** Queries with both attributes having values in the top four levels of the hierarchy, *e.g.* (**location:** USA.New York.White Plains.79 North Broadway, **product:** Electronics. Computer.HP.Inkjet Pinter).

- **Q(4,3):** Queries with one attribute having values in the top four levels and the other attribute having values in the top three levels. *e.g.*(**location:** USA.New York.White Plains.79 North Broadway, **product:** Electronics.Computer.HP.*).

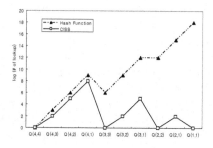

Fig. 11. # of DHT lookups

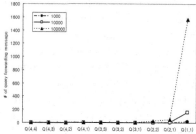

Fig. 12. # of DHT forwarding messages

The other queries Q(4,2), Q(4,1), Q(3,3), Q(3,2), Q(3,1), Q(2,2), Q(2,1) and Q(1,1) are similarly generated. In our experiment, the LPF constructs 24-bit keys. Thus, each attribute is encoded using 12 bits. We simulated all possible combinations for each of the ten queries.

Figure 11 shows the average number of DHT lookups for the ten types of queries in log-scale. When the size of the query range becomes large, the number of DHT lookups is significantly reduced. This is clearly shown from Q(3,3) to Q(1,1) where the difference in the number of lookups required for CISS compared to the hash-based approach is dramatically illustrated. This is achieved due to the object clustering effect of CISS. Queries like Q(3,3), Q(2,2) and Q(1,1) are mapped to one contiguous curve on the Hilbert SFC. For such queries, only one DHT lookup is necessary for query processing in our forwarding-based query routing protocol. However, Q(4,4) is an exact matching query. Thus, in this case the number of DHT lookups required for CISS is the same as that for the hash-based approach. Finally, in cases Q(4,3), Q(4,2) and Q(4,1), one attribute is specified exactly. These results in a decrease in object clustering and therefore decreased performance benefit. Nevertheless, CISS still performs two times better than the hash-based approach for these queries.

Figure 12 shows the average number of query forwarding messages when all peer nodes manage the same size key range. As shown in the figure, the first nine types of queries with 1000 nodes and seven types of queries with 10000 and 100000 nodes do not need query forwarding. The results for these queries can be retrieved from the peer node found out by a DHT lookup. On the other hand, in the cases of Q(1,1) with 1000 nodes and Q(2,2), Q(2,1), Q(1,1) with 10000 and 100000 nodes, query forwarding is necessary because the query range size is larger than the key range size which the peer node manages. However, the forwarding cost is just one message whereas a DHT lookup may cost several messages. Figure 11 and Figure 12 demonstrate that the total number of messages for query processing is significantly reduced in our forwarding-based query routing protocol.

6 Conclusion and Future Work

We have described CISS, *a framework that supports efficient object clustering for DHT-based peer-to-peer applications*, especially data-intensive and multi-dimensional range query-intensive P2P applications. While utilizing a DHT-based overlay network as a scalable and robust lookup layer, CISS uses a Locality Preserving Function (LPF) instead of a hash function. Thus, CISS achieves a high level of object clustering without requiring any changes to existing DHT implementations. Our simulation studies show that a *caching-based update routing protocol* reduces the number of DHT lookups for data updates by up to 93% with 100000 peer nodes, and a *forwarding-based query routing protocol* for multi-dimensional range queries outperforms existing DHT-based P2P systems by up to an order of magnitude. We are currently developing the cluster-preserving load balancing mechanism in detail.

References

[1] A. Andrzejak and Z. Xu, "Scalable, Efficient Range Queries for Grid Information Services", In *Proceedings of IEEE P2P*, Sweden, September 2002

[2] T.Asano, D.Ranjan, T.Roose,E. Welzl and P.Widmaier, "Space Filling Curves and Their Use in Geometric Data Structures", *Theoretical Computing Science*, 181, 1997, pp.3-15

[3] A.R. Bharambe, S. Rao and S. Seshan, "Mercury: A Scalable Publish-Subscribe System for Internet Games", In *Proceedings of NetGames*, Germany, April 2002

[4] J. Byers, J. Considine and M. Mitzenmacher, "Simple Load Balancing for Distributed Hash Tables", In *Proceedings of IPTPS*, CA, USA, February 2003

[5] F. Dabek, M. F. Kaashoek, D. Karger, R. Morris and I. Stoica, "Wide-area cooperative storage with CFS", In *Proceedings of SOSP*, Canada, October 2001

[6] K. Fall and K. Varadhan. NS Manual

[7] A. Gupta, D. Agrawal and A. El Abbadi, "Approximate Range Selection Queries in Peer-to-Peer Systems",In *Proceedings of CIDR*, CA, USA, January 2003

[8] M. Harren, J.M. Hellerstein, R. Huebsch, B.T. Loo, S. Shenker and I. Stoica, "Complex Queries in DHT-based Peer-to-Peer Networks", In *Proceedings of IPTPS*, MA, USA, March 2002

[9] R. Huebsch, J.M. Hellerstein, N. Lanham, B.T. Loo, S. Shenker and I. Stoica, "Querying the Internet with PIER", In *Proceedings of VLDB*, Berlin, September 2003

[10] B. Knutsson, H. Lu, W. Xu and B. Hopkins, "Peer-to-Peer Support for Massively Multiplayer Games", In *Proceedings of INFOCOM*, Hong Kong, China, March 2004

[11] A. Kothari, D. Agrawal, A. Gupta and Subhash Suri, "Range Addressable Network: A P2P Cache Architecture for Data Ranges", In *Proceedings of IEEE P2P*, Sweden, September 2003

[12] A. Misra, P. Castro and J. Lee, "CLASH: A Protocol for Internet-Scale Utility-Oriented Distributed Computing", In *Proceedings of ICDCS*, Japan, March 2004

[13] V. Papadimos, D. Maier and K. Tufte, "Distributed Query Processing and Catalogs for Peer-to-Peer Systems", In *Proceedings of CIDR*, CA, USA, January 2003

[14] A. Rao, K. Lakshminarayanan, S. Surana, R. Karp and I. Stoica, "Load Balancing in Structured P2P Systems", In *Proceedings of IPTPS*, CA, USA, February 2003

[15] S. Ratnasamy, P. Francis, M. Handley, R. Karp and S. Shenker, "A Scalable Content-Addressable Network", In *Proceedings of SIGCOMM*, CA, USA, August 2001

[16] S. Ratnasamy, J. M. Hellerstein and S. Shenker, "Range Queries over DHTs", *IRB-TR-03-009*, June 2003

[17] A. Rowstron and P. Druschel, "Pastry: Scalable, distributed object location and routing for large-scale peer-to-peer systems", In *Proceedings of IFIP/ACM International Conference on Distributed Systems Platforms (Middleware)*, Germany, November 2001

[18] O. Sahin, A. Gupta, D. Agrawal and A. El Abbadi , "A Peer-to-peer Framework for Caching Range Queries", In *Proceedings of ICDE*, MA, USA, March 2004

[19] C. Schmidt and M. Parashar, "Flexible Information Discovery in Decentralized Distributed Systems", In *Proceedings of HPDC*, WA, USA June 2003

[20] I. Stoica, R. Morris, D. Karger, M.F. Kaashoek and H. Balakrishnan, "Chord: A Scalable Peer-to-Peer Lookup Service for Internet Applications", In *Proceedings of SIGCOMM*, CA, USA, August 2001

[21] B. Y. Zhao, J. Kubiatowicz and A. Joseph, "Tapestry: An Infrastructure for Fault-tolerant Wide-area Location and Routing", *UCB Tech. Report UCB/CSD-01-1141*

Author Index

Lecture Notes in Computer Science

For information about Vols. 1–3327

please contact your bookseller or Springer